A KIRGHIZ READER

Indiana University Uralic and Altaic Series
Denis Sinor, *Editor*
Volume 154

A KIRGHIZ
READER

BY

Hu Zhen-hua and Guy Imart

INDIANA UNIVERSITY
Research Institute for Inner Asian Studies
Bloomington, Indiana
1989

Library of Congress Catalog Card Number: 89-085859
ISBN 0-933070-24-1

- T A B L E   O F   C O N T E N T S -

F O R E W O R D

The idea of compiling a modern Kirghiz Reader arose out of quite different motivations and necessities.

Initially, one of the authors collected some relatively short texts so as to create a linguistic corpus diversified enough to serve, within the framework of a University thesis, the purpose of a collection of samples for grammatical parsing.

Little by little, however, it clearly appeared that an exclusively linguistic approach to (Soviet) "Literary Kirghiz" left too many questions unresolved. A preliminary sociolinguistic analysis of the conditions and ways of development of this "Literary Kirghiz" was necessary. This in turn proved to be more than a shift from a synchronic to a diachronic or from a static to a dynamic viewpoint: ultimately from an "Anthology" to a "Chrestomathy".

The new approach necessarily included such problems as the evolution of the alphabetical/ orthographical systems used to transcribe Kirghiz, the exploration of the various linguistic "levels" and, also, a necessary extension of the quest outside the linguistically artificial limits of the soviet Kirghiz SSR.

But the mere illustration of this last aspect required that documentation be collected from at least three different countries (not counting the production of Kirghiz in exile) at a time when one of these countries was barely reestablishing contacts with the outside world and the third one cutting them off.

When at long last the documents were obtained, they often demanded, in order to be fully understood, explanations which by far exceeded the initial as well as the revised aims. The "treasure hunt" threatened to evolve into a fully-fledged history of the development of the Kirghiz language which, as every sociolinguist knows, would have been nothing else than the history of the Kirghiz people as reflected in its tongue...

Since such an undertaking would have demanded more texts, more analysis, etc., a way out of this vicious circle had to be found. Together

with my colleague from Peking who had provided me
with the material necessary for the geographical
extension of this work, we decided
    - to extend its range and conception beyond
the scope of its first ancestor: a "Kirgizskaja
Khrestomatija (Sbornik obrazcov narodnoj
literatury Turkestanskogo kraja)", published in
Tashkent in 1883,
    - to limit it to the dimensions of a reader
which would provide the beginner and/or the
turcologist with two kinds of opportunities:
    . that of getting acquainted with the
different "external" forms of Kirghiz in use
among different native speakers,
    . that of getting acquainted, through parsing,
with the "internal" structure of a language which
still remains outside the main stream of interest
of most linguists and even that of Turcologists.
    For the Turcologists, texts have been
presented in a historical/geographical
perspective (with a few chronological disruptions
due to the irregular acquisition of new
documents).
    For the beginners, texts were selected
according to their difficulty - from primers to
historical documents.
    In order to make parsing easier and more
rational, systematic reference has been made to
the only existing studies to my knowledge
available in the West:
    1) Guy IMART: Le Kirghiz, (Publication de
l'Université de Provence, Aix-en-Provence 1981),
2 vol.
References to this work will be given hereafter
as K + the number of the paragraph where
grammatical explanations can be found, and
    2) Guy IMART: Le Chardon Déchiqueté
(Publication de l'Université de Provence, Aix-
en-Provence, 1982), quoted hereafter as C + the
number of the page where sociolinguistic
explanations are given.
    Lexical and idiomatic problems have been dealt
with in reference to a third, indispensable
instrument for the study of Kirghiz: K.K.
Yudakhin: Kirgiz-Oruscha sözdük, (Sovetskaja
Enciklopedija Basmasi, Moskva 1965), quoted
hereafter as Y + the page number. Only those

(rare) lexical units which cannot be found there have been given in the "Comments" sections.

When the original is in Arabic script, each Kirghiz text has been provided with a transliteration into Latin script.

A translation into English is given for all texts. As a working instrument, this translation aims more for literal accuracy (in order to facilitate parsing) than for literary elegance.

Great care has been taken to provide the student with an interpretation of the original as faithful as possible - a commitment which was not always easy to uphold, especially with early, pre-literary texts. In such cases, the authors have sought the advice of various native speakers and turcologists but accept full responsibility for the variant ultimately proposed.

Last but not least, it goes without saying that the choice of texts has been dictated primarily by their linguistic and/or sociolinguistic interest, secondarily by their value as representative samples and never with any, approving or disapproving, view on their ideological content - a vain endeavor at best since most of these texts speak for themselves.

Roughly speaking, Prof. Hu prepared most of the literary and lexicological comments and myself most of the grammatical, historical and sociolinguistic ones.

At a time when their goal is in sight despite a 14,000 kms separation, the authors want to express their deep gratitude to all those who participated in this truly international and interdisciplinary "joint venture" and more particularly to:

P. Abolgassemi - Lecturer in Persian, Universite de Provence
A. Altay - Radio Liberty, Munich
N.A. Baskakov - Institut Tjurkologii, Moskva
L. Bazin - Institut d'Etudes Turques, Paris
E. Boev - Sofia University, Bulgaria
S. Crisp - Institute for Bible Translation, England/Sweden
B. Cvetkova - History Department, Sofia University, Bulgaria
P. Destenay - Chinese department, Universite de Provence
R. Dor - Institut d'Etudes Turques, Paris

N. Dutrait - Chinese Department, Universite de Provence
J.A. Hudayar - New York
K. Karpat - History Department, University of Wisconsin
A. Khoudjet el-Khil, Islamic Department, Universite de Provence
R. Mantran - Turkish Department, Universite de Provence
O. Pritsak - Ukrainian Research Institute, Cambridge, Massachusetts
Ch. Zheng - Chinese Department, Universite de Provence
    Special thanks are due to Mrs. V. Aymard (English Department, Université de Provence) who presided with great tact efficiency and patience over the "englishing" of the following text, freeing thus the authors from their doubts and qualms, as well as to Professors Denis Sinor and J.R. Krueger and to the Indiana University Research Institute for Inner Asian Studies for their decisive help in Publishing this Reader.
    I would also wish to thank April Younger whose word-processing skills and patience were instrumental in the preparation of the final copy.

HU Zhen-hua
Kirghiz Department
The Central Institute for National Minorities
Peking, CHINA

Guy G. IMART
Slavic Department
Universite de Provence
Aix- en -Provence
FRANCE

THE ALPHABETICAL SYSTEMS OF KIRGHIZ

(PHONOLOGICAL/PHONETICAL VALUES AND TRANSLITERATION)

The transliteration systems used here are different from those adopted in K and C, except for Arabic (cf. AFNOR NFZ 46002) and Chinese (Pinyin).

Russian words have been transcribed in conformity with the norms of the Library of Congress.

The following synoptic table provides the necessary grapheme-to-grapheme correspondence between all alphabetical systems successively used for putting Kirghiz into writing.

Cyrillic ë is /yod + o/, ю /yod + u/, and я /yod + a/. The following Cyrillic graphemes are used only in foreign (mainly Russian) loanwords:
В = v; Ф = f; Ц = ts; Щ = shch, Ъ = "; Ь = C+' (cf. K-547).

Kirghiz long vowels are indicated by V+V, but Radlov has V̄.

The following Arabic graphemes are no more in use, except - rarely - in loanwords:
'ayn: ع (translit. as ε); ۋ = v w; ṭ'ā: ط ; fā': ف ; ḫā: خ ; ẓā': ظ ; ḥā': ح (translit. as x); ṣād: ص ; ḍād: ض ; d̲āl: ذ .

PHONEMES	CYRILLIC SCRIPT		ARABIC SCRIPT	
	Official	Radlov's	Reformed	Xinjian
p	П		پ	
b	Б		ب	
t	Т		ت	
d	Д		د	
s	С		س	
z	З		ز	
š	Ш		ش	
k + back V	k	ʼk	ڠ	
+ front V		К	ک	
g + back V	Г	ҕ	غ	
+ front V		Г	ک	
č	Ч		ج	
ǰ	Ж	j	چ	
j	Й	i	ي	
l	Л	back Л / front ľ	ل	
r	Р		ر	
m	М		م	
n	Н		ن	
ŋ	Ҥ		نڭ	
a	а		ا	
ï	ы		ى	
u	у		و ʼ (ا)	ʼو
o	о		و	
e	Э initial / е non initial	ä	ﻪ ◦ (ا)	
i	И	i	ى (ﻪ)	
ü	Y	ÿ	وʼ (ﻪ)	ۇ
ö	ө	ö	ﻪوʼ) ~(ﻪ)	♦

| LATIN SCRIPT | | | TRANSLITERATION |
1927	1928 - 41	Xinjiang	
p			p
	B	b	b = [ɓ ~ ʙ]
t			t
d			d
s			s
z			z
ʒ	ş	x	sh
	q (Fuyü:)	G	k (q)
	k	g	(ҡ)
ʔ	ꝙ		g (ġ) = [ʁ]
	g		(g)
ɾ	c	q	ch
c	ç	j	j = [dzh]
y	j	y	y =
l			l
r			r
m			m
n			n
	ŋ	ng	ng
a			a
ə	ь	e	ı (Turkish ı)
u			u
o			o
e		ê	e
ˇ	i		i
ˇu	y	ü	ü
ˇo	ө		ö

A - THE PRE-LITERARY LANGUAGE

a) THE ORAL TRADITION: THE MANAS EPIC I-A

> "In a way, scanned speech is the
> written language before written
> language" *

Two excerpts:

I-A(a)
The "Exhortation" (Jomok bashı), as recorded
from Jüsüp Mamay, a native of the Cherik clan,
born in 1919 in Ak-Chü (Xin-jiang) and a well-
known 'Manaschı' (bard).
Published first in <u>Shınjang Qırgız Adabiyatı</u>,
Urumqi, 1981, I, pp. 12-14 **

I-A(b)
"The Handing-over of Power to Manas", as
published in <u>Manas</u> (I-chi bölüp, I-chi kitep),
Kırgızmambas, Frunze 1958, p. 59...

* P. Chaunu: Histoire et décadence, Librairie
Académique Perrin, Paris 1981, p. 148.

** cf. Hu Djen-hua et R. Dor: "Manas chez les
Kirghiz du Xinjiang", <u>Turcica</u>, 1984, XVI, pp. 30-
50.

╼╾╼╾╼╾╼╾╼╾╼╾╼╾╼╾╼╾╼╾╼╾╼╾╼╾

«ماناس» ءبۇسۇنان ۆزۈندۈ

ماناسچى جۇسۇپ ماماي

جوموق باشى

•.....•....•...ي ايتايىن بااتىر ماناستى،

انىن ارباقتارى قولدوسو،

ايتقانىم جالعان بولبوسو،

جارسى توكۆن جارسى جن،

جاراندار دىن كوۈنۈۆۈن،   5

جانىندا تۇرعان كىشى جوق،

جالعانى مەنەن ئىشى جوق،

كوبۇ توكۇن كوبۇ چىن،
كوپچۇلۇكتۇن كوونۇۇچۇن.
10 كورۇپ تۇرعان كشى جوق،
كوبويتكون مەنەن ئۇمشى جوق.
كۇبۇلدوتۇپ سەرداساق،
كوپچۇۇكتۇن كوونۇ توق.
اتاعاردىن جوموعۇ.
15 ايتباي قويسوق بولوبۇ؟
اتادان مىراس نر بولاۇپ،
ايتىپ قالدىق وشونۇ،
ايتىپ قۇمار جازباساق،
ايعابابىز تولوبۇ؟
20 باباعاردىن جوموعۇ،
باشتاساق كەلەر ورولۇ،
باشتاباساق بولوبۇ؟
بابابىزدان قالعان كەپ،
باارى جوقتون ۇلۇۇكەپ،
25 بايىشچەكەي سۇلۇۇكەپ،
بايىرقدان قالعان كەپ،
بالدارى جىناپ العان كەپ.
ۇرۇقتاپ ۇلام ونگۇن كەپ،
ۇرماتتاپ ەلى كونگۇن كەپ.
30 ۇلام بىركە جۇققان كەپ،
قارلار ايتىپ بەرگەن كەپ،
قالتىرباي، بىروون تەرگەن كەپ،
قانچا قەلىم وتودا،
قالباي بىركە كەلگەن كەپ.
35 اسماندا كۇندون نۇردۇۇ كەپ.
الامدەن اشقان سۇردۇۇ كەپ!

ایدان اچقی تۆرعان كەپ،
ایتا بەرسە تۆگونبوس،
ارتی ارتىنان تۆۇعان كەپ.
40 اندان بەری قاراتا،
الدا نەچە ەل ۆتتۇ،
ازار تۆمون جىل ۆتتۇ،
پئلگە مئنگەن شەر ۆتتۇ،
بەلگى كۆچتۇ مر ۆتتۇ،
45 ۈنۈتۈلباي مستەلىپ،
ماناس ۆڭدۈۇ مر ۆتتۇ،
وشۇندۇن بەری قاراتا،
تۇۇ ۈيۈراپ جەر بولدۇ،
جەر جمرتملمپ ساي بولدۇ،
50 ساي تۆبۈلۈپ ساز بولدۇ،
اتابىز ماناس سـیاقتۇ،
ايتلىپ كەلگەن از بولدۇ،
چۇل قوزعولۈپ كۇل بولدۇ،
كۇل تۆگۈنۈپ چۇل بولدۇ،
55 ادسـرلۈۇ جەرلەر قوو بولدۇ،
اق مۇڭگۈلۈر بۈزۈلدۇ،
ارستان ماناس جۇمۇعۇ،
ازىرعا چەيىن سۇزۈلدۇ.
بۈزۈدان ماناس جۇمۇعۇ،
60 بۈزۈلباعان ەل مەنەن،
بۈرعاناقتۇۇ جەل مەنەن،
بۈزلۈلداي تاتتۇ تئل مەنەن،
بۈزۈلۈقباعان ۆن مەنەن،
اجداالرداي سۆر مەنەن،
65 ارقراعان سەل مەنەن،
اچ قیقىرىق چۇۇ مەنەن،

اسمان جارعان دۇۇ مەنەن،
ات جـارىشىپ كەلگەن سوز.
ارتىشان قۇزۇپ جەتـە الاي،
70   اسمائدا بۇلۇت شاشقان سوز.
سىر دەڭىزىن كەچكەن سوز،
مردىن بەرمەت شۇرۇسۇن،
اقىندار اندان تەرگەن سوز.
بالدان تاتتۇۇ نەتكەن سوز،
75   بـاارىن باسىپ كەتكەن سوز.
بەلەس بەلدەن بوروۇندوپ،
بەش ۇدۇرعۇپ ۇتكون سوز.
بۇل جومۇقتۇن ئچىندە،
اياری كوپ البى كوپ.
80   ايتىپ بولعۇس سالتى كوپ،
ابايلاپ ۇق قالايىق،
اپرتىپ ايتقان قالپى كوپ،
التىنى كوپ كۇمۇش كوپ.
اتتانسپ جووعو جۇرۇش كوپ،
85   جاپا! تارتقان قوردۇق كوپ،
جانعا باتقان زوردۇق كوپ،
شامالدان كۇلۇك اتى كوپ.
سايدىرسپ ئىمەي ساتى كوپ
وق وتبوكون تونۇ كوپ.
90   وبۇل توودوي چوكۇ كوپ،
وق تشتەمەي انتى كوپ،
ويدۇ ـ قايقى مانىتى كوپ.
چىرپىق قىرقماق شارتى كوپ،
ايتىپ ادام بئلگەسىز:
95   جاراعىنىن اتى كوپ.
اقىلى كوپ ۇلكۇ كوپ.

ناسااتی كوپ كۇلكۇ كوپ،
تواكوچۇ كوپ ئزچی كوپ،
جەجەنی كوپ، سىنچی كوپ،
100 بوز تورعويدوي ببجراپ،
پوورۇزمداپ ايتقان مرچی كوپ،
اي ـ الالمعا سيباغان،
ارتۇردۇنەچــەن مۇلكۇ كوپ،
بەندەدەن ارتقان ۇزۇ كوپ،
105 پەربدەن العان قزی كوپ،
قۇبۇلۇپ كەتمەي ئشی كوپ،
ولبوي جۇركون كشی كوپ،
ساعدورۇ التىن قۇشۇ كۇپ،
سايداعى قۇمدان سانى كوپ،
110 ساقتالىپ كەلگەن ۇشۇ كەپ.
قىرعىزدىن ساقتاپ كەلگەنى،
سالتاناتتۇ قارا كوك.
جۇز جەلدا بولوت جەر جاعى،
ەلۇۇ جەلدا ەل جاعى،
115 ۇلام ۇقىا ـ ۇقىام دەپ،
ۇققان ساين كەپ جاعى.
نەچەن زامان وتىودا،
مىكربەي كەبى بوزورىبوي،
ەمگەچەكتى ەلگ جاعى،
120 مۇنۇ مىداي تاشتايلى،
انداي بولىو قالايىق،
جولىورىس ماناس وزۇنۇن،
جومبوغۇنان باشتايلى.

"Manas" eposunan üzündü
Manaschı Jusup Mamay
Jomok bashı

1   E...e...e...aytayın baatır Manasti
    Anın arbaktari koldoso,
    Aytkanım jalgan bolboso,
    Jarımı tögün, jarımı chin,
5   Jarandardın köönü üchün,
    Janında turgan kishi jok,
    Jalganı menen ishi jok,
    Köbü tögün, köbü chın,
    Köpchülüktün köönü üchün.
10 Körüp turgan kishi jok
    Köböytkön menen ishi jok.
    Küpüldötüp ırdasak,
    Köpchülüktün köönü tok.
    Atangardin jomogu,
15 Aytpay koysok bolobu ?
    Atadan mıras ir bolup,
    Aytıp kalgan oshonu,
    Aytıp kumar jazbasak,
    Aygababız tolobu ?
20 Babalardin jomogu,
    Bashtasak keler orolu,
    Bashtabasak bolobu ?
    Bababızdan kalgan kep,
    Baarı jokton uluu kep,
25 Bajchechekey suluu kep,
    Bayirkıdan kalgan kep,
    Baldan jiynap algan kep.
    Uruktap ulam öngön kep,
    Urmattap eli köngön kep,
30 Ulam birge jukkan kep,

p.2
    Karılar aytip bergen kep,
    Kaltırbay biröön tergen kep.
    Kancha kılim ötsö da,
    Kalbay birge kelgen kep,
35 Asmanda kündön nurduu kep,
    Aalamdan ashkan sürdüü kep!
    Aydan achık turgan kep,
    Ayta berse tügönbös,

Arti-artinan tuugan kep.
40   Andan beri karata,
Alda neche el öttü
Azar tümön jıl öttü
Pilge mingen sher öttü
Bilegi küchtüü er öttü,
45   Unutulbay estelip,
Manas öngdüü er öttü.
Oshondon beri karata,
Too upurap jer boldu,
Jer jirtılıp say boldu,
50   Say kubulup saz boldu.
Atabız Manas sıyaktuu,
Aytılıp kelgen az boldu,
Chöl kozgolup köl boldu,
Köl tügönüp chöl boldu,
55   Adırluu jerler koo boldu
Ak mönggülör buzuldu
Arıstan Manas jomogu,
Azırga cheyin sozuldu;
Buudan Manas jomogu,
60   Burulbagan el menen,
Burganaktuu jel menen,
Bulbulday tattuu til menen,
Buulukbagan ün menen,
Ajidaarday sür menen,
65   Arkıragan sel menen,
Ach kıykırık chuu menen,
Asman jargan duu menen.
At jarıshıp kelgen söz.
Artınan kuup jete albay,
70   Asmanda bulut shashkan söz.
Ir dengizin kechken söz,
Irdın bermet shurusun,
Akındar andan tergen söz.
Baldan tattuu netken söz
75   Baarin basıp ketken söz.
Beles belden boroondop,
Besh udurgup ötkön söz.
Bul jomoktun ichinde,
Ajarı köp aldi köp.
80   Aytip bolgus saltı köp,
Abaylap uk, kalayık!
Apırtıp aytkan kalpı köp,
Altini köp, kümüsh köp,
Attanip joogo jürüsh köp,
85   Japaa tartkan korduk köp
Janga batkan zorduk köp,

Shamaldan külük ati köp,
Sayditip iymey saatı köp,
Ok ötpögön tonu köp,
90 Opol toodoy chongu köp,
Ok tishtemey antı köp,
Oydu kayki manitı köp
Chırpik kirkmak shartı köp,
Aytip adam belgisiz,
95 Jaragının ati köp,
Akılı köp ülgü köp,

p.3
Nasaatı köp, kUlkü köp,
Tölgöchü köp, izchi köp,
100 Boz torgoydoy bıjırap,
Poorumdap aytkan ırchı köp,
Ay-aalamga siybagan,
Ar türdüü nechen mülkü köp
Bendeden artkan uzu köp,
105 Periden algan kızı köp,
Kubulup ketmey ishi köp,
Ölböy jürgön kishi köp,
Sangdoru altın kushu köp,
Saydagı kumdan sanı köp,
110 Saktalip kelgen ushu köp,
Kırgizdın saktap kelgeni,
Saltanattuu kara kök.
Jüz jılda bolot jer jangı,
Elüü jilda el jangi,
115 Ulam uksa-uksam dep,
Ukkan sayın kep jangı.
Nechen zaman ötsö da,
Eskirbey kebi bozorboy,
Emgechekti eng jangı.
120 Munu mınday tashtalı,
Anday bolso kalayık,
Jolbors Manas özünün,
Jomogunan bashtali!

EXHORTATION

1   Ah.... let me sing of Manas the Brave!
    If his ancestor's Manes come to my aid,
    Then my tale is not to be deceptive.
    Half will be truth, and half ballyhoo:

5   I sing to warm all my friends' heart
    No one witnessed when happened then;
    This is no place for spuriousness,
    Much is drivel and much is truth,
    I sing to warm the audience's heart.

10   No living soul ever saw it,
    This is no place for boastfulness;
    So, if we sing in a loud voice,
    We shall fill everybody's heart.
    Our forefathers' tale...

15   Can we really remain silent?
    This epic, bequeathed to us of old,
    If we fail to pass it on,
    And yield not to the urge to sing,
    Could we exhaust our remorse?

20   Our ancestor's tale,
    We'll begin it advisedly;
    If we do not, would it be right?
    O words, bequeathed to us by men of old,
    Words greater than all that existed

25   Words sweeter than the first snowdrops,
    Words handed down from days of yore,
    O words collected by the young,
    O words which grow and multiply,
    O words familiar and worshipped by the
       people,

30   Words that adhere to each of us,
    Words that old men passed on to us,
    Words picked one by one yet none is
       overlooked,
    How many centuries continued to roll by?
    They still go on trickling,

35   O words brighter than the sun in the sky,
    Words whose magnificence outmatches the
       whole world,

Words more radiant than the moon -
One can recite them endlessly:
Each word in turn begets a word.

40   And since these days of yore,
Nobody knows how many people passed
How many thousands of years flew by!
Lions that set up on elephants vanished,
As did sturdy, gallant heroes;

45   Unforgetably unforgotten,
Passed Manas, the soul-subduing knight;
And after,
The mountain crumbled, the Earth came into
    being;
The Earth began to crack and formed a
    river-bed,

50   The river shifted its course and formed a
    marsh.
Likewise, about our ancestor Manas,
Little remained of what was told,
The desert changed and turned into a lake,
The lake vanished and turned into desert,

55   The hills became shallows,
The white glaciers became murky.
But the tale of Manas-the-Lion
Is still told until now.
The tale of Manas the Hero

60   Remains unchanged with his nation,
Whirling-howling as a snowstorm,
Sweet as a nightingale's song,
In a sober, steady voice,
Formidable as a dragon,

65   Thundering as a river in spate,
Roaring in a heart-rending shriek,
With a sky-piercing strident cry
Each word is a gallopping stallion,
In vain following hot on others' heels,

70   Or a cloud that drifts in the sky
And sets sail on the poem's ocean -
Coral pearls of the Song
That bards collect and assemble -
Would a word be sweeter than honey,

14

75   It then crushes all,
      It rages like a blizzard on a mountain
         slope,
      It is a force that sweeps by.
      In this tale
      Are many sorcerers and several giants,

80   A whole array of inexpressible facts.
      O my people, listen carefully!
      There are many extravagant lies
      And much silver, masses of gold,
      Many troopers charging the enemy,

85   Much sorrow-bringing humiliation,
      Much violence that scars one's soul,
      Many steeds too, faster than wind,
      Many obstacles that were overcome,
      Many cloaks that no arrow can pierce,

90   Many grandees, august as Mount Opol,
      Many pledges not even made on a bitten
         arrow,
      Many a devious trick,
      Many agreements sworn on a broken stick;
      Man, upon reciting, becomes an erudite:

95   There are so many names of weapons,
      So many feats and so much wit;
      Many admonishments and much laughter,
      Many a soothsayer and many track-finders,
      Many a fine talker and many connoisseurs,

100   And, wittering like pearly larks,
      Many rhapsodes who embellish their song;
      So many things alien to the world here
         below,
      And how much wealth of different sorts!
      Besides the common herd, many are skilled
         masters,

105   Many brides are good fairies,
      Many feats have unequal results,
      Many people are immortals
      And there are birds with golden feathers
      More numerous than grains of sand in a
         river-bed...

110 And all these words came down to us,
Preserved as the Kirghiz' treasure,
As a stately black stallion -
It takes a century for the ground to
  revive,
And fifty years for a people to come back
  to life.

115 The more you hear this tale, the more you
  wish to hear it,
Its words sound new as you hear them again;
No matter how much time flies by
Without waning or growing old,
It remained ever fresh until now.

120 But let us leave it at that,
And as things stand, o my people,
About Manas-the-Tiger himself,
Let us begin the tale.

16

TEXT 1-A(a)TEXT 1-A(a)

COMMENTS

Style

       This passage, in Jusup Mamay's poetic ver-
sion, is one of the most popular in the whole Manas cycle.
       The versification system is simple and
'classic', based on a fixed number of syllables
(usually 7 or 8 in the recitative, sometimes 9 -
cf. line 2 - in the transitional passages) with a
caesura after the fourth or the fifth syllable.
Rhymes are usually initial, each verse beginning
with the same sound (from line 1 to line 27: 3A,
4J,6K,6A,7B, etc.). However, a complementary and
complex system of internal and/or final (consecutive or alternate) rhymes, of rich alliterations
and repetitions as well as the recurrent use of
labial/non labial or front/back vowels gives the
bard much freedom. He can thus underline in each
passage the most appropriate rhythm.
       He is even free during each performance
to adapt it in accordance with
  - those passages of the Epic he chooses to
recite (each time inserting them at a different
place),
  - his own corporal attitudes and the musical
accompaniment he likes best (a 'manaschı' always
is a mimer and a musician),
  - his own intonational pattern, intonation in
oral (pre-literary) Kirghiz being pivotal for a
correct understanding of simply juxtaposed sequences.
       Such freedom in the handling of a basical-
ly unstable text explains many of the difficulties
encountered upon translating excerpts from Manas.
These texts do not only display a great wealth of
morphological or lexicological archaisms, of eth-
nographic realia with no exact equivalent in
Western languages, of comparisons and associations
of ideas hardly understandable to the non-initia-
ted. Since a bard always may, at will, add or
transfer or omit a verse or a series of verses,
the 'junctures' which thus inevitably result often
appear as syntactic fault lines, as breaks in the

linguistic and logical continuity of the phrase.
      This is most probably what happened on
line 71 and 94, for example. Such a break can be
camouflaged easily during an oral performance,
but becomes obvious in a written version.
      In this respect, the texts included in
this Anthology, because they are given in chronological order, allow us to become aware of one of
the basic transformations consecutive to the sociolinguistic shift from an almost exclusively oral
tongue to a written language - and that is the
growing importance of the syntactic/logical factor.
      Unfortunately, the gradual disappearance
in now currently published versions of the Epic of
these syntactic/logical gaps signals generally a
parallel decrease in the authenticity of the texts.
When these gaps lack almost entirely (as in text
1-A(b) and contrary to text 1-C), it means that
the recorded, oral version has been 'revised' by
some 'redaktor' - and no one can tell then what
were his criteria, nor what was the exact extent
of his 'sollicitude' for the modern reader. Cf.
for example in 1-A(b)-12 an obvious russianism:
Manjurya.

      Note the succession of, and the opposition
between, those passages which are essential to the
development of the tale and the 'purple passages'
(for ex. lines 23-39) which are for the bard what
a solo is for the musician.
      Cf. text XVI for comments on the Arabic
alphabet used here.
      Some difficult morphological and lexico-
logical points are discussed below:

1. 19: aygababız: our remorse. Corresponds to
      Soviet literary Kirghiz aykap → aykabıbız:
      malice (Y-30)
1. 62: tattu: lit. tattuu : sweet cf. 1. 74.
1. 63: buulukbagan: lit. buulukpagan. Here: not
      'to make jerky movements' as in sov. lit.
      kirg. (Y-164 under buuluk-) but, as in the
      Issik-köl dialect: to stammer, to mumble +
      Neg.: in a steady voice.
1. 80: aytıp bolgus cf. Y-142: what cannot be ex-
      pressed. This 'gus' suffix is improductive
      in lit. kirg. (cf. buzulgus: unbreakable,
      inviolable; K-1186 and Von Gabain: - u+suz
      pp. 72-78.
1. 88, 91, 106: saydırıp iymey, ok tishtemey,

kubulup ket<u>mey</u>. Most probably, the Neg. suffix
with an initial m + a Gerund form.
The problem here is twofold:
- the m- form is archaic and would be termed
today 'not typical for Kirghiz'. It may have
been kept in the Epic for metrical reasons.
- in modern lit, kirg. as well as in Old
Turkic a Gerund cannot appear as a determiner
cf. A. von Gabain: Alttürkische Grammatik,
O. Harrassowitz, Wiesbaden, 3° Auflage, 1974,
p. 122: "Ganz selten findet sich dies Konver-
bium scheinbar auch als Attribut, also Nominal, ein Gebrauch, der wohl als ein Rest aus
einer älteren sprachlichen Gewohnheit zu be-
trachten ist").
l. 90: Opol: a mountain south of Kashgar.
l. 91, 93: ok tishtemey antı; chırpık kırkmak
sartı: Y-564, also ok tishtemish: 'the biting
of the arrow' and Y-880: chırpık ~chıbık kırk-:
to split a twig. Two traditional ways of
making a solemn oath, sealing an agreement.
Ok tishte<u>mey</u> (with a Neg. suffix), as opposed
to ok tishtesh(ip): Y-739) could signal a further degree in disloyalty: the 'traitor' has
not even accomplished the sacred act of the
'biting of the arrow' so that he could more
easily betray his oath - revealing thus pre-
meditation (an interesting interpretation
kindly suggested by Prof. L. Bazin.)
l. 92: Y-561 gives oyk<u>u</u>-kaygı.
l. 101: poorumdap: from rus. for<u>m</u>a, reinterpreted
as 'beauty'.
l. 108: sangdoru corresponds most probably to lit.
sangoor: Y-634.
l. 112: kara kök: this 'Homeric epithet' - dark
grey (as the coat of a stallion) generally
applies to the hero - Manæs - and not, as here,
to the Epic itself. It may also mean (Y-418)
dauntless. Although there is nothing strange
in comparing the Epic to a stallion, this is
probably one more example of an imperfect
'juncture'.
l. 119: emgechekti: Y-951: emg<u>i</u>chekti.

CONTENT:

The monumental Manas Epic is for the Kirghiz
at the same time a national Iliad and Odyssey, a
lyric poem and a classical tragedy, an encyclopae-
dia, the Sacred Book of national Wisdom, a historical chronicle and many other things. Reciting it
triggers the same instinctive emotion as singing
the national anthem elsewhere and the less 'rational' the verses, the stronger their emotional
appeal. In this respect such passages as:
1. 42   Azar tümön jıl öttü
         Pilge mingen sher öttü, etc.
should be compared to Pushkin's 'Ruslan and Liud-
mila':

> У лукоморья дуб зелёный,
> Златая цепь на дубе том...

But the Manas Epic is more than a national
sacred myth: it testifies to the durability and cohe-
sion, against all the odds, of a 'small' people
who knows that, without it and the keen sense of
self-awareness it provides, its name and its life
might turn at any time into one more historical
wreck and become at best a lifeless item in some
treatise on Ethnology. P. Chaunu writes (Histoire
et Décadence, Paris 1981, p. 213):
"Because we have two memories, a biological
memory and a cultural memory linked with language.
As we are not masters of our biological memory,
everything logically depends on our capacity to
keep, to communicate and to transmit the cultural
heritage. The loss of memory (...) is, together
with death, Sapiens sapiens' great existential fear.
Remember the Maori bard's terrible dread at the
beginning of Victor Segalen's 'Les Immémoriaux'
when memory fails him. This dread, which resembles
the dread of death, is common to all custodians of
the community's saga before writing existed."
The manaschı's knowledge, inviolable in an
inviolated traditional society, evaporates when
the latter breaks - or is broken - down. In this
respect, R. Dor's testimony on the dismal wreckage
of the Manas Epic among the (ex-)Afghan Kirghiz
(Central Asiatic Journal, 1982, vol. 26, n° 1-2,
pp. 1-55) is telling.
In both Soviet and Chinese Kirghizstan and in
spite of various dramatic episodes (in 1949-52 in

the USSR, during the 1966-76 'Cultural Revolution'
in the PRC) when this great cultural monument was
subjected to a harsh, totally unscientific and
injurious criticism, the bard's words have proven
to be true: 'Elüü jılda el jangı' and serious
efforts have been made to save this knowledge and
this art. Manaschı have been recorded, their texts
have been and are still being edited, eliminating
thus, at least for part of the Epic*, the risk of
sinking into oblivion. But, as stated above, a new
danger arises out of our very sollicitude - and
technology: that of petrifying what was a living,
breathing, growing organism.
        Cf. also text XV.

*: What is the exact extent of this epic cycle?
The figure usually cited (around half a million
verses) is purely hypothetical. Chinese specialists
insist on the fact that to the three parts known
in the USSR (Manas, Semetey, Seytek) five other
should be added: Kenenim, Seit, Asılbacha-Bekbacha,
Sombilek and Kigitey.

МАНАСКА ТИЗГИН БЕРИЛИШИ

I   Камбарбоздун үйрүнөн
Кармап алып тогузду,
Баарын бирдей сойдуруп,
Жер очогун ойдуруп,
5   Ата уулдан түк койбой,
Алтайлыктын элинен
Алды Манас чакырып
Азы менен көбүнөн.

Башка уруктан маңгул бар,
10   Баатыр Жайсаң дагы бар.
Күлдүр, Калдар беги бар,
Манжурия журтунан
Бала Мажик эри бар.
Баштадан Дөгөн кары бар.
I5   Андан бөлөк бул жакта
Алтайлыктын баары бар.
Алчын, Үйшүн, Найман бар,
Аргын, Кара кожо бар,
Абактардын ичинде
20   Айдаркан баатыр кошо бар.
Абасы Бай башында,
Жакып менен Акбалта
Дагы олтурат кашында.

Ушул жерде Бай экен
25   Күмүш сакал карысы,
Күтүп турган чагы экен,
Күлдү кыргыз баарысы.
Эми абасы Бай кеп баштайт,
Кеп баштаса, деп баштайт:
30   "Төгөректүн баарынан
Түрө келдиң калайык,
Айлананын баарынан
Арбын келдиң, калайык.
Эсен кандан кол келип,
35   Эчен кайта мол келип,
Ортодон чыгып жоо болдук,
Ошо камаса, кайдан соо болдук.
Тукум калбай кырылып,
Тумшугубуз катпайлык.
40   Түюкта минтип жатпайлык.
Ургаачыңды күң кылып,
Таң атпаган түн кылып,
Эркегиңди Эсен кан

Таманга басып жүн кылып,
45 Сатыкка салып кул кылып,
Сандыкка салып пул кылып,
Санабай малың айдатып,
Сайкашканды жайлатып,
Айдап жүрүп кырбасын,
50 Ар тарапка сайлатып.

"Баарыңарга эп болсо,
Бай абаң айткан кеп болсо,
Камданаган болуп калалык;
Кашыңа келсе зордукчу,
55 Каяша кылып туралык.
Балдар, башчысы болбой марыбайт,
Баш—аламан жарыбайт.
Камдуу журт жоого кор болбойт,
Жарактуу киши зар болбойт
60 Жайыт болбой мал болбойт,
Жабылса душман жан койбойт.
Калкалайым десең жаныңды,
Калдайган журтум биригип,
Көтөрүңөр каныңды.
65 Кандуу журт болуп калалык,
Калаба кылса кытайлар,
Кайрат кылган бололук.
Өлүп калсак кокустан,
Бир чукурга тололук.
70 Тирүү болсок баарыбыз
Бир дөбөдө бололук.
Бели катуу бирөөнү
Бек көтөрүп коёлук.
Калкка кабар салалык,
75 Кайраты бар бирөөнү
Кан көтөрүп алалык.
Калмак, кытай кол салса,
Каруу — жарак асынып,
Каршысына баралык."
80 Бай аба мындай дегенде,
Жандын баары күңгүрөп,
"Жакшы кеп!" —— деп дүңгүрөп.
"Бара келде эп экен,
Бай абаң айтар кеп экен!
85 Кана чыгыңарчы, каныңар,
Чыгым тозор жаныңар!

Чыңданыңар баарыңар:
Беттешкен жоого белдүүңөр,
Айтарга сөзү эмдүүңөр
90 Өткүр чечен тилдүүңөр,
Өкмөт жөнүн билчүүңөр!"
Улуу-кичүү баарысы,
Ушуну айтып салышты.

"Кан боломун калкка, - деп,-
95 Кандай болсо чыдаймын,
Калак башкарган наркка" - деп,
Айтар адам жок болуп,
Акылдашып токтолуп,
Калың журт карап калганы.
100 Бая аң уулаган сексен төрт
Калкка көзүн салганы.
"Камалышың кандай?" - деп,
Бай аба элден сурап калганы.
Боз балдар анда кеп айтат,
105 Болгон ишти эми айтат:
"Аң ууладык баарыбыз,
Арада жок силердей,
Ак сакалдуу карыбыз.
Көпчүлүк сени билбейбиз,
110 Биздин көтөрүлгөн каныбыз!"
Айнакул бала кеп айтат:
"Ай, калайык, - деп айтат, -
Чеге минген Ак башты
Ай талаада сойгонбуз,
115 Манас деген баланы
Кан көтөрүп койгонбуз.
Биз кан көтөрдүк теги, - деп -,
Биз көтөргөн каныбыз,
Аяк менен башыңа,
120 Карың менен жашыңа,
Келер бекен эби?" - деп,
Саламаттын Айнакул
Сан журтка айткан сөзү бул.

Кары, жашы күңгүрөп,
125 "Каныбыз Манас болсун" - деш
Калктын баары дүңгүрөп,
Шапырт айта салганы,
Көпчүлүк топук кылганы.
"Карап турган калайык,

```
130  Көрүп турат көзүңөр.
     Кан кылбайбыз дегениң
     Азыр чыксын сөзүңөр.
     Айлыңдан арман калбасын,
     Атап коюп кандыкка,
135  Артынан калбаа салбасын.
     Ата уулудан барсыңар,
     "Аны кылбайт элек" – деп,
     Арманың ичте болбосун!"
     Акбалта айтып мындай кеп,
140  Айгайды журтка салганы.
     Арыстан Манас жаш бала
     Жыйынга басып барганы:
     "Менин астымда болгон ага жок,
     Ажал келсе, дабаа жок.
145  Артымда иним жаш жатыр,
     Акылга дыйкан көй баатыр
     Айтууга менде сөз жатыр.
     Сууруп алар азаптан,
     Сүрү катуу тууган жок,
150  Карып калган жакыпта
     Кайрат кылар шайман жок.
     Казак, кыргыз бир тууган,
     Кан болуучу жан болсо,
     Бирөө чыксын бел бууган!
155  "Талаада атым сойдум, – деп,
     Кан көтөрүп койдум" – деп,
     Өз напсиме тартпаймын.
     Тоодой токонаалатты
     Өз мойнума артпаймын.
160  Келип турган көпчүлүк,
     Калмагың бар, маңгул бар,
     Казагың бар, кыргыз бар,
     Бел байлаган болсун, – деп,
     Мени боштон койсун" – деп,
165  Бала Манас айтат кеп.


     Калк камалып калганы:
     "Ырас айткан сөзүң, –деп
     Кан болууга бул журтка
     Ылайыксын өзүң" – деп,
170  Көпчүлүк ичин жыйбады,
     Өңгөсүнүн баарысы
     Бир-бирине кыйбады.
     Калктын баары күңгүрөп,
```

Кайраттанып дүңгүрөп,
175 "Көпчүлүк ою тынды, - деп,
Көтөрөлүк канды" - деп,
Алты кулач ак кийиз
Астына алып салышып,
Арыстан Манас баланы
180 Акбалта менен Айнакул
Жетелешип алышып,
Казак, кыргыз чогулуп,
Калмак, маңгул жабылып,
Ак кийизге Манасты
185 Олтургузуп алганы.
Журт көтөрүп калганы,
Алиги турган жыйынды
Жети айлантып барганы.
Ороздунун көк туусун
190 Эми Жакып оболотуп аштады,
Тойду жаңы баштады.
Онолду Жакып карыя,
Абалкы бейлин таштады.
"Кайрат кылчу душманга
195 Манаска бийилик бердик" - деп,
Келгендер кетти жайына
"Кандуу журт болуп калдык" - деп.

THE HANDING-OVER OF POWER TO MANAS

1   From the herd of Kambar's favourites,
Having caught nine stallions
He had them all slaughtered
And had a hearth dug out.

5   Without neglecting in the least fathers and
       sons
From the (whole) Altay people
Manas invited
Everyone, young and old.
From other clans, there were Manguls,

10   And so there was Jaisang the Brave,
Küldür as well as Kaldar-beg;
And from the Manjur nation
There was Majik, the young hero
And at their head the old Dögön.

15   Besides all these in this same place
There were the Altays all,
The Alchyns, Üyshüns and Naimans,
Argyn and Kara-hoja
And among the Abaktars

20   Was Aydarkan the Brave in unison
With Bay the Patriarch seated at their
      head;
Jakip with Akbalta
Sat by his side as well.
And in this place Bay was indeed

25   The old man with a silver beard.
It was the time indeed awaited long
The entire Kirghiz multitude -
Now Bay the Patriarch took the floor
And beginning his speech, he started by
      saying:

30   "From all precincts around
You flocked hither, o my people,
From the surroundings all
You came in a body, o my people!
A party sent by Esen khan assailed us

35 And once more, after so many times before,
        attacked in force
    While enmity broke out among ourselves.
    If we are all at daggers drawn, where will
        the cure come from?
    May we not be exterminated without issue!
    May our mouths not harden!

40 Let's not linger in this dead-end!
    Turning your wifes into his slaves,
    And making nights that have no dawn
    That Esen khan transforms your sons
    Into sheer felt, trampled underfoot,

45 Into bondmen meant to be sold
    And puts the money in his chest.
    He carelessly drives out your cattle,
    Murders your best leaders.
    Let him not stamp and hound us out,

50 Scattering us to the four winds.
    If this sounds right to all of you,
    If what Bay said is serious talk,
    Let us be ready promptly;
    If the oppressor comes near by,

55 Let us dig in and bare our teeth!
    My friends: no leader - no reward;
    People in disarray score no success.
    A provident people is not the enemy's
        laughing stock,
    A man in readiness is not a man in need.

60 There can be no cattle without pasture
        land:
    If the enemy swoops down on us, not a soul
        will survive.
    If thou sayest: "Let's save our souls!"
    My people that has grown so big, unite then
    And choose your khan!

65 Let us be a nation endowed with a khan.
    Should the Kitays pick a quarrel with us,
    Let us march into battle.
    And should be perish suddenly,
    Let us fill the same grave!

70   Should we remain alive,
       Let us all sit on the same hill.
       The sturdiest fellow among us,
       Let us make him our beg.
       Let's inform the whole nation,

75   And the strongest among us,
       Let us make him our khan!
       Should Kalmuks and Kitays swoop on us,
       Let us don our suits of armor
       And rush upon the enemy!"

80   Thus spoke Bay Patriarch
       And all began to buzz
       And hail: "Well said
       A clever thought, indeed;
       Such words are worthy of our Patriarch.

85   Come out now, our khans, assert your
         rights,
       All you dignitaries who paid your share.
       Let all of us brace up:
       Those of you strong enough to pit
         themselves against our foes
       And those of you whose speech is efficient

90   And those of you whose tongue is convincing
         and bold,
       Those of you skilled to rule!"
       Then all of them, young and old,
       Began to quibble and argue.
       But none saying: "I shall be khan over
         this nation

95   I shall hold out, whatever might happen and
         rule as custom has it!"
       Ever came to the fore.
       Having thus quibbled to its heart's content
       The thronging crowd then stood and gaped.

100   Then Bay who for eighty four years had been
         a hunter
       Looked toward the people:
       "What's your predicament?"
       Asked the multitude Bay the Patriarch.
       The youngest lads then took the floor

105 And sketched the matter as follows:
    "We've all been hunting,
    But among us, there is no one like you,
    Our white-bearded elder.
    We do not know your assembly's choice,

110 But our khan, we've chosen him!"
    The young Aynakul then began to speak:
    "Now, my people, says he
    We selected White Head, the stallion fitted
        with a studded saddle,
    And slew it on a lea.

115 Manas, the gallant sire
    We've elected to be our khan.
    We did elect him our khan, he said,
    But this khan whom we have chosen,
    The have-nots and the haves,

120 The elders and the young,
    Will he suit them?" - said he.
    Such was Aynakul's welcome speech
    To the inumerable throng;
    Elders and youngsters create a din:

125 Saying: "Let Manas be khan over us!"
    The whole people in an uproar
    Trumpets in unison,
    And then calms down.
    "O people, thou hast witnessed,

130 Thy eyes can see.
    Let those who say: "We won't make him our
        khan!"
    Express their view right now!
    Let there be no regrets from any of your
        camps
    Regarding this poll to khanhood;

135 Let no quarrel subsequently break out
    Among you all, fathers and sons;
    May no one say: "We should not have done
        that"
    May no resent live in your heart!"
    Having thus spoken, Akbalta

140 Raised the alarm for everyone.
    Manas the Lion, the young brave

Made his way toward the council:
"I have no elder brother before me,
And if Death comes, no remedy.

145   Behind me comes my younger brother -
A distinguished hero, endowed with
   cleverness -
I have something to say:
To get me out of trouble
I have no awe-inspiring kin;

150   Jakıp, who's now grown old
Is no more help to keep the foe at bay.
Kazakhs and Kirghiz are kinsmen;
If someone's apt to be a khan,
Let him speak out who will tackle this
   task!

155   Saying: "I slew my horse on the lea",
Saying: "I chose a khan",
I shall not act selfishly;
A shame as big as a mountain
May I not hang around my neck!

160   The whole nation has come hither,
The Kalmaks, the Manguls,
The Kirghiz and Kazakhs.
So let me take the work into my hands
And act all on my own".

165   So spoke the young Manas.
The crowd surrounds him then
Saying "You're right,
Being the khan over this people
Is befitting to you!"

170   The people does not stint his praise
And no one to the very last
Rebelled against any one.
The whole assembly makes a din
Regaining faith in a loud voice.

175   Having said "The people's mind's now calm
Let us ordain the Khan!"
A six-'kulach' long piece of felt
They spread out before him.
Manas the Lion, the young brave,

180   And Akbalta with Aynakul
       Taking his arm, led him forward
       While Kazakhs and Kirghiz joined in,
       While Kalmaks and Manguls followed;
       And Manas on the long white felt

185   They helped to sit.
       The people lifted him off the ground
       And round the greeting assembly
       Carried him seven times.
       Orozdu's blue standard

190   Jakip then raised and drove into the ground
       And the banquet began anew.
       The old man Jakip livened up,
       Forgot his past worries.
       "So as to face up to the enemy

195   We've handed over the power to Manas"
       Said those who had came upon leaving.
       "We're now a nation with its own Khan!"

COMMENTS

STYLE (Morphology and Lexicology)

l. 1: Kambar: in the pre-Islamic Kirghiz pantheon,
the protector of horses.

l. 2: K-1602, 1680   l. 58,59: Y-336
l. 11,14,19,20: K-2840   l. 60: K-1579
l. 19: abaktar or arbaktar?   l. 65: K-1590
l. 24: K-1786   l. 67: K-1382
l. 24,26: K-2051   l. 68: K-1739,1866,
                                      2455
l. 28: K-1799   l. 81: Y-468
l.31: K-1680   l. 86: Y-741
l. 34,35: K-1602   l. 88,89: Y-951
l. 37: K-1866   l. 89: K-1311
l. 38,39: Y-765   l. 93: K-1778
l. 40: K-1890   l. 97: K-1391
l. 48,49: Y-622   l. 99,101,103,etc.:
                                      K-1239
l. 52: K-1866   l. 103: K-1712
l. 55: K-1747   l. 115: K-1347

l. 113: chege mingen: the exact meaning of chege
is a moot point. If it is not a hero's name,
cf. the typological parallelism with Manas on
l. 115 , it could be
- either: chek- (Y-854 VII or V): to harness
or to pull away from a post = to untie, hence
'the horse he was about to ride'
- (suggestion of a native speaker): "Chege -
demek mıktalgan eer. Eerdin üstünö ten koyup,
anı mılk menen chegeleyt": a studded saddle.
A hide is laid on the saddle and decorated with
studs (köör chegele- : Y-854).

l. 116: K-1712,1741   l. 147: K-1818,1270
l. 121: K-2059   l. 150: Jakıp: Manas'
                                      father
l. 125,126: Y-203   l. 152: K-1324
l. 134: K-1895   l. 156: K-1741
l. 137: K-1226,2035,(1243)   l. 157: Y-552
l. 145: K-1815   l. 160: K-1747,1588
l. 146: Y-205   l. 164: Y-149,K-1895

l. 161,162: The 2nd pers. possessive suffix with

a collective proper noun has approximatively
the same hypocoristic value as +ke (K-1045).

l. 189: Orozdu: Jakıp's father and Manas' grand
father
l. 192: K-2455   l. 194: K-1218
l. 197: K-1778

CONTENT

It is probably not by sheer chance if this
excerpt so much resembles several passages from
the Orkhon Inscriptions. The last verse: Kanduu
jurt bolup kaldık almost literally corresponds to
l. 9 on the Kul Tigin's Inscription 'East side):
'qaγanlïq bodun ärtim': We used to be a people who
had its own khan (cf. T. Tekin: A Grammar of Orkhon Turkic, Indiana University Publications,
Bloomington, 1968, pp. 233/265).
The persistence over about 1,000 years of
the same theme - the necessity to gain access to,
and preserve independence through statehood is
remarkable in history.
The relative scarcity of Arab loanwords and
of Islamic references (l. 18: kojo; l. 174: ajal,
dabaa) indicate that the proto-text of this passage
however frequently re-edited later on, dates back
probably to the 18th century.

b)   EARLY   WRITTEN   DOCUMENTS   1-B

A letter from Karabek-uulu Jantay (a clan chieftain in Northern Kirghizstan) to the Russian military administration of the West Siberian 'liniya'.

First published by V. Ploskikh: U istokov druzhby, Izd. Kırgızstan, Frunze 1972, p. 80-81.

Probably written in the 1820s.

Письмо кыргызов западносибирским властям

TRANSLITERATION   TEXT 1-B

First deciphered and transliterated by Prof.
Emil Boev and B. Tsvetaeva (Sofia); revised and
completed by Prof. Hu Zhen hua.

Cf. below for an analysis of the graphic system

1   ayrub alursızmu üch jüz orus bilen qazaqqa
     suranchı baturni

2   qosub buyurub bersengiz. eger bizge ol aytqan
     bilen suranchı bat...

3   (ur)nı bersengiz, jawlo bolgon qırgizların
     chabıb bermesem, saqalım kesilesün. oshol
     waqıtta

4   bizni ayurub alsangız ol ölgenche padshahga
     xismat qilmasam jantay atım qurusun.

5   soltı bolsa, hem suranchı baturni inilerin
     tüshürüb algan. sarıbagısh bolsa hem chapub

6   berürmin. chaprastı bilen tınaydın biri birige
     alıshı araz bolmasqa qolnı tez chıgaringız

7   bul xatnı jazguchu qarabeg oglı jantay möhrimni
     bastım.

1 Айырып аласызбы? Үч жүз орус менен казакка
   Суранчы баатырды

2 кошуп буюруп берсеңиз! Эгерде бизге ал айткан
   орус менен Суранчы баатыр-

3 ды берсеңиз, жоолап болгон кыргыздарын чаап
   бербесем, сакалым кесилсин! Ошол убакытта

4 бизди айырып этсеңиз! Ал өлгөнчө падышага
   кызмат кылбасам, Жантай атым курусун!

5 Солто болсо, Суранчы баатырдын инилерин түшү-
   рүп алган, Сары Багыш болсо чаап

6 берермин. Чапрасты менен Тынайдын бир бирине
   алышы араз болбоско, колду тез чыгарыңыз!

7 Бил катты жазуучу Карабек-уулу Жантай мөөрдү
   басным.

Can you separate us? Please order a 300 Russian Cossack-strong (detachment) (to come) together with Suranchı baatır.

If you send us the (above) mentioned Russians together with Suranchı baatır, may my beard be cut off if I do not bring to heel those Kirghiz who rebelled. At that time, please help us.

If I do not serve the Padısha (the Tsar) until my death, may my name Jantay perish! As to the Solto (clan), they took Suranchı baatır's younger brothers as hostages; as to the Sari Bagısh (clan), I'll annihilate (them myself).

Dispatch rapidly reinforcements before the Chaprastı and Tınay (clans) quarrel.

I, Jantay, Karabek's son, having written this epistle affixed my seal.

COMMENTS

STYLE and SCRIPT:

        This is one of the oldest documents now avai-
lable, written in a language form that can definite-
ly be termed 'kirghiz'.
        Many similar (and even slightly older) 'busi-
ness letters' are known to exist, but they remain
unpublished or buried in various local archives.
        Most probably, the scribe's intention was to
use the only written form known at that time in
Central Asia: the traditional literary 'Chagatay'
language. Note, for example, the use of 'hem': and,
of a Gen. case in -ni (instead of lit. kirg.: nın)
on l. 5, of the interrogative form in m- and such
non-harmonic forms as mohrim, uğli, yazğuchi, etc.
        He allowed however colloquial, informal lin-
guistic features to slip into this hastily jotted
down note, most of which are typically Kirghiz
(initial j-, labial harmony, d- variant of the
/NIn/ suffix (K-417), while a few others would be
called 'Kazakh' in today's terminology: jawlo (lit.
kirg.: joola), qosub (lit. kirg.: koshup). For
yazğuchu, cf. K-1221.
        The very 'inacurracy' of the Arabic script
(cf. below) allows however these heterogeneous peculiarities to remain unnoticed, each reader having
the possibility (especially as far as vowels are
concerned) to decipher the text in accordance with
his own personal phonetic and harmonic system.
        This means that the ethnolinguistic (morpho-
phonological) and stylistic heterogeneity of the
text, thus obvious from the encoder's viewpoint,
is perceived by the decoder as a mere stylistic
diversity: the one resulting from the juxtaposition
of petrified/learned formulae (l. 7) and colloquial
turns of speech (l. 3).
        This in turn points to the necessity of avoi-
ding what would be a typical anachronism. The kind
of language used here should not be interpreted as
'bad' Chagatay, written by a provincial scribe in-
dulging unconsciously in dialectisms, nor is it an
attempt to 'democratize' an aristocratic, urban

language and even less a conscious effort to shift
from an artificial lingua franca to a 'purer' form
of Kirghiz. No one at that time was aware of what
a 'national' language is supposed to be because no
one imagined there should be a bilateral correspondence between an ethnic group (they all were non-
discrete and became delimited in an authoritarian,
bureaucratic way only a full century later) and a
given set of phonological/morphological features.

It seems more correct to say that the professional scribes, because of a common, supra-ethnic
system of education, were then involved (some cons-
ciously and others not) into a dynamic process that
could have given birth ultimately to a 'pan-Turkes-
tanian' koine. The constitutive elements of this
'national' language in the making were, on the one
hand, the underlined learned lingua franca of a scholarly
trained, even if limited, social layer (this element
providing syntactic flexibility, lexicological
adaptability to modernization and a minimum of
standardization) and, on the other hand, a great
variety of colloquial, spoken features of multiple
ethnic and geographical origins which ensured the
expressive ability of the language and warranted
its 'natural' character.

The sole, but important, justification for
the use of the very inacurrate Arabic script in
writing down such a language was precisely the need
to 'conceal' the still apparent junctures and make
the diversity of all its constituents appear as
blurred as possible.

Of course, only extra-linguistic factors
(more diversified, wider economic relations between
various parts of the country, a web of schools, an
administrative system using this language - in a
word: national statehood) could have ultimately
welded together all these elements and rooted the
new linguistic form.

This is precisely what the Soviet linguistic
policy prevented through the implementation of
various local, 'literary' languages. In any case,
this text does not exemplify a 'geological' section
showing a pre-literary stratum, but rather a biological section showing a linguistic embryo before
a forced termination of pregnancy.

A second point is worth noting. Even if only
a minute fraction of the population - professional

scribes/clerics in charge of the main manaps' rudi-
mentary administration - was able to read and write,
it is a non-innocent inacurracy to state that "Kirghiz was not a written language before 1917".
 V.M.Ploskikh himself in various works (cf.
Kirgizy i Kokandskoe Khanstvo, Frunze 1977) speaks
of written documents and mentions small personal
'libraries' containing 'kurjun's (leather-bound
manuscripts). Up to now, each new 'archeological
expedition' brings to light written documents not
only from long forgotten local archives, but also
from family treasure-troves in distant, God-forsaken
places.

 The Persian handwritten variant of the Arabic
script used here comprises 22 graphemes:

آ	initial a or e	آگر eger	
ب	initial b and final p		
پ	irregularly, initial p bilen	پلان plan = but باتور batur	
ت ظ	not always clearly distinguished		
ج	j ج : ch	س :s ش : sh	
ک	k,g	گەسىلسون kesilsün	
ع	instead of غ : [ɤ]	ف : q	
ن and ن	at the end of a word: n	ﻫ : h	
نک	ligature n + k: ng		
او	o,u,ö,ü (initial); elsewhere: w		
ی	i,ı (often not written in the middle of a word)		
ي	i, y		

 Of course, transliterating a text written in
such a system always implies a certain amount of
interpretation as well.

CONTENT:

 Although extremely short, this text illustrates very accurately the mechanism which presided

over the conquest of Northern Kirghizstan.

At the beginning of the 19th century, the
Kirghiz people - an already linguistically and
culturally cohesive force - is rapidly recovering
after the 18th century Oirat invasions. These Oi-
rats have been defeated by the Chinese Qing who
now control Kashgaria. After an unsuccessful revolt against them in 1825, Northern Kirghiz migrate
toward the North West through what is stil a
'Power vacuum zone'.

However, as soon as 1813, they are in contact
with the advanced posts of the Russian 'Sibirskaia
Liniia'. Russia at that time is busy waging wars
in Europe. She is not yet able to take advantage
of the very favorable conditions resulting, first,
from the Kokand/Qing feud over the control of the
eastern slopes of the Tien Shan and then from a
'gentlemen's agreement' between these two powers
at the Kirghiz' expense. But the prey has been
identified and selected.

Waiting for more propitious times, the Russians shift to a policy of slow implantation based
- as shown by this document - on local selective
alliances and manipulation of tribal rivalries.
Twenty five years later, around 1850, this system
has already evolved into a covert protectorate, the
'pacified' tribes being used against the 'rebels'.

Such tactics make the most of a double evolution inside the Kirghiz tribes themselves:

- a social evolution resulting from a gradual
shift of power from the 'biy's (hereditary chieftains) to the 'manaps' which add economic wealth
(they own numerous herds of animals and control
poor people), military force (they are able to keep
a small 'army') and the old baatır's (heroes)
prestige to their newly acquired clanic legitimacy.

- a political evolution: this concentration of
power - parallel to the on-going process of ethnic
integration - aims at securing for the Kirghiz people full independence from whatever alien forces.
This process clashes however with an ancient tradition of tribal and even clanic autonomy.

As a result, intertribal rivalries are exa-
cerbated and tribal wars flare up, opposing, especially, the two most powerful tribes: the Bugus and
the Sarı Bagısh.

Each warring party looks for outside help -
which can come only from Kokand or Russia - thus

ruining the initial project of national consolida-
tion and reinforcement and playing into the hands
of those against whom each one intended to guard
oneself.

Paradoxically but logically, when the external pressure mounts (for example, during the Kokan-
dese expedition under Madali Khan), the tendency
toward unification - through submission of the
weakest - increases (cf. the 'Declaration of Independence' by Ormon Khan around 1840 and then by
Alimkul) while 'foreign' ties (with Russia) evolve
into a de facto protectorate ('officialized' in
1862) at the same rhythm as Kokand sinks into a
terminal 'Time of Troubles'. Russia's strategy here
is parallel to Britain's (in India) or France's
(in Morocco) and appears as an early version of
the modern 'domino theory'.

Whether the sender of this letter can be
equated with the 'Jantay, Karabeg's son' mentioned
in a poem recorded by V.V.Radlov in his Proben...
remains a moot point.

The Sari Bagish confederation of tribes under
the Shabdans' 'dynasty' was the first one to accept
Russian vassalage in 1862, but also the first one
to revolt in 1916 (cf. T.R.Ryskulov: Kirgizstan,
Moscow 1935).

For a while, toward the end of the 1870s,
British and Ottoman diplomatic circles seem to have
envisaged the creation of a buffer-state - a kind
of Greater Afghanistan before the term existed -
which would have included most of Kirghizia. But
in 1895 at the 'Colonial Conference' in London,
the three competing Empires put an end to the Scramble for Asia by jointing, along boundaries which
meet in Central Pamir, one of the last 'white spots'
on world maps - an alleged 'res nullius' which,
for the Kirghiz, meant unity and autonomy.

The severe condemnation of intertribal squab-
bles and of the subsequent 'Call to the Russians'
was going to be a favorite theme for most of the
19th century akins as well as for the first representatives of the young Kirghiz intelligentsia at
the beginning of the 20th century (cf. D. Aitmambe-
tov: Kul'tura Kirgizskogo naroda v vtoroi polovine
19-ogo veka i nachale 20-ogo veka, Izd. Ilim,
Frunze 1967).

It is interesting to note that this text shows no sign of Islamic influence. At the very same time neighboring 'Kazakhs' were petitioning Nicolai I not to build any new mosque on their territory (cf. V. Cherevanskii: <u>Zapiski po delam very musul'man-sunnitov</u>, Skt Petersburg 1906, p. 34).

44

b) EARLY WRITTEN DOCUMENTS TEXT I-C

Beginning (Jomok bashı) of the epic poem 'Semetey'
(the second part of the Manas Trilogy) in Borzu-
uulu Moldobay's manuscript, dated 1864. (The
copyist most probably was a native of the Talas
valley)

From the 'Fond Rukopisey' of the Institut Yazyka i
Literatury Akademii Nauk Kirgizskoy SSR.

مه‌سه‌له پیسماناتای بوترفرز

1	ایلیدارکی ایلیدسیوی مجدماغی آته ‌ی کیلاتارو ای رالو	17
2	معناآنیوب مرکانذ میہ تودمدینی ینیے قو رادکا	18
3	مجدماتانلیب رتیشودمیپ تودرزاتعی جبورو ر دوکی	19
4	باطردسبہ روغلادونی نجاگاظ کرتیسے عدانے بور ار مو	20
5	ایلیارکی ایلیدسیوی مناذری یادقعو رغلاسنا فوا بیسا	21
6	مجدماتابرلعانی روا ی یس بجری نیگودکتان یسا	22
7	جبردوب تالعانی نوغایعیہ بعتمانیں اردع بطا یسیح	23
8	غمدناع ربولعابپ تالعانذ دریبہ اوعوغارہ مسلدنینی	24
9	لنزیعیت بلکتاغر غواوبنینگ کولومونی یوعتورکانغندری	25
10	بومجیبسیارہ سبدکانینگ موردغو نوغایعتان نوورغم	26
11	رشتمای تالعانی بطا یس غوای یلایت یبلیہ بومیس	27
12	کود تونلون کدبج بجیہ کردرغبکیلگارہ مندرک یوعکا	28
13	کوی تاستعم سنداونیزداوغو جارمی تونلوں ھارسو جبیہ	29
14	ھابسندرباتعرفانی بنشرینوعکا میراسدا ردسیہ نوزارو جبوری	30
15	آباجایہ فرانسدانسبب ارقدمہ خالقیہ نوغای دسیب اوعردما	31
16	سبمرونتاسبداسیب ادقدمع ماللیتے نوغای دسیب اوعنا	32

Qissa-i Sematay bot(u)rd(u)r

1 Ilgerki eldin jomaǧɪ
   Munɪ aytub b(e)rgenden
   Jomaq qɪlɪb aytsun deb
   Batɪrdɪn oǧlɪ Kök jaldɪ
5 Ilgerki eldin Manazɪ
   Jomaq bolǧan awasɪ
   Jerdeb qalǧan Noǧayqa
   Künam bolub qalqanɪ
   Sharɪǧat pilgen Xudaynɪng
10 Bu s(e)bebden b(e)dening
   Jetmay qalǧan chamasɪ
   Köbi tögün köbi chɪn
   Köy qasqanɪn köni üchün
   Janɪnda turǧan kishi joq
15 Aba jan qara tashdan keb uqtum
   S(a)rɪ tashdan keb uqtum
   Aytsa kelet oralu
   Ad(a)mdɪn nesi quradɪ
   Ad(a)mzatqa jorodu
20 Aytsa köni bolamu
   Jaw qachurǧannɪn awasɪ
   Jeri keng qol talasɪ
   Jetmayt ad(a)m chamasɪ
   D(a)rs oquǧan m(o)ll(o)nɪng
25 Qol(u)nda joqtur kaǧazɪ
   Nurǧu Noǧay qanqorǧo
   Xuday bilet chɪn bolsa
   Körüb kelgen b(e)nde joq
   Jarmi tögün jarmɪ chɪn
30 Jerenlerdin köni üchün
   Xalqɪm Noǧay deb uqtum
   Saltɪm Noǧay deb uqtum.

This is the Tale of Semetey the Hero

1   This is the tale of the people of yore:
Rather than keeping on narrating it,
Let us sing so as to make a tale,
Of the Grey-Maned, the son of a hero:

5   Manas of the people of yore.
The rumor (of his deeds) has become a tale.
To those Nogays who settled down
This has become doubtful;
To God who knows the shariyat

10   And therefore to a simple mortal,
It remains unfathomable.
Part is fancy and part is truth.
(I sing) to please the initiates.
There was no witness then.

15   I've heard it from mylord Black Scalp,
I've heard it from mylord Red Scalp.
When I recite, it'll be the perfect time.
Which man ever stood aloof (from it)?
It has been intended for all human beings.

20   When it'll be told, can it satisfy them?
His fame puts the enemy to flight
His land is the steppe of Kengkol;
(But) human shrewdness cannot reach that.
(Even) the learned who attends lectures

25   Had no paper at hand (to write it down).
For the Hero of the Nogay clan
God knows whether it's true.
No mortal witnessed it,
Half is fancy and half is truth;

30   (I sing) for stalwart lads
I heard that my people is Nogay,
I heard that our customs are Nogay.

TEXT I-C

COMMENTS

Style and Script

The alphabetical system in use here (the di-vāni style) is the same as in Text I-B, the possible confusions being also identical, especially for such vowels as u/ü (written as w, although ڤ is sometimes used in this last case) and i/ı, written as yod:ى . اى irregularly stands for initial e. As far as consonants are concerned, ب is b and p; s and t are written س or ص/ت or ط; ش is sh (no example in this passage).

Even more clearly than in I-B, the language used here tends to be a 'neutral', supra-ethnic form of 'Chagatay'. But this general framework is adapted, at each linguistic (lexical, phonetical, morphological) level to the actual peculiarities of both the narrator's and the copyist's own speech.

Both are undoubtedly Kirghiz - hence the initial j, the Gen. in -din (instead of -ning) which contrast with such 'learned' or 'bookish' forms as Plur. yerenler (instead of erender), oğlı, joq or the many non-harmonic forms.

On the other hand, and since we know that Moldobay was a native of Northern Kirghizia, other 'spoken' features such as final -s (1. 6: awası, lit. kirg.: abaz), the -z- realization of /(s)I/: K-43,845 (1. 5, 25, but -s-: 1. 6, 22) and the awası form (with a ڤ noting a [ß] realization of /b/ suggest that the narrator probably was a native of the South.

l. 6, 21: awası from abaz: voice; is given by
         Y-17 as "rare".
l. 9: sherɛ at pilgen: for bilgen: a sandhi
         phenomenon.
l. 10: bende: is given by Y-128 as "archaic":
         man as a feeble creature.
l. 8: lit. kirg.: künöm: doubt.
l. 13: köy kashka: from köy: exceptional and
         kashka: (a horse) with a star on his
         forehead: pure; chieftain → remarkable
         Y-417.
         köni: lit. kirg.: köön~ köngül
l. 15,16: Kara Taz, Sarı Taz: the Black/Red-haired

one with ringworm: referential characters in the
Kirghiz oral literature.
1. 17:   oralu: lit. kirg.: orun
1. 21:   jaw: lit. kirg.: joo
1. 30:   yerenlerdin: the initial yod does not
           point to a Kirghiz form in j-. Y-960
           gives eren: strong; hero. This is proba-
           bly a phonetic transcription: K-209.
Note on 1. 2: aytub ber-: K-1682.

Content

        This second part of the Trilogy, dealing with
the feats of Manas' son, is as 'classical' a text
as I-A with which it shares (as it is normal in
oral literature) a great number of interchangeable
'chevilles' (pivot verses, such as 1. 12, cf. I-A(a)
1. 8).
        The interest of such manuscripts is twofold:
 - they provide us with an authentic, untampered
version of the Epic (even if the very use of the
Arabic script makes it impossible for us to restore
its actual pronunciation),
 - they signal among the native intelligentsia,
at a very critical moment (the Russian protectorate
over Northern Kirghizia was established in 1863) a
keen desire to record - and thus save - texts considered to be symbolically important for 'kirghizity'. (Radlov's assembling of 'folkloristic' texts
is slightly posterior).

NB! 1. 13: another possible reading is kök kashka:
        Y-363: grey-haired with bald spots; pure;
        leader.
A native speaker suggests another possible meaning:
confidant (sırdash), hence: initiate. As with eren
(1. 30), one can hesitate: does the bard sing for
the powerful or for the connoisseurs and the dared ?
The last solution is more plausible.

b) EARLY WRITTEN DOCUMENTS TEXT I-D

An excerpt from the "Koshoktor" (Laments), in Proben der Volksliteratur der Nördlichen Türkischen Stämme, Gesammelt und übersetzt von Dr. W. Radloff, V. Theil, Dialekt der Kara-Kirgisen, Sankt-Petersburg, 1885.

This test was collected around 1866.

К У Л   М Ы Р С А

I Бір аі<u>к</u>ырнын ӳрӳ баітал jо<u>ҕ</u>ол<u>ҕ</u>он екäн,
Кул Мырса істägäн екäн. Кул Мырса баі
ды<u>ҕ</u>ына 'кон<u>ҕ</u>он екäн, бу баідын сулӯ 'кы-
сынын коі<u>ҕ</u>уна Кул Мырса кіргäн екäн.
Кыстын атасы бычак мінäн Кул Мырсаны
jӳрöккö салыптыр, Кул Мырса чалкасынан
5 кет іп öлӳп калыптыр. Кул Мырса ӳjӳнö
ка іт па<u>ҕ</u>анда Кул Мырсанын атасы Кубат
ӯлӯн куатістäп. Баідын ӳjӳнö кеісä, баі-
дан сурады. Ба і "jок, кöрбöдӳм" деді.
Оі нош бол<u>ҕ</u>он сулӯ кыс турду, ешіктäн
чыкты су<u>ҕ</u>а барды Кубаттын jолун тосту
ырдады:
10 Кубаттын ӯл'аі Кул Мырса, досӯм,
Чöнтöгӳн тол<u>ҕ</u>он был Мырса, досӯм,
Jатыр едіҥ jес бурап, досӯм,
Jетіп келдіҥ jок сурап, досӯм,
Аламын дедіҥ, алдадыҥ, досӯм,
15 А'к дамбалым 'калдадыҥ, досӯм,
Ал боі салбаі 'кар<u>ҕ</u>ылдыҥ, досӯм,
Сулӯ кысты сар'кылдыҥ, досӯм,
Атäкäн соjуп коіду біläк'аі, досӯм,
Таjып кетті 'кара jӳрöк' аі, досӯм,
20 Саі<u>ҕ</u>ан бір jердäн 'кан чыкт'аі, досӯм,
Чірäніп jатып jан чыкт' аі, досӯм,
Ешіктін асты кӳрöнд'аі, досӯм,
Кул Мырсаны сӳрöнд'аі, досӯм,
Кӳн маҥдаілӯ кӳрöҥ ат, досӯм,
25 Кӳндӳ кöстöп 'каҥтарсын, досӯм,

Кӱ Jӧр атаӊ Кубат'аі, досӱм,
Кӱрӧндӱнӱ̆ аӊтарсын, досӱм !
Аі маӊдаілӱ̄ кӱрӧӊ ат, досӱм,
Аі тӱбӱн кӧстӧп ќаӊтарсын, досӱм !
30 Ал атäкäн, ал Кубат, досӱм,
Кӱрӧндӱнӱ̆ аӊтарсын, досӱм !
Сені ӧlтӱргӧн атäкäн, досӱм,
Тӱбӱнӧ кемä̆ ќалбаі курусун, досӱм !
Сені ӧlтӱргӧн атäкäн, досӱм,
35 Атäкäн jатып ќурусун, досӱм !

Атасы укту, ӱ̆jӱнӧ барды, колду курады,
келді баіды чапты, сулӱ̄ кысты алды. Кул
Мырсаны кунун алды. Кул Мырсанын сӧ̄гӱн
кӱрӧндӱдӧн суруп алды.

K U L   M I R S A

1   A mare (apparently) disappeared from a herd
of colts; Kul Mırsa tracked it. Kul Mırsa
put up at a rich man's camp; Kul Mırsa is
said to have gained admittance to the womb
of this bay's beautiful girl. The girl's
father stuck a knife in Kul Mirsa's heart,
Kul Mirsa

5   fell backwards and dropped stone dead. When
Kul Mırsa did not come back home, Kubat,
Kul Mırsa's father, set out looking for
him. When he came to the bay's camp, he
asked him. The bay said: "No, I haven't
seen him". The pretty girl who had been his
mistress stook up, stepped across the door,
went for water, crossed Kubat's path and
sang:

10   Kubat's son, alas, Kul Mirsa, my friend,
This Mırsa had his pockets full, my friend,
You lived fiddling with copper coins, my
    friend,
You came asking for what is forbidden, my
    friend

15   You messed my white drawers, my friend,
You didn't care for it, and despised me, my
    friend,
You kept the pretty girl languishing, my
    friend,
My father tore up your forearm, my friend,
Your black heart failed you, alas, my
    friend,

20   Blood gushed out of the ripped side, alas
    my friend,
You spread out at full length, your soul
    left you, alas, my friend,
In front of our door is a garbage heap, my
    friend,
Call there for Kul Mırsa, alas, my friend,
His bright-headed brown stallion, my
    friend,

25 Let it rake through towards the sun, my
          friend,
     Your grieving father Kubat, alas, my
          friend,
     Let him rummage in the dunghill, my friend,
     Alas, the broad-headed brown stallion, my
          friend,
     Alas, let it rake through towards the
          bottom, my friend,

30 So this father Kubat, my friend,
     Let him rummage in the dungheap, my friend,
     My father who killed you, my friend,
     Let him dry unburied at the bottom, my
          friend,
     My father who killed you, my friend,

35 Let him lie and dry, my friend,
     His (Kul Mirsa's) father heard (it), went
     back home, assembled troops, came back, put
     the bay to the sword, took away the pretty
     girl. He avenged Kul Mirsa. He dug out
     Kul Mirsa's bones from the garbage heap and
     took them.

TEXT I-D

COMMENTS

The alphabetical system used here (based on the Cyrillic script) is not only V.V.Radlov's own. With minor changes, it is that of the 19th century Russian school of Turcology and has been kept up to now
- as the de facto basis of the 'new orthography' imposed on all Turkic languages of the USSR in the early 1940s (C-160),
- as one of the (both phonetical and phonological) transcription and transliteration systems used in the USSR together with the IPA:
'i' is both i and yod   'ÿ' is ü
In lit. kirg. the distinction e/ä (now noted ə for the Southern dialects) is not phonologically relevant.
ᵕ on a vowel indicates that it is ultra-short and tends toward zero.
Consonants have the same value as in modern Kirghiz (C-25,26) and Radlov's innovations note only phonetic realizations (K-503-516):

/g/	г	[g]	before front vowel
	ҥ		before back vowel
/k/	к	[[k]	before front vowel
	ҟ	[q]	before back vowel
/l/	l	[ɭ]	before front vowel
	л	[ɣ]	before back vowel

'j' most probably stands for j when initial but its exact value between vowels is not clear (it is yod in modern Kirghiz).

This text has obviously been collected in a 's'-dialect zone:
    iстӓ, кӧстӧп, кыс   lit. kirg.: izde, közdöp, kiz

1. 1: Kul̲ Mırsa: in spite of Radlov's ᵤ, Y-547 mentions gül or kül mırza: "This is how

women mourners call the deceased in their
dirge".
ürü: lit. kirg.: üyürsü, where ṻ > üyü:
K-187-192, 202
jogolgon eken: K-1973-1982,2051
l. 2: baidıgına: K-1069
l. 4-5:chalkasınan ketti: to fall back dead K-840
ölüp kalıptır: K-1825,1739
l. 6: kuat istäp: Radlov's punctuation is not
reliable enough to parse this passage:
istäp may be a circumstancial gerund or
an apocopated form of /(I)ptIr/. Kuat
probably stands for kubat > kuu: Y-454.
l. 12: jatır eding. This form has no equivalent
in lit. kirg. K-1952-6.
l. 16: Radlov's notation албаі салбаі should
probably be corrected so as to read: al
boi salbai: Y-139: boy sal: to be nice to
somebody.
kargıldıng: kar + kıl-: Y-345: to humiliate
with a phonetic notation of the sandhi
phenomenon.
l. 17: sarkilding: lit. kirg.: zarık-: to languish
to pine for.
l. 18: soyup koydu: K-1741
l. 19: tayıp ketti: (your heart) slipped away =
failed.
l. 23: süröndöö: to utter the war cry.
l. 32: ätäkän: atakem in the Russian edition of
1886.
l. 33: tübünö: from tüp: the bottom; jer tübünö:
underground.
kemä: kömö, from köm-: to bury.
l. 37: kun: the 'wergeld'.
l. 38: sürüp: lit. kirg.: suur-: to dig out.

Note the complex rhythmic scheme based on
alternate sequences of 8 or 7 syllables culminating
on verse 33 (10 syllables) with the girl's curse.
The exclamatory 'ai' as well as the final
'dosum' are certainly related to the musical accompaniment and the narrator's gestures.

b) EARLY WRITTEN DOCUMENTS TEXTS I-E

Moldo Kılıch:

- Cover of the first edition of Qıssa-i Zilzala,
  Kazan' 1911.

- E. Arabay-uulu's foreword   Text I-E(a)

- Beginning of the poem   Text I-E(b)

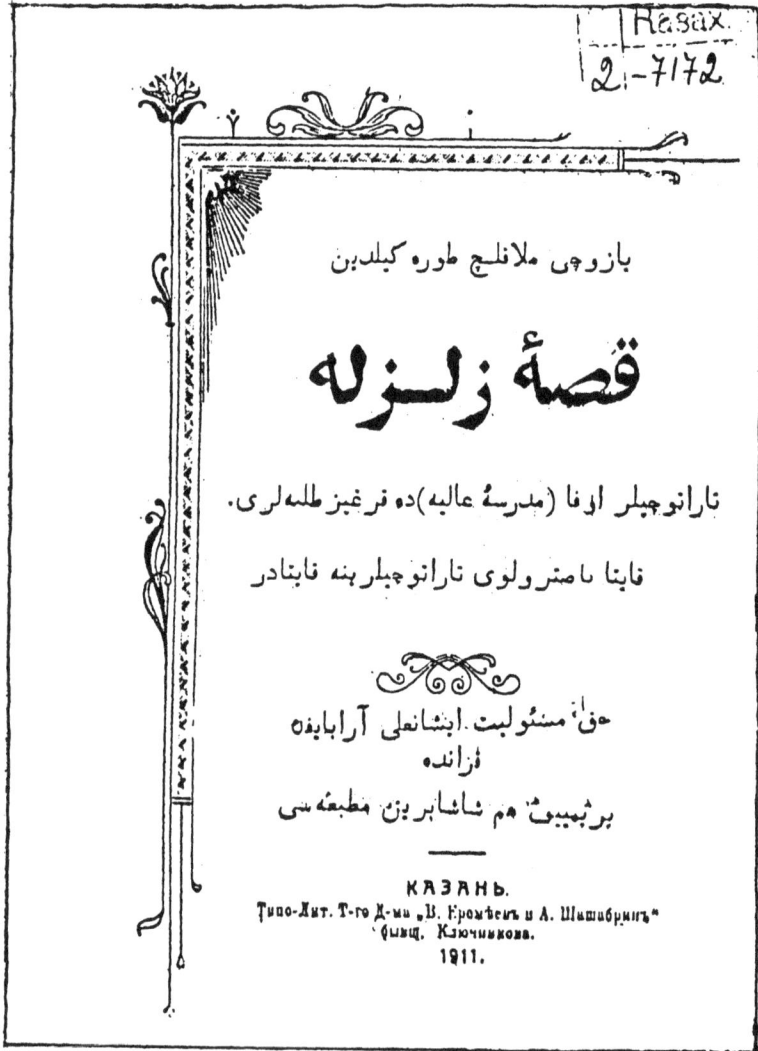

بازوچی ملانلنچ طوره کیلدبن

قصهٔ زلزله

تاراتوچیلر اوفا (مدرسهٔ عالیه)ده ترغیز طلبه لری.

قایتا باصترولوی تاراتوچیلربنه قایتادر.

حقٔ مسئولیت ابشانعلی آرابایده اوزانده

برتیبیت هم ناشابرین مطبعه سی

КАЗАНЬ.
Типо-Лит. Т-го Д-ма „В. Еромѣевъ и А. Шашабринъ"
филц. Ключникова.
1911.

TRANSLITERATION   TEXT 1-E

          Yazuchi mla qlch ţure kildin
          Qşe zlzle
          taratuchilr ufa (mdrse ġalie)de qrġiz
                                        tlbelri
          qaita bastruluy taratuchilrine qaitadr
          hq msulit aishn ġli arabayfde
          qzande
          yrimiif hm shashabrin mţbᵋesi

TRANSLATION

          Author: Moldo Kılıch Törö Kildin
          STORY OF THE EARTHQUAKE
          Distributors: The Kirghiz students at
                  the Galiye medresseh in Ufa
          Second edition by the same distributors
          Editor-in-chief Ishan Gali Arabayev
          in Kazan
          Typography Eremeev and Shashabrin

(in Russian): Kazan'
          Cooperative Typolithography firm
                  'V. Eremeev and A. Shashabrin'
          formerly Klyuchnikov
          1911

TEXT I-E(a)

Foreword to Qissa-i Zilzala
by E. Arabay-uulu

١ آلغی سوز: صاربانش روغندن،

٢ صانی نلدك نونيفندنفارا اوجفار نوريغندىن حققان مشبور

٣ ىابر (آخن) ملانلج نك ٢٠ مه جلدن برلى آخندق منان

٤ كوب غزال بازب جيفارغان ابدى. خيران كتابچەلاردى

٥ باصمه خانه براى بولفاندن مبج برن باصنرالماى قول مين

٦ بازب ئل منان سوبلب جورتقه كورسەتوجى ابدى، بزدك

٧ قرغيزدن باصمه خانه نىكورگان بر آدم بولماىنورغان

٨ ابدى، بز دبر ابلدە جورگاندە. ملانلجنك غزالن اشنوب

٩ براز حيات كوكل كونارلب بوعالمدە نبلر بار ابكانى كوز

١٠ آلدىمزغه كىلوجى ابدى. اوبلاوجى ابدم-قاب سىنى خداى

١١ تعالى بزدى بارق دنباغه جيفارسە نلج نك (سارزمانن)

١٢ باسترسەم خلقىه نراتسەم دجو ابدم ممدە بالدارىغه الفبا

١٣ اوفؤنب بالدار معناسن بيلمى ملا آ كه بونه دىبكان سوز

١٤ دبب صورافانده اوزبىزدە معناسن بيلمى فالفاندن نه

١٥ آبنارىدى بيلمىنچه آلدابفنه برجواب بىرب بالدار كىنوب

١٦ بالغز فالفاندە كوزلر بزدن باشلر چفقان وقتى بولفان

١٧ ابدى. آنااوز نلمزدە بالالر اوفورلق كناب باسنرىسانىاى

١٨ ... دىب. مؤنه بوجلداردە انشاءالله آزى كوب اورنا

١٩ (مدرسهٔ عالیه)دە اوتوب بانتان قرغيز (قزاق) شاگردلرى

٢٠ شول اوبلارمزدى جيفارىغه كرىشكان ابدك؛ ملا نلج

٢١ بزدك حرىكتنى اوعب اوشبو «قصهٔ زلزله» دىبكان غزالدى

٢٢ بازب برب جبارگان، كوز منان كورگان وانه تاريخ

٢٣ بولب فالسون دبب بازغان ابكەن!

1	alği suz: şarbağsh ruğndn
2	şaf tlnng tuniğndn qara quchqar turuğndn chqqan mshhur
3	shair (aḫn) mal qlchnng 20ma jldn brli aḫndq mnan
4	kub ğzal iazb chiğarğan aidi. ḫiran ktabchelardi
5	başme ḫane iraq bulğandn hich brn baştr almai qul min
6	iazb tl mnan suilb jurtqe kursetuchi aidi, bzdng
7	qrğizdn başme ḫaneni kurğan br adm bulmai turğan
8	aidi, bzdir ailde jurgande mla qlchnng ğzaln ashtub
9	br az hiat kungl kutarlb bu almde nilr bar aikani kuz
10	aldimzge kiluchi aidi. auilanchi aidm qab sini ḥdai
11	tɛali bźdi iarq dniɛe chiğarse qlchnng (sar zmann)
12	baştrsem ḫlqme tratsem dchu aidm. hmde baldarğe alfba
13	auqutb baldar mɛnasn bilmi mla ake bu ne dikan suz
14	dib şurağande auzibzde mɛnasm bilmi qalğan-dqdn ne
15	aitardi bilminche alda bğne br juab birb baldar kitub
16	ialğz qalğande kuzlr bzdn iashlr chqqan uqti bulğan
17	aidi - ata auz tlmzde balalr auqurlq ktab baştrsaqai
18	dib. mune jldarde ansha ɛalle azi kub aufa
19	(mdrse ɛalie)de auqub iatqan qrğiz (qzaq) shagrdlri
20	shul auilarmzdi chiğaruğe krshkan aidk; mla qlch
21	bzdng hrktti auğba ushbu "qşa zlzle" dikan ğzaldi
22	iazb brb jbrgan kuz mnan kurğan uaqɛe tariḫ
23	bulb qalsun dib iazğan aikan!

62

ADAPTATION in modern literary Kirghiz

I   Баш сөз — Сарбагыш уруусунан
таза тилдин тунугунан, Кара Кочкор турагы-
нан чыккан белгилүү шайыр акын Молдо Кылыч.
Жыйырма жылдан бери акынцык менен көп ыр
5 жазып чыгарган эле. Кайран китепчелерин
басмакана ыраак болгондуктан эч бирин бас-
тыра албай кол менен жазып, тил менен сүйлөп журтка көрсөтүүчү эле. Биздин кыргыз-
дан басмакананы көргөн бир да адам болгон
эмес эле. Биз элде жүргөндө Молдо Кылычтын
ырын укканда бир аз көңүлүбүз көтөрүлүп,
бу дүйнөдө эмнелер бар экени көз алдыбызга
10 келүүчү эле. Ойлочу элем, кап, сени кудай
таала бизди жарык дүнүйөгө чыгарса, Кылычтын "Зар Заманын" бастырсам, калкыма
таратсам дечү элем, жана да балдарга алипе
окутуп балдар мазмунун билбей Молдо аке
бул эмне сөз деп сураганда өзүбүз да мазмунун билбей калгандыктан эмне айтарды
15 билимейинче, алдап гана бир жооп берип,
балдар кетип, жалгыз калганда көздөрүбүз-
дөн жаштар чыккан убакыты болгон эле. Ата
өз тилибизде балдар окурлук китеп бастыр-
сак ээ! деп, мына бул жылдарда кудайга
ыракмат азы көп Уфа жогорку диний мектепте
окуп жаткан кыргыз студенттери ошол ойлору-
20 бузду чыгарууга киришкен элек; Молдо Кылыч
биздин аракетти угуп, ушул бу "Жер титирөө"
деген ырды жазып берип жиберген, көз менен
көргөн окуя тарых болуп калсын деп жазган
экен.

TRANSLATION   TEXT I - E(a)

1   Preface: (For being) a native of the Sari
     Bagish clan, thanks to the limpidity of a
     pure tongue, originating from the Kara
     Kochkor encampment, the remarkable poet
     (bard) Moldo Kılıch, during twenty years of
     poetical activity, composed many gazals.
     These dear old booklets,

5   as he was far away from a printing house,
     he couldn't have printed (and) copying them
     out by hand, declaiming them orally, he
     displayed them to the people. Among us,
     Kirghiz, no one had ever seen a printing
     house (and) when we moved about among our
     people, upon hearing one of Moldo Kılıch's
     gazal performed, our heart somehow rejoiced
     (and) everything in this world

10   arose in front of us. I used to think:
     "Bless my soul! If God the Most High
     (could) lead us to a world of light,
     Kilich's 'Time of Sorrow' I would pring
     (and) spread among my people" - I used to
     say. And when we taught the alphabet to the
     children (and when) the children, because
     they didn't know its meaning, "Teacher,
     what does this word means?" asked, because
     we didn't know its meaning ourselves,

15   unaware of what we should say, we gave them
     a deceiving answer, (then) once the
     children were gone, and we remained alone,
     came the time when tears poured out of our
     eyes. "Alas! if only we could publish a
     primer in our tongue!" we would say... such
     were during these years the thoughts which
     began to express those few Kirghiz students
     which studied, God willing, at the Galiye
     medresseh in Ufa;

20   Moldo Kılıch, having heard about our
     efforts, immediately volunteered this poem
     "Story of the Earthquake" and wrote it so
     that events he had witnessed remained
     historical facts.

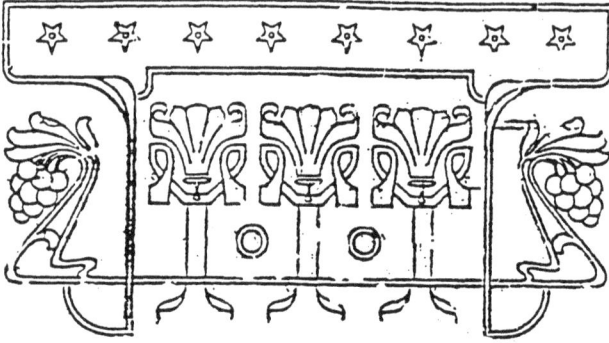

بسم ———— الله الرحمن الرحيم

1 اوّل سوزوم بسم الله 2 آبتدا برسهك سوز موندە

3 كاب چيغاردم جا كندان، 4 كبلگين اوردهك بزنورنه

5 كنابلردە بزبول جدل 6 قورتنج بولار يوز يلدە

7 تور محمد پيغمبر 8 اومت كارمزكوب جانلر

9 اوريلاب قارا آرينگدى 10 آنى مانالدى نارغانلر

11 كوروب كالدك نالابدى 12 اوزاق بشاب بارغانلر

13 صوتون ايتلر كوبابدى 14 سوزگە قولاى عالغانلر

15 ابلگار كبلير بر بزروم 16 اوز ايركنچه بولفانون

17 زار زمانغە سوزبلادم 18 مربزرومو بولجه لون

19 الله تعالى هراشتى 20 اوزك توزوب اوكندەقون

TEXT I-E (b)

TRANSLITERATION

      Bismin alla alrahman alrahym

1 Awal sözüm "Bismin Alla"
   Ayta bersek söz munda
   Keb chygardym jangydan
   Kelgin ördek biz turna
5 Kitablarda bir boljel
   Qorgunch bolar yüz jylda
   Nur Muhammed paygamber
   Ümitkerimiz köb janlar
   Oylab qara artyngdy
10 Aq saqarduu qaryganlar
   Körüb kelding talaydy
   Uzaq yashab barganlar
   Sonun ishler köbeydi
   Sözge qulaq salganlar
15 Aylager keler bir boorum
   Öz erkinche bolgonun
   Zar zamanga süyledim
   Xer boorumo boljelun
   Alla tagaly xer ishdi
20 Özing tüzeb ongdogun

Шапкаттуу жана мээримдүү кудайдын аты менен!

I   Абал сөзүм "Кудайдын аты менен!"
     Айта берсек сөз мында
     Кеп чыгардым жаңыдан
     Келгин өрдөк биз турна
5   Китептерде бир болжол
     Коркунч болор жүз жылда
     Нур Мукаммед байгамбар
     Үмүткөрүбүз көп жандар
     Ойлоп кара артыңды
I0   Ак сакалдуу карыгандар
     Көрүп келдиң далайды
     Узак жашап баргандар
     Сонун иштер көбөйдү
     Сөзгө кулак салгандар
I5   Айлагер келер бир боорум
     Өз эркинче болгонун
     Зар заманга сүйлөдүм
     Ар боорума болжолун
     Алда-таала ар ишти
20   Өзүң түзөп оңдогун

TEXT I-E(b)

TRANSLATION

In the name of Allah, the Benefactor,
the Merciful.

1 My first word is: "In the name of God",
Such is the message I keep on proclaiming.
I declare anew:
Let the ducks come - we are (immortal) cranes;
5 There is a warning in the Books,
Fearsome things (as happens once) in a century
will take place
Nur (radiant)-Muhammad-the-Prophet
(Is) our hope (for) the multitude.
Keep in mind what (you will leave) behind you,
10 You, white-bearded old men;
You have witnessed so much,
(You) who lived on for so long.
Wonderful things grew in number
(For) those who lent an ear to the message
15 (But) my contemporaries' self-conceit (is) a
baneful doing;
I announce the time fixed for sorrow
For each one of my contemporaries.
Allah the Most high! everything
20 May Thou correct (and) put right !

PARSING

Qysa-i Zilzala: a good example of Chagatay-
like, 'learned' mixed tongue in favor among the
literati at that time; it comprises two Arabic
lexical units (qiṣāᵗ: narrative; zilzāl:earth-
quake) syntactically linked through a Persian
izafat construction

Bismin... : a ritual phrase in Arabic

11 awal: ar. awwal = first. Sometimes written
abal/aval/obol/obolu. Present meaning: earlier,
before.

12 ayta bersek: note the Modality form in /A ~ j/
ber- (K-1729). Since ayta ber<u>sek</u> is obviously
the (nominal) determiner of sȫz, the -sek
element cannot be interpreted as /sA/-k (1st
pers. Plur. Conditional), but rather as the
archaic sᵒq ~ sᵒk suffix mentioned by A. von
Gabain ("Deverbale Adjektive") in <u>Alttürkische</u>
<u>Grammatik</u> (3. Auflage, Wiesbaden,O.Harrassowitz
1974, pp. 75,80.)

14 ördök... turuna: Possibly, an allusion to one
of the mythic "copper-winged", "sharp-eared
guards" of Kongurbay (a hero of the Manas Epos)
called (kuu-)ördök, (kuu-)Kulja and (kuu-)
tülkü. But a more earthly (and sarcastic) allusion to the Russians cannot be totally excluded.

15 boljol: the time fixed (by God) for punishment.
Hence: warning

111 talay = dalay: a lot of

115 kylyr?/keler? or a typo for kylym ?: deed,
action - or century, world ? cf.J-488. This
verse is not clear:
a) Ilger keler bir boorum = my predecessors =
(relatives coming before)
b) Ilger kylym bir boorum = my relatives from

the last century
c) Aylager kylym (l 16) bir boorum = cf. the
translation above.
The syntactical construction would then be:
... bolgonun ... bir boorum (inversion)
bir boorum : my close relative, my people

119 Alda taala: ar. Allah taⁱālā, same meaning.

This is certainly the most difficult text. In
    fact, many native speakers of Kirghiz confessed
    that they could hardly understand it and the
    translation proposed above remains uncertain:
    l 4,6,15-16 . This is not only due to the
    lexical and morphological archaisms, but mainly
    to an 'asyntactic syntax', the logical links
    between the verses being secured (orally) by
    intonation rather than through linguistic units.
    Moreover, an effort is necessary to reconstruct
    both the author's philosophy and the historical
    circumstances which prompted him to write these
    verses. Cf. Comments below.

Besides the usual inaccuracy in rendering most
    vowels, it is interesting to note the author's
    (or the Tatar printer's ?) inconsistency in
    noting the initial /j/ which is given as ⋗ in
    jangydan (clearly j) and boljel (l. 3,5,18) but
    as ⁚ (/y/?) in l. 6.

COMMENTS

STYLE and SCRIPT:

These texts provide a good example of the
graphic system used in Kazakhstan/Kirghizstan at
the turn of the century among the 'learned', i.e.
among those people who had studied at the Tatar-
speaking medressehs of Ufa, Kazan or, to a lesser
extent, in Orenburg.
        Basically, the typographical set in use here
is the same as the one used in Ottoman Turkey or
for Crimean Tatar. The Arabic alphabet has been
kept in full, as well as the two 'Persian' graphemes پ : p and چ : ch. ng is rendered through
a three-dotted kaf instead of the nun + kaf liga-
ture. Typically 'Arab' graphemes such as 'ayn, ḥa,
ḫa, fa which are useless in Turkic for lack of
corresponding phonèmes have been kept in Arab
loan-words.
        Consonants:

ب	: p and b	ج	: j	ر	: r
ط ت	: t	د	: d	ز	: z
ص س	: s (cf. Texts 1-B,C)			ش	: sh
ل	: l	م	: m	ن	: n
ك	: ng	ع	: 'ayn		
ق	:[q] ↘			ك	:[g]↘
ك	:[k] → /k/			غ	:[ʀ]↗ /g/
ح	:[h] ↗				

        Vowels:

ٱ	: a	ي	: i,ı,y	و	: all
ه ه	: e	ى	: final i		labials
					+[w/β]

        A further distinction among front/back and
high/low labials (u,o,ö,ü) is irregularly and indirectly suggested through the use of a prefixed

alif and/or through such oppositions as qaf versus kaf. But the vocalization of the text, especially of the final (suffixal) segments is incomplete or even lacking.

A comparison between the transliterated text and the modern vocalized version of it (which, for a given native Kirghiz reader probably did not change much since that time) gives a good idea of the extreme inadequacy and gratuitous complexity of this traditional system: it had at the same time too many graphemes (all the emphatics are useless) and too little of them since no distinction was made between labials and between i and ı.

One can quote in this respect a well-known Arabist's jest: 'You have to read in order to understand, but you must understand in order to read'. Besides, one must count also with orthographical/ morphological irregularities (1. 12, 17: baldar/ baladar), a more or less successful tendency to imitate now the Chagatay and now the Kazan Tatar written norm and some (conscious or unconscious) 'corrections' made by the Tatar-speaking editor or printer.

All these distorting lenses intervene successively between the oral reality and the written text, each one tending to eliminate local peculiarities and to let filter only what is common to all forms of 'Turkic' involved.

The result is as impenetrable as the 1820 or 1864 texts and may look extremely imperfect to a modern reader used to graphic transparency and a normalized morphology.

It must be clear however that, back in 1911, this system was considered (and probably still is by trained intellectuals) to be satisfactory and, therefore, that our modern reaction is an anachronism. The system's very lack of precision in rendering the various writers' phonetic (essentially vocalic) peculiarities allowed the integrated social group of intellectuals with a supra-ethnic ideology to act as if an equally supra-ethnic, integrated 'pan-Turkic' koine already existed or, more exactly, to prepare and accelerate its implementation.

Taking advantage of a lesser than in Indo-European languages linguistic diversification, this system tended to transform a situation of passive linguistic 'joint ownership' (C-69) into an active one and therefore provided for each local (or,

often, social) variant not a clearly contrasted
photograph 'of flesh and blood', but a kind of X-
ray picture, limited to the bare essentials which
each reader was free to interpret and put into
shape in his own image, i.e. in accordance with his
own ethnolinguistic and/or social code.

The cultural/political advantages of this
'semitic script system' in a multiethnic society
have been particularly well defined by Prof. O.
Pritsak (The Origin of Rus', Harvard Ukrainian
Research Institute, t. 1, Cambridge, Mass. 1981,
p. 91-92):

"They (the Arabic, Aramean and Sogdian scripts
- GI) owed their popularity to the fact that they
generally indicate only the type of vocalic pho-
neme involved and, in rendering consonants, often
do not give specific features (e.g. voiced/unvoiced).
Thus, the script could show just the outline of a
word, and the speaker could pronounce it according
to the phonemic rules of his own dialect. Because
steppe empires included speakers of many dialects
and related languages, they found the Semitic
script to be an ideal communication medium".

But this traditional system was also quite
attractive for modern-minded intellectuals: it was
as much prospective, i.e. aimed at the future as
it was tributary of the past (cf. Comments on text
1-G).

It tended in any case to understate precisely
those residual features which would have enabled
us to determine the geographical, social and ethnic
origin of the author: initial suffixal consonant
in /d,t/ resulting from /L/, /D/ or /N/ archiphone-
mes (K-245), verbs conjugated in Modality (K-1478)
or such 'dialectal' features as initial s- (instead
of lit. kirg. z-: sar/zar: K-43).

Under these conditions, it seems rather vain
to try to track down 'Kirghiz' or 'Kazakh', 'Tatar'
or 'Chagatay' elements: the author does not make such
a distinction (in order to do so he would have had
to anticipate   a largely artificial and bureaucratic opposition imposed by the Russians in the
late 1920s and - which is more important - he does
not want to make it).

His intentions, shared by the vast majority
of Kazakh/Kirghiz intellectuals before their 'physical liquidation' in the early 1930s, was:

- to use such a language that could be spontaneously understood and yet sound as natural through-
out the vast territory stretching between the purely 'Tatar' and 'Uzbek' zones,
- and thus to facilitate the formation of a koine
so designed as to integrate most of the local
('dialectal') variants, perpetuate and root these
possibilities of inter-dialectal/inter-regional
understanding which already existed between 'learned'
people, clear the way for a possible and future
linguistic integration on a regional and even pan-
Turkic scale.

The 'ortok til' (C-152) thus aimed at was
supposed to play an active role in Turkestan,
'lifting up' the popular culture and ethnic awareness to the level already reached by the intellectuals instead of downgrading the written language
to the cultural level of the common people and
limiting its scope to their local/tribal/professio-
nal horizon.

Such a lofty aim maybe was surrealistic and
in any case hard to attain: it demanded time and
above all a wide autonomy in cultural and educational matters. The impending historical events were
to show that this was precisely what the Kazakh-
Kirghiz intellectuals lacked or, more exactly, what
they were denied.

x

A few remarks on non-literary forms and
various grammatical points:
1. 1: algı söz: lit. kirg.: bash söz (cf. however
   text XV-B)
      ruğ: lit. kirg.: uruk: clan (cf. 1-G,15:
   ruu)
1. 2: şaf: lit. kirg.: sap (ar. through tatar)
      tlng: lit. kirg.: tildin. cf. also 1. 6:
   bzdng, 1. 8: qlchnng: Gen. in ng: a feature
   common to Chagatay, Tatar and Kazakh.
      turnğudn: lit kirg.: turaginan, from turak:
   encampment
      mshhur: mashhur: remarkable, well-known
1. 3: shair < ar. through tat.: this word was obviously unknown in Kirghizstan and is explai-
   ned through a better known quasi-synonym:
   akın: bard. This was a commonly used pedago-

74

gical method for 'enriching' and standardizing the vocabulary.

jldn: cf. 1. 6: jurtqe, 1. 8: jurġande,
1. 15: juab, but 1. 11: iarq, 1. 16: ialġz,
iashlr: note the irregular notation of one of
the most distinctive features of Kirghiz: the
initial j- (K-54).

1. 4: molla: in spoken kirg.: moldo with a -ll-<
-ld- dissimilation (K-352)
iazb chiġarġan aidi = jazıp chıgargan edi:
(K-1445, 1971)
ḥiran: lit. kirg.: kayran: Y-321.

1. 5: başme ḥane: lit. kirg.: basmakana. Note
on the cover the ar./tat. equivalent: mtbεe
almai: cf. 1. 7: bulmai turġan, 1. 13,15:
the m- realization of /BĀ/: K-2072 is not typical for Kirghiz where it appears only in the
petrified form /mAjInČA/: K-1234.

1. 6, 10: körsötüchü edi, kelüchü edi: K-1217

1. 8: ashtub: lit. kirg.: eshitüp < eshit-: to
hear: Y-970.

1. 9: ḥiat < ar.: life. A chag. idiomatic expression where 'life' is used as an incidence to
'heart': my heart being somewhat lifted as far
as life is concerned.

1. 10:kap seni: Y-342

1. 11: tεali < ar; lit. kirg.: taala: the Most
High
sar: lit. kirg.: zar < pers.: sadness,
sob (cf. below)

1. 12: hmde: xam da < pers.: what's more

1. 13: mlaake: lit. kirg.: moldo ke ~ moldo ake:
K-1045, Y-38.

1. 16: iashlr: an obviously non Kirghiz form.
lit. kirg.: jashtar

1. 17: ata: Y-78.
bastraqai: lit. kirg.: bastırsak, ee
cf. Text 1-D: ai and Y-971.

1. 18: εalle: lit. kirg.: alda: Y-48

1. 19: shaġrdlri: lit. kirg.: shakirt: Y-897.

1. 22: uaqεe: lit. kirg.: okuya.

CONTENT:

Although quite short, this preface by a well-
known pedagogue (cf. Text 1-G) to a famous poem of

the 'classical' poet Moldo Kılich Shamırgan (1866-1917) provides a good introduction to the intellectual life of the Kirghiz intelligentsia between 1898 and 1916, i.e. after the failure of the Andijan insurrection and before the 'Great Headlong Flight'.

The author realistically depicts the harsh material conditions which prevailed then in Kirghizstan and made particularly uneasy all attempts to develop any modern form of intellectual life: a country isolated by huge distances and high mountains from the main cultural centers, an almost complete lack of schools, of qualified teachers, of printing houses, books and even primers, a population unable in its overwhelming majority to read and write, locked in the ghetto of limited dialects and limited contacts with the outside world.

These are typical 'Third World' conditions, as we would say today and the rural teacher's despair around 1910, his sorrowful impotence to cope with a jammed situation contrasting with his passionate desire to 'enlighten' his people corresponds very exactly to the feelings of Ch. Aitmatov's 'First Teacher': little had changed in 1924.

But the important point is that, as stressed by Arabay-uulu, to the "Aufklärer's" striving for cultural preaching corresponded, deep in the masses, a reciprocal and equally unquenched thirst for learning. This will express itself through, and secure the success of, the mainly spontaneous - and not state-inspired - 'Likbez' movement of 1920-1934.

Such a historically induced social 'dead end' and the generalized frustration it develops is, for Arabay-uulu, the logical result of concrete circumstances, the key to the understanding of which is to be found in Moldo Kılich's poem.

This latter author, now considered 'reactionary' and 'decadent' because of his 'historical pessimism', was born at the very time when Kirghizstan was losing her age-old independence. He lived through the difficult years that followed Yakub beg's failure to prevent the dividing out of the once Power vacuum zone during the final stage of the 'Scramble for Asia'; he knew then the long 'Time of Troubles' by which the stormy existence of the Kokand khanate came to an end; he then experienced the relentless drive of the Tsarist army, the filtering deep inside the country of the Tsarist 'chinovniki', the unending and useless insurrections flaring up here and there, down to the blood-filled drama of the submission of the last strongholds in Southern Kirghizia.

Then came, during the 1880-90s, the successive waves of Slavic colonists whose agricultural methods ruined the traditional pastoral life, the modern techniques and ways of life of whom, even when they appealed to the natives and improved their daily conditions, shattered their self-esteem and every aspect of their Weltanschauung. Lastly came, during the last year of his life, the drama of 1916, the repression, the mass 'ürkün' (flight) toward Eastern Kirghizstan.

His whole life thus passed in a heavily wounded, bewildered country, where all traditional (tribal) and rather recently imported (Muslim) values were losing their self-evident, soothing aspects and crumbled while, from all four cardinal points, the mountainous stronghold where his people had so often sought refuge and found shelter, was being invested.

No wonder if, in such conditions (clearly reminiscent of those of today's Afghanistan), the poet adheres to a philosophical trend known as the 'Zar Zaman' (The Time of Sorrow) or 'Zamana' (The Tragic Epoch).

This trend, the initiator of which had been, during the second part of the 19th century, Kalıgul Bay-uulu (1785-1855) and Arstan Bek-uulu (1824-78), presents itself as the systematization of themes linked to Ahmed Yassavi's sufi (mystic) pessimism.

In today's USSR, this trend is presented as expressing the ideology of the old 'feudal' order with its politico-religious illusions and its 'reactionary' hostility toward everything 'kaapır', i.e. kafir.

There is no doubt that the majority's feelings towards the Slavs were probably not running very high, especially in the 'rebel' zones and that Islam (political, theocratic Islam rather than the strictly religious one) appeared to many as a self-sufficient system providing all with an explanation of the national tragedy and a program for overcoming it.

However, if some believed they could find in the first Four Caliphs' ideal a structure more

efficient for that goal than the traditional tribal
squabbling, others, upon considering how the ultra-
orthodox Kokand had collapsed when challenged by
Russia, rejected precisely as inefficient the ideology and the daily way of life of that 'real Islam',
considered to be a dangerous, deceptive cocoon.

Besides, this kadymist form of Islam was a
system yet uncompletely assimilated by the ethnic
body and still felt as partially alien because
suspiciously typical for these half prestigious
and half despised neighbors: the Sarts of the plain
down below.

Another trend was thus developing at the turn
of the century which came from the intellectual
circles of Kazan and Ufa: under the pretence of
religious reform and philosophical modernism, it
promoted an entirely new ideal, more 'nationalist'
and 'öz türk' than Islamic, more oriented toward
European science - and political liberalism - than
toward Oriental wisdom - and despotism, scholasticism -, ready to accept, even from the Slavs,
everything capable of triggering an ethnic Renaissance.

As an up-to-date, secularized pedagogue, eager
to publish the works of his traditionalist master,
Arabay-uulu clearly demonstrates that in Kazakhstan/
Kirghizstan, especially among those people who,
long after their school years, maintained regular
contacts with their Alma Mater through a whole web
of 'jadid' schools, of local 'clubs', through
reviews published in Tatar, Kazakh or Uzbek, there
was no contradiction nor incompatibility between
these two trends.

The prevailing disarray doubtlessly concerned
the solution that should be chosen, but not the
aim to be attained: an ethnic renewal warranting
ethnic autonomy.

This is precisely the goal Arabay-uulu buckles
down to with contagious enthusiasm and with that
kind of 'practical idealism' so similar to that of
France's Third Republic school teachers or Russia's
advocates of 'malye dela' (little steps). We know,
thanks to modern studies*, the 'the masses' heeded
this appeal.

Moldo Kilich's book, published in Kazan in
1911 at a time when Tatars had recently been deprived of the right to preach, teach and publish in
Turkestan in their own language, symbolizes quite

perfectly the emergence among the Kirghiz/Kazakh
intellectuals of an ethnic awareness. It will be
logically completed in 1913 by a Primer edited by
the same Arabay-uulu (cf. text 1-G).

Two other books, Osmanalı Sadıq-uulu's "Tarıh-ı Qırgıziyya" in 1915 and Manap Shabdan's
"Tarıh-ı Qırgız Shabdaniyya" in 1914 were to mark
the modest start of a Kirghizo-Kazakh written language, the ultimate traces of which, after the
Moscow-induced ethnolinguistic restructurating of
the 1920s (C-85) are, sadly enough, to be found
in Text XV.

All of them in some way ask the same agonized
question about the future of a people who did not
know yet with which 'traumatizing stimulation'**
he was going to be confronted once more but who
rightly trusted in its ability to overcome it.

*: D. Aytmambetov: Kul'tura Kirgizskogo naroda v
   vtoroi polovine 19-ogo i nachala 20-ogo vekov,
   Izd. Ilim, Frunze 1967.
**: cf. Carlos Rangel: L'Occident et le Tiers-
   Monde, Laffont, Paris 1982.

c) TOWARD MODERN KIRGHIZ TEXT I-F

Togolok Moldo:

Nasıyat (Excerpt). Published in Moscow in 1925
in the so-called 'reformed' Arabic alphabet.

Compare with a later edition in Cyrillic script:
Togolok Moldo: Chıgarmalar, Kırgızstan Basması,
Frunze 1960, pp. 261-270.

1 قالام آلدم مەن قولغو
قابار بەرەم اوڭ سولغو
قارا تامان كەدەيلەر
جالپى تۈشكۈن اوڭ جولغو!

5 قارا تامان كەدەيسڭ
كەدەيلەرم نە دەيسڭ!
جابىرڭدى اويلونۈب،
جايڭدن قامن جەكەيسڭ!

زالم اوكۈمۆت تۇشۇندا،
10 جابىر كۆردۈڭ اۇشۇندا،
چوكويۇڭ حوق بۇتۇڭدا،
اۇتۇن آلدڭ قىشندا!
جالپى جۈردۈڭ آلدانب!
جايى قىشى جابرقاب،
15 ايلاب جۈردۈڭ زارلانب!

پايدا تاب بايلاردان،
قالغانڭ جوق مالدانب.
اورۇ گۆرۆشتۈن تۇشۇندا،
باينا جۈربە قارمالب!

НАСИЯТ

Калем алам оң колго,
Кабар берем оң-солго.
Кара таман кедейлер,
Жалпы түшкүн оң жолго!

Кара таман кедейсиң,
Кедейлерим не дейсиң?
Жабырыңды ойлонуп,
Жайыңдын камын жегейсиң!

Залим өкмөт тушунда,
Жабыр көрдүң ушунда.
Чокоюң жок бутунда,
Отун алдың кышында.

Жалчы жүрдүң алданып,
Жайы-кышы жабыркап
Ыйлап жүрдүң зарланып.
Пайда таап байлардан,
Калганың жок малданып.
Өзгөрүштүн тушунда
Байга жүрбө кармалып.
Кара таман кедейлер.
Акыл ойлоп камданып,
Алга чыккын шанданып!

Edifying Poem

1   I take the pen into my hand (I put pen to
       paper)
    I proclaim it from the rooftops:
    You, beggars with dirty feet,
    Follow you all the right path

5   You, poor villein with dirty feet!
    Miserable wretch, what do you say?
    You keep turning over your enslavement (in
       your mind)
    Pay attention to your condition! (Be class-
       conscious!)
    At the time of the oppressive rule,

10   You experienced subjection;
    You had no shoddy shoes on your feet
    And yet gathered firewood in winter;
    You worked as a hired man, always deceived,
    Tormented in summer, tormented in winter,

15   Always crying in despair.
    From the rich you drew no benefit
    Although you toiled as a beast of burden;
    In these revolutionary times
    Don't wait on bays as a captive.
    You beggars with dirty feet
    Think it over, be on the alert
    And march forward with majesty!

TEXT I-F

COMMENTS

This poem was written in 1922. Later normalized versions in Cyrillic script slightly differ from
the original in Arabic script:
1. 1: Kalem alam men kolgo / Kalem alam ong kolgo
        I take the pen in my / right hand
The 'men' version provides an alliteration
with ber_em while the 'ong' one sounds more like an
interpolation with 1. 2.
    Conversely, the text in Arabic script is pro-
bably faulty on 1. 13 where jalpı jürüng... has
been corrected into jalchı jürüng... (confusion _ِ_/
؟- ?) in the 1960 text. 'Your whole people' is im-
probable because of d and of 1. 15.
    The alphabetical/orthographical system used
here gives a good example of the early stage of
what was called in the late 1920s the 'modified
Arabic alphabet':
    - all emphatics have been eliminated
    - ng is ﻧﮓ
    - a first attempt is made to match phonemic and
graphemic relevant features in distinguishing, for
example, open and closed labials:
        ﻭﺍ : o or ö   ﻭ' u or ü
    - the system takes advantage of the laws of
synharmony to suggest a further distinction between
front and back vowels:
    1. 2: ﻭ is necessarily o and not ö because _ﻎ_
= [ɣ] > /g/ admits only back vowels
    1. 19: ﻭ'is ü because of ﻪ = e
(cf. Text I-G for the 'kıbachı' system).
    - ı and i are still often omitted, while a and
e are better noted
    This script is thus halfway between the tradi-
tional system and the one later introduced in the
USSR and still in use in Xinjiang (cf. Texts 1-A(a)
and XVI).
    Note some set phrases such as: ong-solgo: to
the right and to the left, i.e. to the two 'wings'
(the traditional subdivision of tribes)= to everyone; or kam je-: to eat the worry = to mind (for
/GAj/: desiderative: K-2043 and A. von Gabain, p.
111). In lit. kirg. /GAj/ is used mainly in corre-

lation with ...ele and not, as here, with an Exhortative form: K-1877.

Some dialectal (northern) features can be detected in the non-normalized version:

ne: lit. kirg.: emne: what

jürbe: non-harmonic, lit. kirg.: jürbö

chokoy: a kind of ankle boot with an upward curved end.

But the main interest of this text lies in its vocabulary and in the author's effort to promote socio-political terms and to find appropriate translations for Russian Marxist catchwords:

l. 4: ong jol, for example, is both the traditional 'right path' to happiness and, ideologically, the 'correct line'.

l. 7: jabır is harassment and 'oppression'

l. 8: jay is position - and social condition. What this whole verse tries to convey is: Be class conscious! (in lit. kirg.: taptık ang-sezimdüü bol)

l. 9: zalım ökmöt is a tyrannical government - and autocracy

l. 18: özgörüsh means 'upheaval' (from özgör-: to change) but is an interesting case also: it corresponds to ar. ınkılap (same original meaning) and was introduced in the early 1920s as the political term for 'Revolution' as well as a Turkic (and Kazakh/Kirghiz) purism in lieu of the pre-1917, 'panislamic' (and Uzbek-Tatar) ınkılap. Nevertheless, it was soon repelled from the politically orthodox vocabulary and replaced by 'revolyutsiya' so as to make it clear that the Great October Revolution had not been a mere upheaval: a clear example of 'orthoglossy' (C-181). Köngtörüsh: a coup, had the same meaning - and the same fate: both are now classified as 'obsolete' by Y-588, 423, but köngtörüsh is still in use in Xinjiang Kirghiz (cf. texts XVI).

The 'classical' 7-syllable verses with initial, final and internal rhymes exhibit only apparent exceptions:

l. 8,9: a reduced diphtong and an ultra-short vowel: ökümöt

l. 16: taap: an 'irregular' gerund of tap-. The evolution of *tabıp into taap is incomplete: one must scan ta + ap (in fact: taβap).

Togolok Moldo (cf. Text II-A), a classic (and
'progressive') poet relies here on one of the traditional genres of religious 'edifying' poetry to
convey a new, revolutionary catechism. The intrusion of political mottos and of a would-be revolutionary jargon testifying to the desire to have an
up-to-date political national tongue contrasts with
the imported, 'Gorky-ist' proletarian inspiration
and transforms, as it happens often in literature
with lofty feelings, a genuine, moving concern for
the God-forsaken ones into a homily.

c) TOWARD MODERN KIRGHIZ TEXTS I-G

Three documents:

- Eshenalı Arabay-uulu's foreword to his <u>Kırgız
  Alipbesi</u> (Kirghiz Primer), Sredneaziatskoe
  gosudarstvennoe izdatel'stvo, Tashkent 1924,
  pp. I,II,III. (4,000 copies)

  Text I-G

- Same document: covers of the first and second
  edition

  Texts I-G(a)$_{1,2}$

- First issue of the first Kirghiz newspaper:

  Erkin Too (The Free Mountain), November 7,

  1924.

  Text I-G(b)

TEXT I-G(a)$_1$

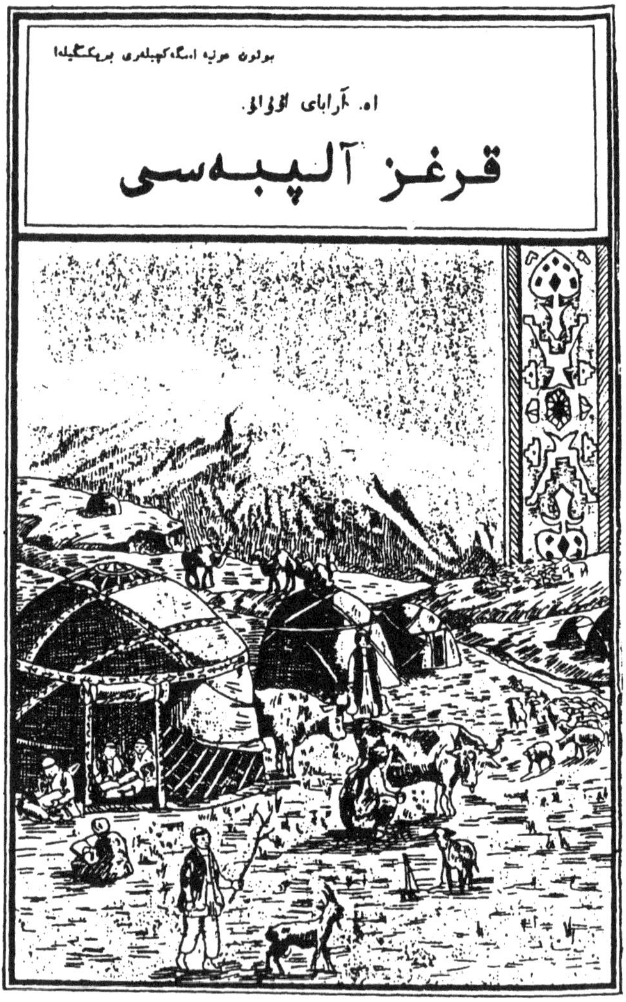

بۇتۇن دۇنیو اسکگدکچىلەرى بىرىككىلە!

اه. آرابای اوزولو

قرغز آلپبه‌سی

اكنچى: جول باسلدى

س.س.س.ر. قالقتارىن بوربوز باسما ماحكەمەسى
١٩٢٦

TRANSLITERATION/TRANSLATION   TEXT 1-G(a)$_1$

Bütün dunya emgekchileri, birikkile!
Workers from the whole world, unite!

Q(i)rg(i)z al(i)pbesi
A Kirghiz Primer

TRANSLITERATION/TRANSLATION   TEXT 1-G(a)$_2$

Bütün dunye emgekchileri, birikkile!
Workers from the whole world, unite!

E. Arabay uulu
Q(i)rg(i)z al(i)pbesi
ek(i)nchi jol bas(1)ld1

Second edition

SSSR qalqtarin(1)n borbor basma mahkemesi

Central Publishing House of the Peoples
of the USSR   1925

باشقى ئسوز.

I

1 — آر ِبر اؤلؤت اوزىنه انجىلؤؤ ِتىبلى بولبوى اؤلؤت بولالابات. انجكنتز

2 تىبلى جوق اؤلؤت مادانيباتتان، ماعار فنان نؤرؤؤ فالؤؤندا ِشكك جوق، حافيقات

3 زامانبيز مادانيبات هم ماعارى زامانى بولغوندؤقنىان آر ِبر اؤلؤت ئاؤز

4 ئانه تىبلى مەنەن امزلگكن امگكەجبلمرىنه تارىبه بەرب هم كەدمبدن كەلمر

5 دەگى جانش مؤزندارن ئانه تىبلىنده مكتەب، كىتتەبنىر دابارلاب شؤنؤ مەنەن

6 تارىبا فيلؤؤ تيش.

7 منا بؤ امك كەرەكنؤؤ كە كؤجىلكنى كەكمش حوكؤمانى كەمزنؤس بارتباسى

8 جولدؤ كە كبر مجا ئب بەرب اولنؤرات.

9 آل ئه مى انداى بولغوندؤ فرغز بولغون جمرى ئاوزنجــه ِبر اؤلؤ ت

10 اؤكنبيز ده نالش جوق بر ـ اوق نؤركسنەندەگى باشقا اؤلؤتنلردان نل جوززنده

11 بزدن آبر ما بار بى؟ دەگەن ِبر سؤال بار! جوبوب آچق آلبەتنه بار.

12 1 — موندان مملك جلرم جلدان بەرى ئسؤيلنوب كىلنگكن فرغز تىبلى

13 باشقا نلكگه فاتشباستان ساقتالب كەلدى دەب آبنؤؤغا هەج كم تالاشىدا. (برمە

14 سلارام كرگكەنى بولسو فرغز بوركؤن كىگكەن جيغار). ِمبسالى اوززبەك، ذتار

15 وا باشقا تؤرؤك رؤزلاربىن تىلن آلساقى آرابى، فارسى نلمر كؤب فاتشقا

16 ندان اؤكنجىدەن لؤغات هم شىؤادا كؤب باشقالق بولغوندون جالبى تؤشنؤؤ

17 مؤمكن امەس.

18 II — بزگه امك جاقن نل فازاقى ِتىبلى بر ـ اوق آنداد لؤغات، شىؤ اجاغبنان

19 زور آبر ما بار اؤكنجى تؤرده آبنفاندا ِتابش هم ئاؤن جاغبنان جانا اولار غاقو بولا

20 نؤركغان نامغا جاغبنان آبر ما كؤب. شؤنك ئاپجؤن فازاقى تىبلن فرغزغا ئانه

21 تىبلى اور دؤنا ابتەرب كؤز جؤەؤب جؤر گؤزا دؤرؤس امەس.

22 ِمبسال، كؤرسونؤب اولنؤرؤ آجات امەس تىبلگكەن آدام بولسو منا بؤل

23 فرغز آلبەمسـن آلب باشقا نؤرك رؤزلاربىن آلبەمسى مەنەن سـالشتنبر ــا

24 جەەت دەبىز.

25 جانادا امسكمرنب اونؤگكه بولودؤ: منا بؤ فرغز الببەسى نارتب فلنؤزدا

26 ِتبلبيزگكه امك جاقن بولغون فازاقى آلبەمسىنن نارتبنى آلندى هم جالغز

27 جوغورزدا آبنلغاندى لؤغات شىؤ اجاغندا جانادا نوبؤش هام ئاون جاغنداغى

28 آبر ملار ئوبغو آلنب اوزكمرنبلب نبزلدى.

29 ِسقاسن آبنفاندا تؤمانى فرغزجا نه گمرەك نەبىنەى جاسالدى

II

مندان بيلابغى "تل فورالدارى هم باشفا اوفۇۇ كيتەبنەرى اوشول جول
مەنەن بلرەاقچى.

1 مۇعاللەمدەرگە امسكەرنۇۇ: فرغز تيلدەكى ۵ (بەش) "اوندۇۇ نبىشنتار
ارفابسيبسى اكيبدەن سوزلۇغا مۇمكن «نوو، جوو؛ بۇۇ؛ جوۇ؛ ساان، تاان؛
امەك، جەمەك؛ جيبين، قيبين، سيباتنۇ.

II «آ» فرغز نيلدە ەمج ۇانت امكە اپنلبابت جاغنى ٠٠ نىۇاچى
اجكەرتە الباپت.

III "سوز اباقتارندەاغى « ى » مەنەن « ۇ » نون فازراق نيلندەگبدەبى
"دودر مولدزك فرغز نيلندە كوبونجو اچز امشينلەت.
شوندۇفتان اچزىامشىنلكەنجە الماشترباي جازرۇۇ كەرمك.

"سوز باشندا «و» جاكى «ۇ» بولسو اباقى "اۇندۇۇ نبىشدا" كوبولنجو
«و» جاكى «ز» بولماقچى. ميساللى. اوشو، اۇشۇ، قوروو، بۇروو،
توفموق، اۇفۇرزق، نۇندۇك، سيباتنۇۇلار.

VI بولاردان باشفا "سوز اباغندەاغى جارزناى، جالفووولوردو «ت، د» آب
اچز امشىنلكەنجە جازلۇ نبش تابلدى. تابلغان كەمجبلكە كيبن تل فورالدارى
نارتب فيلنفبجا نەكشەرلب نولۇفتانماقچى.

7 البىمە اورنو آرىتن سۆرەنى كورسەتلبدى اوغون نۇبنۇ اجــات
نۇشبەكەنەكتەن. اول البىمەنجازلبازناان اچز كورنۇب اولتورات. شونزك
سيباتنۇ اباقفا جازبلا نۇرغان «ع غ» تامغاسبدا كورسوتۇلبدەي فرغز نيلندە
اپنلاغاندەفتان.

IV بۇ البىمە هام بلشفا اوفۇۇ كيتەبنەرى جانادا فرغزدن كورككم خالق
ادابيباتنارى ناىكەنت شالرندەاغى فرغز جاشتارنىن مادانى هام ماعارف
اۇبۇمۇنۇن هام فرغز ــ فازراق "بلم كەمىسبەسنن تابشيرۇۇ بوبۇنجا اۇشولور-
دۇن فار اماغينان اونۇز ماماال كەت "بلم كە كەمشىنن فابلدومەنەن باسنبربلب
اولتزرات. هام باسنبرلماقچى.

منا بۇل البىمەنك كەم كەنبگن تاالب جول جوبوو كورسو نكون داغدبلۇز
مۇعالمەدمربيز بولوۇغالسا، راهمان آبنب كەلگەن جەرندە اەكنجى بالسلۇدا
اۇكدوب باسنبرابز.

ابرنجا فرغز مەكتەبنەرندە منا البىمەنى اوفۇزتقان مۇعاللەمدەرمەن اۇمۇت
اتنەبز، اەمە نبلن نزبۇزنەننزۇرە فاراپ نەكشەرب «اوز ھبكرلەرن كور-
سۇنزلەرن.

III

1   ۷II اوسكهرتۇۇ: منا بۇ آلىبەنى اشقچ رەۇتنە جازدىق فا۔

2   را قىرغىز كەمسىبمىسى آبرم بولبوسنون مورۇن؛ شونوڭ ٬ اۇچۇن

3   ٬ سوز آباغنداغى آرپ تاماغلارى قرغىز تىلىنە كەلمە گەنجەرلە۔

4   ربدا بار اول خانالق بول آلىبەنىن مبناۇ باسلوۇزىندا آشا نەۀ۔

5   شەرلبهدى آنداى كەمجىلىكتىرەدەن بارن تەئشەمرپ كىتنەبنتەربىزدەن

6   اۀنچى باسلوۇزىنـدا جولغو قوبوبوز. بول برنجى آدمدا بوتون

7   اۇرگورنۇپ جىبمەرۇگە قولابىز بولغون سەبەبتنەر بار: ١) مۇعا۔

8   اللمدمەربىزدەن دافقدىسى آزدق ٢) قرغىزداغى قالام تاراراق

9   اوقۇغاندارىبىزدەن جاناادا مۇعاللمدمەربىزدەن نالقوسونا توشبەكەندك

10   ٣) ناشكەنـدەگى خزماتىجىلاربىزدەن كوچونون آزدىغى بولدى.

11   شونوڭ اۇچون بۇ جلقى باسنبىرلغان كىتنەبنتەربىزدى ٬ اولجوب

12   برجلفا جەتمەلك غانا باستبىرپ اولتوراۇيز.

13   اە. آراباي اوۇولو.

14   ٢٤ جل. ١نجى مارت.

TRANSLITERATION

bashqi ^suz

1	ar^br ulut ozine enchiluu ^tili bolboy ulut bolalbait. enchiktu
2	^tili joq ulut madaniiattan, maɛarftan quruu qaluunda shek joq, ḥaqiqat
3	zamanibz madaniiat hem maɛarf zamani bolĝonduqtan ar ^br ulut ^oz
4	ene tili menen ezlgen emgekchilerine tarbie berb hem kedeidn keler
5	degi jash muundarn ene tilnde mektep, kitebter daiarlap shonu menen
6	tarbia qiluu tish.
7	mna bu eng kerektuu kengchilkti kengesh ḥukumati kemunus partiasi
8	joldu kengir echaab berb olturat.
9	al emi anday bolĝondo qrĝz bolĝon jari ^oznche ^br ulut
10	ekenibzde talash joq br-oq turkstendegi bashqa uluttardan tl juzunde
11	^bzdn airma barbi? degen ^br sual bar! jobob achq albette bar.
12	mundan ^mng jarm jldan beri ^suilnob kilngen qrĝz ^tili
13	bashqa tlge qatshbastan saqtalb keldi deb aituuĝa hech km talashbas. (brem-
14	saram krgeni bolso qrĝz borkun kigen chigar). ^misali ozbek, tatar
15	wa bashqa turqk ruularinn tili alsaq arabi, farsi, tlder kob qatshq-
16	ndan eknchiden luĝat hem siwada kob bashqalq bolĝondon jalpi tushnuu
17	mumkn emes.
18	bzge eng jaqn tl qazaq ^tili br-oq andada luĝat, siwa jaĝinan
19	zor airma bar eknchi turde aitqanda tabsh hem ^un jaĝindan jana olarĝa qoiula
20	turĝan tamga jaĝinan airma kob. shunng ^uchun qazaq tiln qrĝzĝa ene
21	tili orduna aiterb koz jumub ^jurguzu durus emes.
22	^misali, korsotub olturnu ajat emes

TEXT 1-G(a)*


```
        tilegen adam bolso mna bul
23      qrǵz alpbesn alb bashqa turq ruularinn
        alpbesi menen salshtirsa
24      jetet deibz.
25      janada eskertb otuge bolobu: mna bu qrǵz
        alpbesi tartb qlnuuda
26      ^tilibzge eng jaǵin bolǵon qazaq alpbesinn
        tartibi alndi hem jalǵz
27      joǵoruda aitlǵanday luǵat shiwa jaǵnda
        janada tobush hem ^un jaǵndaǵi
28      airmalar oiǵo alnb ozkertilb tizldi.
29      qsqsn aitqanda tumaq qrǵzcha tegerek tebe-
        tei jasaldi.
```

TRANSLITERATION   TEXT 1-G(a)**

1   mndan bilaiği ^tl quraldari hem bashqa oquu
     kitepteri oshol jol
2   menen barmaqchi.
3   I - muğallmderge eskertuu: qrğz tilndeki
     5 (besh) ^unduu tibshtar
4   ar qaisisi ekiden sozluğa mumkn 'too', 'buu',
     'juu', 'saan', 'taan',
5   'eek','jeek', 'jiin', 'qiin' siiaqtu.
6   II - 'a' qrğz tilnde hech waqt achke aitl-
     bait jağni " ϟ " (^) qiwachi
7   achkerte albait.
8   III - ^soz aiaqtarndği 'i' menen 'u' nun
     qazaq tilndeidei
9   ^dodomolduk qrğz tilnde kobuncho achq
     eshitlet.
10   shonduqtan achq eshitlkenche almashtrbai
     jazuu kerek.
11   ^soz bashnda 'o' jaki 'u' bolso aiaği
     ^unduu tibshda kobuncho
12   'o' jaki 'u' bolmaqchi. misali: 'osho',
     'ushu', 'qoroo', 'turoo',
13   'toqmoq', 'uquruq', 'tunduq', siiaqtular.
14   IV - bolardan bashqa, ^soz aiağndaği jarnaq,
     jalğoolordo 't', 'd', ab
15   achq eshitlkenchi jazlu tish tabldi. tabl-
     ğan kemchilk kiin tl quraldari
16   tartb qilnqicha teksherlb toluqtanmaqchi.
17   V - alpbesi orto arptn sureti korsetlbedi.
     oğon tubtu ajat
18   tushbegendkten. ol alpbeni jazilunan achq
     kornub olturat. shonung
19   siiaqtu aiaqqa jazila turğan 'ğ' tamğasida
     korsotulbedi qrğz tilnde
20   aitlbağandqtan.
21   VI - bw alpbe ham bashqa okuu kitebteri
     janada qrğzda korkom ḥalq
22   adabiiattari tashkent shaardaği qrğz
     jashtarnin madani ham maɛarf
23   ^oinmunun ham qrğz-qazaq ^blm kemesiesnn
     tabshiruu boiuncha osholor-
24   dun qaramağinan ^otub mamaleket ^blm
     kengesinn qabldo menen bashtirilb
25   olturat. ham bashtirlmaqchi.
26   mna bwl alpbening kem ketign taab jol joboo
     korsotkon dağdiluu

TEXT l-G(a)**

27   muǵalmderibz bolo ǵalsa, rahmat aitb ebi
       kelgen jernda eknchi basluda
28   ongdob bashtirabz.
29   airqcha qrǵz mektebternde mna alpbeni
       oqutqan muǵallmderden umut
30   etebz, ene tiln tubunen ture qarab teksherb
       ^oz pikrlern kor-
31   sotulern.

1   VII - eskertuu: mna bu alpbeni ashqch
      rette jazdq, qa-
2   ra qrģz kemesiesi airm bolboston murun,
      shonung ^uchun
3   ^soz aiaģndaģi arp tamģalari qrģz tline
      kelmegen jerle-
4   rida bar ol ḥatalq bul alpbeni mina bu
      basluunda asha tek-
5   sherlbedi. andai kemchilkterden barn
      teksherb kitebteribzden
6   eknchi basluunda jolģo qoiobuz. bul brnchi
      admda butun
7   orgorttub jiberuge qolaisz bolģon sebebter
      bar: 1) muģa-
8   llmderibzden daģdisi azdq 2) qrģzdaģi
      qalam tartarlq
9   oquģandaribzdn janada muģallmderibzdn
      talqusuna tushbegendk
10   3) tashkendegi ḥzmatchilaribzdn kuchunun
      azdiģi boldu.
11   shonung uchun bu jlqi bastirlģan kitebte-
      ribzdn ^olchob
12   br jlga jeterlk gana bastirb olturabz.
13   e. arabai uulu
14   24 jl 1-nchi mart

ADAPTATION in modern literary Kirghiz proposed
by a contemporary Soviet native speaker showing the
linguistic discrepancies with the pre-literary tongue and the way such a text is understood now.

БАШКЫ СӨЗ

Ар бир улут өзүнүн эне тили болмоюнча улут
боло албайт. Эне тили жок улут маданияттан,
билимден куру калышына шек жок. Акыйкат зама-
ныбыз маданият жана билим болгондуктан, ар бир
улут мектептер, китептер даярдоо менен бирге,
өзүнүн эзилген эмгекчилерине кедейдин келечек-
теги жаш муундарына эне тилинде тарбия берүүгө
тийиш.
Совет өкмөтү, Коммунисттик партия мына ушул
эң керектүү кеңчиликти кеңири жолду чаап берип
отурат.
Мына ошонун негезинде кыргыз эли өз алдынча
улут болуп отурганда шек жок.
I- Мындан бир миң жарым жылдан бери колдонулуп келинген кыргыз тили башка тилге катыш-
пастан сакталып келди деп айтууну эч ким талаш-
пас /бирин-серин киргени болсо, кыргыз бөркүн
кийген чыгар/. Мисалы, өзбек, татар жана башка
түрк элдеринин тилдерин алсак, араб, фарси тил-
дер көп таасир тийгизгендиктен, экинчиден, лек-
сикасы, фонетикасы жана грамматикасы көп башкача болгондуктан, жалпы түшүнүү мүмкүн эмес.
II- Бизге эң жакын тил казак тили, бирок
анда да лексика жагынан зор айырма бар. Экинчиден, тыбышы жагынан жана аларга коюла турган
тамга жагынан айырма көп. Ошол үчүн казак тилин
кыргызга эне тил катары жарайт деп көз жумуп
коюу дурус эмес.
Мисал көрсөтүп отуруу ажат эмес. Аны каалаган адам болсо, мына бул кыргыз алиппесин алып
башка түрк элдеринин алиппеси менен салыштырса
жетет дейбиз.
Жана да эскертип өтүүгө болот: мына бу кыргыз, алиппесин жаратууда тилибизге эң жакын
болгон казак алиппесинин негиз пайдаланылды
жана жогоруда айтылгандай, лексика, тыбыш
жагынан айырмалар ойго алынып өзгөртүлүп тү-
зулду.

Кыскасын айтканда, казактын тумагы кыргызча тегерек тебетей болуп жасалды.

Ошентип, тил боюнча китептер жана куралдар жогоруда айтылган жол менен түзүлүп бармакчы.

I - Мугалимдерге эскертүү: кыргыз тилиндеги беш үндүү тыбыштар ар кайсысы экиден созуулуга мүмкүн: "тоо, жоо, буу, саан, таан, ээк, жээк, жыйын, кыйын", сыяктуу.

II - "а" кыргыз тилинде эч качан ичке айтылбай башкача айтканда аны "ə" ичкерте албайт.

III - Сөз аягында "и" менен "у"нун казак тилиндегидей даана айтылбай калышы кыргыз тилинде көбүнчө ачык угулат.

Ошондуктан аны толук жазуу керек. Сөз башында "о" менен "у" болсо, аяккы үндүү тыбыш да көбүнчө "о" жана "у" болмокчу. Мисалы: ошо, ушу, куруу, буруу, токмок, укрук, түндүк, сыяктуулар.

IУ - Булардан башка сөз аягындагы мүчөлөрдө "т,д" апачык угулганындай жазуу керек деп табылды. Табылган кемчилик кийин тил куралдары тартипке келгенден кийин текшерилип толукталмакчы.

У - Алиппеде орто сүрөтү көрсөтүлбөдү, анткени мунун кажаты жок. Алиппенин жазылуусунан ачык көрүнүп олтурат. Ошол сыяктуу аяккы келе турган "г" тамгасы да көрсөтүлбөдү /кыргыз тилинде жок болгондуктан/.

УI - Бу алиппе жана башка окуу китептери, ошондой эле кыргыздын элдик көркөм адабиятты Ташкент шаарындагы кыргыз жаштарынын маданий жана билим укмунун, кыргыз-казак билим комиссиясынын тапшыруулары боюнча мамлекеттик билим кеңешинин карамагына өтүп, анын чечими боюнча бастырылып отурат.

Мына бул алиппенин кемчилигин көрсөткөн дасыккан мугалимдерибиз болсо, ыразмат айтып, эби келген жеринде, экинчи басылууда оңдоп бастырабыз.

Айрыкча кыргыз мектептеринде мына бу алиппени окуткан эне тилин түбүнөн түрө карап текшерип, өз пикирлерин көрсөткөн мугалимдерден үмүт күтөбүз.

УII - Эскертүү: мына бул алиппени шашылыш түрдө жаздык /кара кыргыз комоссиясы түзүлө электе/, ошондуктан сөз аягында колдонулган кээ бир тамгалар кыргыз тилинде андай

болуп айтылбайт. Ал каталык алиппени мына бул
басылуусунда аша текшерилбеди. Андай кемчилик-
терди жоюп, китебиздин экинчи басылуусунда
жолго коёбуз. Бул биринчи кадамда өзгөртүп
жиберүүгө белгилүү тоскоол болгон себептер бар:
    - мугалимдерибиздин билими төмөндүгү,
    - кыргыздагы кат билген адамдарыбыздын
жана мугалимдерибиздин талкуусуна түшпөгөндүк,
    - Ташкендеги кызматчыларыбыздын күчүнүн
аздыгы болду. Ошон үчүн бул жылкы бастырылган
китептерибизди өлчөп, бир жылга жетерлик гана
бастырып олтурабыз.

                    Э. Арабай уулу.
                    24-жыл, I март.

F O R E W O R D

1   Any people lacking a language of its own cannot be a people.

2   There is no doubt in particular that a people without a language of its own finds itself deprived of culture and education;

3   therefore, taking advantage of our era of justice, culture and education, each people

4   must train, it its own mother tongue, its oppressed toilers

5,6   and educate the have-nots and the young generations of the future by way of developing schools and books in their mother tongue.

7,8   The Soviet government and the Communist Party (created) the necessary opportunities and opened up a broad way.

9,10   This being so, there is no doubt that our Kirghiz land constitutes by itself a nation; but as far as the language (is concerned),

11   is ours different from those of the other nations in Turkestan? This is the question! Let's not beat about the bush. Of course it is.

12   I- This Kirghiz language, spoken for the last 1,500 years,

13   nobody denies that it came down to us and was preserved without becoming stale (even if here and there some new comer has donned the Kirghiz felt cap)

14,15   If we take for example uzbek, tatar and the tongue of the other turk peoples, because they were much under the influence of Arabic and Farsi,

16,17 and, secondly, because of great differences
in vocabulary and pronunciation, they
cannot be understood by all.

18,19 II- For us, Kazakh is a very closely
related tongue; but even there, there is a
huge difference in vocabulary and
pronunciation. In the second place, as far
as sounds and vowels

20,21 and the letters Kazakhs use are concerned,
there are many differences. This is why
proposing Kazakh as a mother tongue for the
Kirghiz while turning a blind eye to these
differences, is not correct;

22-24 There is no need to supply examples. If
somebody wants them, we'll tell him to take
this Kirghiz primer and to compare it with
that of other Turkic peoples.

25 By the way, let us remember that while
composing this Kirghiz primer,

26-28 the pattern of the Kazakh primer so similar
to our language has been kept and, as
stated above, taking only into
consideration the differences concerning
the vocabulary and pronunciation, the
sounds and vowels, it was (accordingly)
changed and adapted.

29 In short, the tumak was tailored into a
round tebetey, a la kirghiz.

- - - - - -

TEXT I - G(a)**

1,2 So, from now on, language handbooks and
other study books will have to follow the
same path.

3-5 I- Reminder for the teachers: each of these
vocalic sounds in Kirghiz must be
pronounced as if doubled: thus 'too'
(mountain), 'joo' (enemy), 'buu' (vapor),
'juu' (to wash), 'saan' (milking), 'taan'

(part), 'eek' (chin), 'jeek' (edge), 'jiin' (harvest), 'kiin' (difficult).

6,7 II- In Kirghiz, 'a' is never pronounced as a front (vowel), in other words the kibachi cannot make it frontal.

8,9 III- The 'i' and 'u' sounds at the end of words which in the Kazakh language remain vague are generally heard clearly in kirghiz.

10 Because of this, they should be written without modification, as they are heard clearly.

11-12 If there is an 'o' or an 'u' at the beginning of a word, the final vocalic sound must usually be 'o' or 'u'. Example: 'osho' (this), 'ushu' (that), 'kuruu' (to build), 'turuu' (to stand),

13 tokmok (mallet), 'ukuruk' (lasso), 'tündük' (nocturnal) and the like.

14-16 IV- What's more, in particles (?) and suffixes at the end of words 't' and 'd' must be kept in writing the way they are very clearly heard. Errors that could be discovered will have to corrected later after checking before normalizing the language handbooks.

17,18 V- In this primer, no model of medium letter is presented. This is because they are absolutely redundant. It can be seen clearly from the way this primer is written.

19,20 In the same way, the final 'g' is not shown here, since it is not pronounced in Kirghiz.

21-25 This primer, as well as other readers and (texts of) Kirghiz folk literature, in conformity with the decision of the pedagogical cultural association of the Kirghiz youth in Tashkent and of the Kirghiz-Kazakh scientific commission and for having fallen within their province are and will continue to be printed with the consent of the State Scientific Council.

26-28 Should there be experienced colleagues of ours capable of finding shortcomings in this primer and of showing the way (to eliminate them), we would thank them and make corrections in accordance, where it is fitting, in the second edition.

29-31 More particularly, we pin all our hopes on those teachers who use this primer in Kirghiz schools and thouroughly analyze and check their mother tongue, as well as on their own opinions and indications.

- - - - - -

TEXT I - G(a)***

1   VII- Reminder: we wrote this primer in haste at a time

2   when there was no special Kara-kirghiz commission; this is

3,4   why there are here and there letters at the end of words which are not suitable for the Kirghiz language. This error has not been eliminated from the present edition of this primer.

5   Thus, after checking all these shortcomings, we'll eliminate them in the second edition of our books.

6,7   There were some ill-timed reasons for (not) succeeding in changing everything at the first attempt:

8,9   1)- the lack of training of our teachers, 2)- the impossibility for our teachers and literate people to exchange opinions,
10   3)- the paucity of collaborators in Tashkent.

11,12 This is why we calculated the number of
copies published this year (so as to) print
only what is necessary for one year.

13   E. Arabay uulu

14   1924, 1 of March.

COMMENTS

WRITTEN FORM:

    One of the main interests of these texts is
the kind of alphabet they are written in. 'Refor-
ming' the Arabic alphabet, i.e. making it less
cumbersome and more readable for the Turkic languages has been since at least the last third of the
19th century one of the main themes of the jadids'
cultural and political platform.
    Just as for the Russian 'progressive' intelli-
gentsia which had a similar problem, this implied
both a basic transformation of the orthographical
system and a simplification of the alphabet itself.
But in Turkic-speaking areas this question was all
the more heatedly debated that
    a) the gap between the traditional written form
and the real pronunciation of the living Turkic
languages was much deeper than in the case of Russian, and that
    b) the reform had become a volatile issue, with
both practical and symbolical consequences.
    When the 'reformed Arabic alphabet' begins to
be used in official publications around 1922-24,
that is after the Bolshevists' take-over, but before
the elimination of the 'national communists', it
signals (C-152) the victory of the native fellow-
travelers over the 'arabists', i.e., lumped together
the real old-style kadymists and those non-socia-
list jadid intellectuals who, as spiritual heirs
to Gaspraly, were attached to the formation of a
literary language common to all Turkic-speaking
peoples of Russia.
    It signals also the victory of those same
fellow-travelers over the 'latinists' (leftist supporters of a radical shift to the Latin alphabet).
Even if the latter were merely expressing another,
equally native, modernistic, secular current going
back to Mirza Fatali Akhundov, they were suspected
of introducing in an underhand manner into the Turkic world a Russian-made machine of war, the ultimate effect of which could be denationalization.

As we know, this centrist tendency triumphed
for less than two or three years, the Latinization
movement (C-164) gaining momentum in 1926, i.e. as
soon as, with the liquidation of the 'national communists' (and Lenin's death), Stalin began to rely
on the last group of natives to establish his own
authority. But this short period was sufficient to
ruin - paradoxically enough - the very hopes that
the 'reform' was supposed to save.

Contrary to the case of Russian - an already
normalized literary language - there was still no
common, 'pan-Turkic' tongue. 'Rationalizing the
orhtography', therefore, was much more than just
a technical problem of written form and script.
In a system which had mechanically, i.e. without
due linguistic justification, transfered to Turkic
the Semitic use of not recording in writing all
vocalic sounds, it meant, basically, introducing
a systematic vocalization of all utterances.

But a text, duly vocalized according to its
author's phonological and morphological system,
automatically brought into the open all the peculiarities opposing this linguistic scheme to that
or those of other readers. More generally (because
similar divisive issues existed at all linguistic -
lexical, morphological, phonetical, syntactical
levels -, 'bringing the written language closer to
the masses' could only mean revealing the existence
of quite different Turkic tongues, ruining the
efforts of past intellectuals to fashion, behind
and thanks to the opacity of an imperfect script,
the beginnings of an 'ortok til', therefore 'objec-
tively' strengthening the argument of the Latini-
zers and, ultimately, allowing the central government to impose its 'Divide et impera' scheme.

Kemal Atatürk's policy in Turkey was soon to
prove that only in an independent country could
Latinization be what it was meant to be: a technical, cultural, modernistic, nationalistic measure.

As a matter of fact, some of the divisive consequences of the reform were perfectly clear to,
and accepted by, that group of Kazakh-Kirghiz intellectuals who wanted to secure their autonomy from
both the Kazan Tatars in the North and the Uzbeks
in the South. Following events were to prove soon
(C-91) that their wishes were going to be over-
fulfilled.

In any case, the reformed alphabet allowed the

implementation of a non-historical, but rather phonological and in some cases even phonetical orthography (cf. ** 1. 19-20: the refusal of such historical and/or foreign features as final ġ, presuma-
bly in such cases as sariġ → sarı: yellow, or *1.
15: (u)ruular(ı)n(ı)n instead of 1-E, 1. 1: (u)ruġ-
(u)nd(a)n.

   After many contradictory and, at times, dramatic episodes and thanks to different political
and cultural conditions, only in Xinjiang has a
variety of this 'reformed' alphabet remained in use
(cf. Texts 1-A(a) and XVI) up to now.

   Technically speaking, the new script, in spite
of an alleged rejection of the middle forms of letters (**1. 17) which in fact is not fully carried
out, remains similar to the one used in 1911 by the
same author (text 1-E) with, however, two important
innovations:
 - a wesla-like diacritic mark written above the
'big' waw allowed a distinction between u and ü: و,
and o and ö: و . But the 'support' alif was still
kept for initial vowels: ‍ا a, ه‍ا e, او : o ö, اُو: u ü.
 - a hamza-like diacritic mark: ء called 'kıbachı'
(literally: an expert) and similar to the ь in Russian, signaled, on the basis of the very strict labial
vowel harmony system (K-369), that all the vowels
of this word were to be read as front ones: ö,ü ,i.
Thus: *** 1. 11: ölchöp = ءاولچوب

   However, the kıbachi was not used if another
grapheme in the word already suggested that all the
vowels were front ones: *1. 2: özine = اوزینه
It was not easily readable or, often, was omitted
altogether: *** 1. 11: üchün = اوُچوُن ; i was
still more often omitted: bir = بر or noted by a
ya which worked as well as yod (NB: the undotted ya
was ı: cf. text 1-E!); the same can be said about
i: *** 1. 1: ashigıch = اشغچ , qırgız: قرغز

   The final p in Gerunds is still written with
a ba and the linguistically redundant, but pedagogically acceptable distinction between [q]: ق and
[k]: ك for /k/ and [g] : گ and [ɣ]: غ for
/g/ is still made, nurturing a dispute which still
lingers on (K-503, 549).

   Note in ** 1. 6: ۋ for b~ w ~β: kıbachı, not
used however for the same sound in suwal ~suβal.

   A certain number of typographical errors (in
**1. 1, 21: bilaigi, bw) are structural and linked
to the number of dots under or above the grapheme.

STYLE:

Three different stylistic tendencies can be discovered in these texts, endowing them for contemporary readers with an awkward heterogeneity which, however, probably was (from the author's viewpoint) a mere attempt at enriching and diversifying the stylistic/expressive capacities of his mother tongue (ene til).

First, some linguistic features denote the author as a Southerner **1. 17: oğon: Dat. of ol: this (Northern variant: al); the shu form (demonstrative) instead of ushul; such lexical units as eshit-, kulay. These features cannot be called 'dialectal' if only because the reference literary norm was established about ten years <u>after</u> this text was first published. They rather illustrate Arabay-uulu's desire to use a language actually understandable to the local illiterates and authentically 'Kirghiz'. This, in turn, suggests that, for him, 'Kirghiz' was something different from both today's 'Kazakh' and 'literary' - that is, in fact, Northern - Kirghiz: something which, as a genuine Southerner, he calls 'kara-kirghiz': ***1. 2.

Secondly, numerous Arabic loanwords, in their traditional spelling, reveal the kind of classical education he received in Ufa. Such items, however, are less numerous than in text I-E and, possibly, play a different role. They tend less to anchor Kirghiz as an 'oriental' language than to provide it with an already commonly shared by other Turkic languages unified terminology. Loanwords of Arabic and Persian origin were indeed considered much in the same way as their Latin and Greek equivalents in Western languages.

This is why two different kinds of 'Arabisms' are freely mixed here:

lexical items such as maɛarif, ḥaqıyqat, ajat, suab ~suwal ~sobol, jağni, which have filtered into Kirghiz through Kazan Tatar,

and items introduced through 'Uzbek': wa, hem, hiğat, shiva.

These can stem from written Chagatay, from spoken Uzbek, the influence of which is particularly strong in Southern Kirghizia and/or from more or less conscious 'corrections' made by the publishers in Tashkent.

It is interesting to note, in the second

edition, the use of basma mahkemesi: printing house.
Although mahkeme (lit. kirg.: mekeme: Y-522) means
'administration, office' and 'tribunal' in Turkish,
Azeri, etc., it has kept here its original meaning
of 'chancellery' while appearing at the same time
as a typical calque of rus. knizhnaia palata (where
'palata' is both 'administration or governmental
institution' and 'judicial division' of a court).

Thirdly, the author's attempts to develop a
terminology goes far beyond the introduction into
a basically spoken language (cf. *l. 13,29) of Arabic words of scholarly origin, which he used in spe-
cialized contexts (luġat is not 'dictionary', but
'vocabulary': lit. kirg.: leksika) or 'explains'
with a native word, the original meaning of which
is thus modified (cf. *** l. 3: arip = tamga: letter, grapheme, originally: a clanic mark. Cf. the
same explanatory technique in 1-E, l. 3: shair =
akın).

New Soviet realia are expressed through Russian loanwords: kemünüs partiyası: Communist Party,
kemesiya: committee and Russian inspired phraseo-
logy (**l. 21-25). However
calques often replace direct lexical loans:
kenges ökümöt: soviet government, from kirg. kenges: council + ar. ökümöt: government.
national linguistic particularism (above all
Vowel Harmony) is respected: kemünüs instead of
lit. kirg;: kommunisttik, which is orthographically,
phonetically and morphologically parallel to rus.
kommunisticheskaia (partiia). Cf. C-167 and K-526,
546, 1102).

The same cautious desire of updating his
native tongue, adapting it to new and wider 'social
functions' without disfiguring it, presides over
his attempts to create a pedagogical and grammatical terminology: ündüü tıbısh: vocalic sound for
'vowel' is still used, as okuu kitep for 'handbook'.
Other items were less successful: jalgoo: affix,
from jalga-: to add is given by Y-221 as 'archaic'
while the exact meaning confered by the author to
such words as jarnak: Y-236: portion = particle?,
or til kuraldı (lit. linguistic weapon): pedagogical material ? (most probably a calque from rus.
uchebnye posobiia) is now unclear.

Such failures do not necessarily point to a
vicious method. A certain amount of linguistic
'purism' was the only conceivable possibility at
a time when the vast majority of the population

knew no other language than their own local dialect.
It had already given positive results in Kazan and
Crimean Tatar. Everywhere, when the experiment had
been allowed to last long enough, when the development of terminology was backed by a web of schools,
by newspapers and by administrative/juridical insti-
tutions using the native language, newly coined
words or 'old' words used in a new meaning had been
adopted.

What gives this text (and most of those written
at that time) the 'strange' and 'outdated' character now underlined by readers educated in accordance
with the 'Soviet norm' (C-195) is not the objective
'failure' of this spontaneous policy which was not
given the time necessary to fail. It is the forced
implementation, from outside, of another policy
which deliberately took an opposite course.

It must be added however that a ponderous, at
times irrational style, aggravated by true archaisms
(enchiktüü: particular ≠ modern kirg.: personal;
daġdilüü; dödömöldük; türük, ruular: peoples instead
of uruktar:tribes, etc.) do, indeed, dishearten
the contemporary reader. The deep syntactical transformations carried out by a contemporary native
speaker when asked to give a modernized version of
this text testifies to the evolution of Kirghiz in
this respect.

All these hardly inevitable shortcomings -
which were to be followed, well into the 1930s, by
worse ones - as well as the obvious defects of the
graphic system were to be overemphasized by official critics when Latinization became, for a while,
the official policy.

Morphology and phonology (including Labial
Vocal Harmony), on the contrary, follow, with a few
exceptions (a -ıng Genitive in *l. 20; a -me Nega-
tive in ***l. 3) the contemporary normative pattern.

Since many of these features are not typical
for the Southern dialect, we have here an additio-
nal proof of the author's desire to design an
'average' norm.

Isolated remarks:

*1.4: ezilgen: an obvious 'ideological' calque:
      oppressed, from ez-: to press, to crush.
 1.5 dayarlab: lit. kirg: dayardap, although there

are numerous cases of /DA/ or /LIk/ being realized
as d or l after r.
1.6: tish: lit. kirg.: tiyish. Compare with **1.5:
jıın, qıın: lit. kirg.: jıyın, kıyın. In this
much debated problem (K-196), the author obviously opts for the existence of long /i/
and /ı/.
1.14: brem-saram: lit. kirg.: berin-serin: a few
1.29: tumaq: a typically Kazakh cap with ear-flaps.
The Kirghiz headdress is called 'ak kalpak'.
**1.2,16: barmaqchı: K-2172, toluqtanmaqchı:K-1207
1.4: most probably, the author refers here to the
long vowels: K-150, 185-195 which are about
twice longer than the short ones. But he for-
got to mention ö and ü.
1.8,9: Unlike their equivalent in Kazakh, they
are not diphtongized: kirg. tirköö/kaz. tirkeü:
to note down.
1.11,12: what the author probably tries to explain
here is the labial harmony phenomenon: K-380.
But he mixes lexemes (toqmoq) which, synchro-
nically speaking, are monolithic with true cases
of synharmonism: tün+/LIk/= tündük and normal
cases of labial harmony with exceptional ones:
/U ~ O/: K-387-400.
1.26: jol-joboo: lit.= (showing) the way-means.
In lit. kirg. jobo is 'plan'.
daġdilüü: K-227
1.27 and ***1.1: rahmat, retter: K-217.

CONTENT:

Thanks to Z. Bektenova:"U istokov Kirgizskogo
bukvaria i pis'mennosti", El Agartuu, 1975,8 we
have some biographical information about the author.
Eshenalı Arabay-uulu was born in 1882 in the
village of Kın-Batısh, Kochkor district in Southern
Kirghizia in a rather poor family. From 1900 until
1910 he works as a country schoolteacher, then goes
to Ufa to study at the prestigious Galiya medresseh.
Together with another (Kazakh) student, he prepares
a first, Kirghiz-Kazakh primer which is published,
in Arabic script, in 1911 in Ufa by the 'Sharq'
publishing house and writes a preface to Moldo
Kılıch's 'Qıssa-i Zilzala' (Text 1-E).
He becomes then conscious of the differences
- quite unimportant as far as understanding is

concerned, but pedagogically troublesome - opposing 'Kazakh/Northern' forms to 'Kirghiz/Southern' ones - a problem which was to reappear around 1924 when a 'basic dialect' had to be chosen for the 'literary norm' in the making.

His 'Kirghiz Primer' (58 pages) was written and published in 1924 in Tashkent. 4,000 copies of this first edition were printed. A second edition was published in 1925. Arabay-uulu is also known to have published a long article in the first issue of 'Erkin Too' (cf. below).

However modest at first sight, all these primers, including Munanwar Qari Abdurrashid Khanogli's 'Adib-i Anwal' for Uzbek in 1901, had for the cultural and national development of the peoples concerned the same symbolical impact as the famous 'Riben bukvar' in Bulgaria.

Without any doubt, the key phrase here, justifying the publication of a Kirghiz primer and expressing the author's philosophy, is "A people without a language of its own cannot be an (autonomous) people". Conspicuously enough, this 'declaration of particularism' sounds exactly like the well-known, 19th century Hungarian motto: 'Nyelvében él a nemzet': A nation lives through its language.

This motto perfectly sums up the first jadid intellectuals' short and long-range program of cultural (much more than administrative and above all political) autonomy from
- the Russians: a claim which was considered sufficiently self-evident not to be specifically stressed,
- the urban/merchant 'Uzbeks' in the plain, among whom the kadymist influence remained strong (in 1924, the Basmachi war was going on) and who were suspected of continuing, within the new Soviet frame, the same policy of cultural assimilation, now centered on Tashkent, as Kokand in a recent past. This choice is mentioned only in passing because the author needs the Tashkent-based typographical infrastructure and also because it obviously plays into the hands of the Russian-controlled new power in Southern Turkestan.
- the Kazan Tatars: the author's stay in Ufa convinced him, as indicated above, that the Tatar-led cultural Renaissance (the Nahada) would yield

positive results only if adapted to local conditions.

But this linguistic regionalism comes up against the classical problem of discretely delimiting the chosen linguistic unit. While the author insists here, for pedagogical reasons, on the necessity to distinguish 'Kirghiz' from 'Kazakh', we learn from Z.Bektenova that "he spoke Kazakh much better". In fact, one should not attach too much linguistic importance to a distinction which was not considered at that time to have dangerous implications for the future and which even now (after having been officialized from above) still allows between speakers of each variant, easy, spontaneous intercommunication.

As an intellectual, the author most probably had adapted his original geographical and social idiolect to the parlance of the numerous and very influential Kazakh reviews and newspapers. But, at the same time, his past experience as a schoolteacher in far-off places had convinced him of the pedagogical necessity of linguistic means of teaching as close as possible to the local dialects. The teaching variants between which he hesitates are thus not ethnolinguistic, but rather sociolinguistic ones.

To be more precise, the contradiction we seem to face here was truly insoluble only inasmuch as the problem was stated in static, strictly synchronical terms.

But, as we know, the Turkic intellectuals' linguistic policy was a prospective one. And so is the author's 'swing-wing' pedagogy: the use of a tribal, grass-root dialect he favors in primary schools should simply facilitate, according to him, a faster access to a first level of knowledge which automatically implies the use of a wider, already 'regional' linguistic form. This second stage, in turn, would permit the student to acquire fluency in a higher, 'pan-Turkic' form. Thus would a projected national 'ortok til' ultimately develop at the same rhythm as a hierchically organized web of schools fostering a pan-national education.

At that time, Arabay-uulu was a 'fellow-traveler' who implicitly rejected both panislamism and panturkism, concentrating on the practical task of educating his people rather than on ideological issues. The 'nationalism' of his first sentence is thus tempered by the second one which clearly shows its humanistic, rather than political content.

We know nothing of Arabay-uulu's further fate, except that he published in 1928 a new primer in Latin script (cf. Text XI-C^2). But by 1926 the sociolinguistic platform he advocates here - moderate lexical 'purism' - was beginning to collide with the official policy.

His name is not recorded in the 1976, 6-volume edition of the 'Kırgız Sovet Enciklopediyası'.

Front page of the 1st issue of 'Erkin Too' (The
Free Mountain)- the 1st Kirghiz-language newspaper.
in Kh. Karasaev: Turmush Kürgüsü (The Mirror of
Life), Kırgızstan Basmasi, Frunze 1966, p. 21.

TEXT 1-G(b)

TRANSLITERATION   ERKN TOO

Bashqarmann adresi
Tashkende lenin-jırak köchölörü
burchunda
oskr esenski basarında qarshı
bashqarma jumushu
saġat 12 hem 3-gechein kelüügö bolot

                Juma 7-nchi nuiabr 1924 jl
                         brnchi jl chgıshı

1 ULUU OKTEBR TONGKORUSHUNUN 7NCHI JLĠI
2 MAIRAMINAN TUULUB OLTURĠAN QRĠZ MAMLEKETNN
3 UIUTQUSU: QRĠZ ARASINAN CHQQAN BATRAQ,
4 KEDEI,DIIQAN QOSHCHULAR

(In contemporary orthography:)

    Улуу Октябрь төңкөрүшүнүн 7-нчи жылкы
        майрамынан
    туулуп олтурган кыргыз мамлекетинин
        уюткусу:
    кыргыз арасынан чыккан батрак,
    кедей, дыйкан кошчулар

TEXT I-G(b)

TRANSLATION

(In Russian): Organ of the
District Committee of the
Russian Communist Party and of
the District Executive Committee of the Kara-Kirghiz Autonomous District.

Office Address:
Tashkent - corner of the Lenin-jɪrak streets
opposite the Oskar Esenski bazaar
Working hours: 12 to 3.

THE FREE MOUNTAIN
Friday, November 7, 1924
First year of publication

THE YEAST OF THE KIRGHIZ STATE
BORN FROM THE 7-TH ANNIVERSARY OF THE
GREAT OCTOBER UPHEAVAL (are) THE
ASSOCIATIONS OF PEASANTS, PAUPERS AND MANUAL
WORKERS (stemming from) INSIDE THE
KIRGHIZ (people)

NB! Almost every word in this splashy headline is
felt today as stylistically obsolete:
    töngkörüsh is now 'upheaval' rather than 'revo-
                lution'
    uyutkɪ is now 'active element'
    kedey and koshchu are not used anymore.

d) FROM TRADITION TO MODERNITY TEXTS II

Togolok Moldo:

- Excerpt from the poem 'Ala Too' (in N. Kangel-
  diev, V.N. Shneydman: <u>Bizdin Adabiyat</u>, segiz
  jıldız jana orto mektepterdin jetinchi klassı
  üchün okuu kitebi, Mektep Basması, Frunze 1970,
  p. 68).
                                        Text II-A

- Excerpt from 'Kıshkı Childe' (in Z. Bektenov,
  J. Temirova: <u>Bizdin Adabiyat</u>, segiz jıldık jana
  orto mektepterdin 5-klasstari üchün, 8-chü
  basılıshı, Mektep Basması, Frunze 1965, p. 105).

NB! Poetry has been selected to illustrate this
transitional period because in the process of
'putting into writing' a hitherto exclusively oral
language, non-rhythmic prose is in itself a rather
late innovation.

Тоголок Молдо   АЛА   ТОО

I Ала-Тоонун арасы
  Жалпы жердин сарасы.
  Айтып өтөм бир катар,
  Аңгемесин карачы.
5 Башы Ак-Сай, Чатыр-Көл,
  Туурасы Торгарт, Жапыз-Бел,
  Ушул жерде жердешип,
  Өсүп-өнгөн кыргыз эл.
  Аягында Арпа бар,
10 Салтанаты канча бар.
  Көрбөгөн жан бир көрсө,
  Көөнү ачылып шаттанар.

  Ак-Сай менен Арпада
  Ар уруу чөптүн кени бар.
15 Абышкасы оштонуп,
  Жигиттен кыйын деми бар.
  Ала-Тоо деп аталып,
  Аягы кетет керилип.
  Албан түрлүү чөптөрү
20 Адамга сонун көрүнүп.
  Ала-Тоодон ар канча
  Сонун тоолор бөлүнүп,
  Атагы дайын билинет,
  Анык көзгө көрүнүп.
25 Түп атагы Тянь-Шань,
  Турган эли бир канча,
  Келгендин баарын батырып,
  Көрүнбөйт көзгө бир жанча.

  Кең өзөн Чүйдү калтырбай,
30 Көрсөтүп өтөр кези бар,
  Баяндоого кең Чүйдү
  Байымбеттин сөзү бар.
  Сонундуктан Чүй жери
  Алтын күрөк аталган.
35 Сары өзөн Чүйдү жердеген
  Адамы калбай катардан.
  Чүйдүн башы Көк-Ойрок,
  Келишкен жайлоо сонуну,
  Айткан менен түгөнбөс

120

40 Ар канчалык форуму.
Соң-Көл деген көлү бар,
Куртка деген бели бар,
Нары жагында Жумгалды
Айтып өтөр жөнү бар.
45 Кара-Кече жеринде
Таш көмүрдүн кени бар.

Солто-Сары, Соку-Таш,
Курттуу-Көл, Балгарт, Кара-Саз,
Нарындын башы Тарагай,
50 Кемир-Кырмак, Кара-Таш.
Сары-Жазы, Ак-Шыйрак,
Уч-Каркыра, Кеген бар,
Ботонун-Сазы деген бар,
Болжолсуз сонун Текес бар.

55 Шарапаттуу Ысык-Көл
Тамашалуу кызык бар.
Кызыл-Кыя кени бар,
Көчмө кыргыз эли бар.
Сыбызгы жумшак жели бар,
60 Жайкалган жатык бели бар.
Эзелден туруп жердеген,
Элет кыргыз эли бар...

1   The heart of Ala Too -
That's the most outstanding place in the
      world.
About it I'll tell you a little,
Listen carefully to the tale.

5   Its far extremities are Ak-Say and lake
      Chatir
And its flanks Torgart and Japız Bel:
It is by dwelling on this land
That the Kirghiz people grew and throve.
At its feet the Arpa spreads -

10   How great is its magnificence!
The heart of whom has never seen this place
Will leap when seeing it, wild with joy.
Along the Arpa, the Ak-Say
What a treasure of different plants!

15   There old men are fit as fiddle
And more vigorous than young lads.
Those mounts are called 'rainbow-colored',
Their foothills spread afar.
A motley wealth of plants

20   Enraptures everybody's sight.
Branching out of Ala Too
How many splendid ranges
The glories of which are renowned
Openly greet our eyes.

25   Its original title to fame is the Mounts of
      Heaven;
Countless are their inhabitants:
They welcomed everyone who came
(And yet) no soul comes in sight.
Without moving away from the broad-bedded
      Chü,

30   It is high time to describe it,
And for praising the wide Chü
Bayımbet* has his own words.
For its beauty, this land of Chü
Is called the 'Golden Spade'.

35   No living soul is to be found
       Who would not live in its golden valleys.
       Kök Oyrok is the river-head,
       Set in lavish mountain pastures
       And, whatever happens, eternal is

40   Their varying glamor.
       There is a lake, called Song köl lake
       And a range too, called Kurtka Range
       And farther on, the Jumgal land
       Is to be cited as well

45   In the country of Kara-Keche
       There is coal aplenty.
       Solton Sarı, Soku Tash,
       Kurttuu köl, Balgart, Kara Saz
       And Taragay, at the Narin river-head,

50   Kemir Kırmak and Kara tash!
       There is also the Sari jaz and Ak-Shıyrak,
       Uch-Kachkira, Kegen
       Botonun Saz
       And the Tekes, of inexpressible grace,

55   There is also the sacred lake:
       Issik-köl, so puzzling and strange;
       The mines at Kızıl-Kıya
       And the Kirghiz, a nomadic people.
       The breeze is gentle there, as a reed pipe,

60   The sloping foothills snake up and down
       And from the beginning of time
       Here dwells the nation of the nomad
          Kirghiz....

*:   The author addresses himself by his own
       name.

Тоголок Молдо

КЫШКЫ ЧИЛДЕ

I Кыш чилдеси кырк күнү
Суук болот күн-түнү.
Бургак болот, мунарык,
Жер көрүнбөйт тунарып.
5 Кысым болот кышында,
Кыш чилденин тушунда.
Малга-жанга көп жабыр.
Кыйын болот ушунда.
Жолдоштору кырк болот,
10 Бу да кыркка жыл толот.
Кырдач деген алты күн
Кыйкырып өтөт кырданып,
Малдын-жандын майын жеп,
Түрүн бузуп сурданып.
15 Апкыт-сапкыт жети күн,
Бу да суук кыш болот.
Ала шалбырт кар эрип,
Түндө тоңуп муз болот.
Анын арка жагынан
20 Адынын келет алты уулу,
Жединин келет жети уулу.
Алты, жети, он үчү,
Чилденин кайрат бел күчү.
Бул он үчтүн артынан,
25 Үйгө түшүп үт келет,
Үткө аралаш жут келет.
Үттүн өзү он беш күн,
Бири калбай бүт келет.
Чилде кымбат кармаса,
30 Малдын майы калбаса,
Жут ушунда башталат.
Малдын кырып арыгын,
Итке сүйрөп ташталат.
Кам кылбаган адамга
35 Мал тукуму аз калат.
Минерине ат калбай,
Ээр-токумун жазданат.

In the Depth of Winter

1   The winter's heart - that's forty days
When cold will rule night and day.
There'll be flurries of snow and mist
The land will wane and disappear.

5   There'll be hardships in wintertime
During the winter's chilliest time.
Cattle and men will bear the brunt of it,
It will be hard indeed.
This stretch of time has forty companions

10   Through them the year comes to its end
During six days (their name's 'kɪrdach')
The cold will sweep along and rumble and
    rattle
Eating away the fat from men and beast
Ruining all things in its wrath.

15   Seven more days - Apkɪt-Sapkɪt -
It's still chilly winter.
The snow melts in piebald spots
Freezing again at night into solid ice.
And then in their footsteps will come

20   Adi's six children
And Jedi's seven sons.
Six, seven, then thirteen days,
The frost again steps up its strength
And when these thirteen days have passed,

25   Bowing down on the yurt, in comes Üt
And in the mist of it, in comes disease.
The 'Üt' itself lasts fifteen days,
No more, no less, quite exactly.
When intense cold descends on all for good

30   When animals have no more fat,
The epizooty swoops down.
One slaughters the scraggy cattle
Hauls it away and throws it to the dogs.
The careless owner will be left

35   With just a few breeders;
And once deprived of mount to ride,
He'll use the saddle as a pillow.

COMMENTS

Togolok Moldo - the 'Plumpish Mollah' - (his
true name is Bayımbet Abdrakhman) was born in 1860
in a locality called Kurtka in the Narın Valley in
a modest rural family. He was educated however by
his father, an 'akın' himself, who introduced him
to the 'minor genres' of the traditional folk poetry:
tales, fables, legends, lyric, occasional poetry,
etc. He began studying to become a mollah but was
forced to break up his studies for lack of money.
He took advantage of these few years to become
acquainted with local history and, above all, with
the national Epic.
        He practiced two main literary genres: tradi-
tional folk poetry - including 'anticlerical' and
'accusatory' themes - and, especially after 1918,
'engagé' poems such as 'Nasiyyat' (cf. I-F).
        These themes earned him the reputation of a
Kirghiz Nekrasov, transforming him readily into
an 'akın-democrat' and his works into a must for
school handbooks.
        The two, half-scholastic, half almanac-like
poems given here testify to the permanence of two
basic themes, indissociable in popular poetry:
the elated worship of the beauties of Nature which
is linked to an old, pre-Islamic shamanistic cult
of the Creation and of the 'Bak' (Joy) God, and
the fervent belief in the necessity of 'Roots'.
        Togolok Moldo died in 1942.

II-A: Ala Too (the 'Piebald Mountain')
        This is the name of a ridge which branches
off the Tian Shan range, stretching westward from
lake Issık-köl toward Chimkent, south of the Chü
bassin and overlooking the capital city of Frunze.
        We can be almost sure that in the original
version the mountain mentioned on l. 25 was not
called 'Tian Shan' (this verse has only 6 syllables
instead of 7) but, most probably, Tengir Too - its
traditional ethnic name, the meaning of which: the
Celestial/Divine Mountain was correctly translated
as Tiān Shān in Chinese: 天 山 and recorded as such

by Russian explorers.

It is impossible to know whether the poet's language presented or not any peculiarities: these have been erased through the double process of trans-literation into the cyrillic alphabet and of adaptation to the modern literary norm, always strictly controlled before inclusion into a school anthology.

One can note however:
- on l. 3,30 and 44: the author seems to have a preference for the verb öt-: to pass, used here as a 'pseudo-auxiliary' expressing continuity: K-1405, 1414,1669 and Y-601: al kul bolup ötkön: he had been a slave (for all his life)
- on l. 40: forumu corresponds to lit. kirg. borum: Y-148: beauty, grace (a Russian/Western loan-word 'форма', with the regular adaptation of foreign 'f' into [φ], orthographically rendered by б in cyrillic script: K-95,498,528). Here ф has been maintained for contradictory reasons: because there certainly was a ف in the original manuscript in Arabic script and because it looks more Russian.

For grammatical explanations, cf.:
l. 4: K-1888   l. 39: K-1819
l. 17: K-1590

II-B: Kıshkı Childe
Childe is a Persian loanword (Y-862) which designates the coldest (kıshki) of the hottest (jaykı) 40-day periods of the year. Cf. childe baba: the Spirit of the Cold, now assimilated to rus. Дед Мороз : Santa Claus. In other Turkic languages, 'çile, çillä refers to a 40-day period after a birth or a death.

The 'childe' period breaks down into
. kırdach: six days: Y-493, cf. kır : a crest, a ridge
. Apkıt-Sapkıt: six days: Y-61: "the period when Winter recedes under the pressure of Spring"
. Adi, Jedi: six days each
. Üt: Fifteen days: Y-826. It is both the 12th month in the solar calendar (Feb. 22-Mar. 21) and the first ray of sun which filters in through the upper opening of the yurt, signalling thus the coming of Spring.
Verses 2 and 16 do have 7 syllables: the word written suuk was most probably written and pronounced as a disyllable: cf. turk. soğuk; kaz. suyk

with a regular VCV → V̄ evolution: K-187.
    Conversely, verses 20 and 21 should be read
as 'ad(ı)nın kelet alt(ı) uulu' with an ultra-short
'ı' in an unstressed position: K-182 and the elision
of 'ı/i' next to a long vowel: K-307.
    1. 30:   K-1857.

d) FROM TRADITION TO MODERNITY TEXTS III

Toktogul Satılganov:

  - Kosh, apake!   Text III-A

  - Aylangan toonun bürkütü   Text III-B

(in N.Kangeldiev, V.N.Shneydman: Bizdin Adabiyat,
Segiz jıldık jana orto mektepterdin jetinchi klassı
üchün okuu kitebi, Mektep Basması, Frunze 1970,
pp. 49,51)

Токтогул Сатылганов

КОШ, АПАКЕ !

I   Боздодуң, апа, боздодуң
    Кайгымды кайра козгодуң.
    Кайрат кылсаң болбойду,
    Тирүүмдө жоктодуң...

5   Ыйладың, апа, ыйладың,
    Ыйлаба, жашың кургасын.
    Убайым тартып ый ыйлап,
    Уулуңду муңдуу кылбагын...
    Айланайын апамсың,
IO Анчалык неге жаш алдың?
    Айдалып барам алыска,
    Азабым тартып жатарсың.

    Карууң кетет, кейибе,
    Кулак сал менин кебиме:
I5 Ажалым жетип өлбөсөм,
    Карчыга куштай айланып,
    Келермин кайра элиме!
    Айланайын апаке,
    Балапандай баккансың.

20 Алпештедиң, апаке,
    Адам кылдың асырап.
    Ачылар бекен кабагым,
    Ушул иштен ажырап?

    Керимбай кылды кесирди,
25 Кекенип мага эсирди.
    Жаш кезимден каршы эле,
    Журтумдан айдап кетирди...

    Айланайын апаке,
    Уккун менин сөзүмдү,
30 Картайгандан көп ыйлап,
    Алдырба муңга көзүңдү.
    Ажалым жетип өлбөсөм,
    Акыр бир күн алармын
    Керимбайдан өчүмдү.

Farewell, Mother!

1   You're sobbing, mother, sobbing
    And start up my sorrow again.
    Can't you really regain courage
    And mourn me not when I am still alive?

5   You're weeping, mother, weeping.
    Don't cry and dry yours tears.
    By living in fear and shedding such tears
    Don't make your son feel so wretched.
    You are my mother, my dearest

10   Why do you shed so many tears?
    I am leaving, driven far away,
    And you'll stay here, grieving for me.
    When your courage deserts you, don't
      grieve,
    And lend an ear to my words:

15   Should I not die and meet my fate,
    I'll soar and wheel round like a hawk
    And I'll come back to my folk!
    Mother, my dearest,
    You cherished me like a fledgling

20   And coddled me, mother,
    Raised me, made me a man.
    Will my brow brighten
    When I come through such a predicament?
    Kerimbay inflicted that affront on me

25   He raves and nurses a grudge against me;
    He kindles his wrath since I was a child,
    He forced, drove me away from my people.
    Mother, my dearest,
    Listen to my words:

30   Don't cry so much in your old age,
    Don't let your eyes be doomed to grieving.
    Should I not die and meet my fate,
    I'll see the end of it
    And take revenge on Kerimbay!

Токтогул Сатылганов

АЙЛАНГАН ТООНУН БҮРКҮТҮ

I Күн тийбес тамда жатамын,
    Күч кетип, эс ооп алсырап,
    Алдымдан нымдуу сыз өтөт,
    Айласыз жатам жалдырап.
5 Козголор менде дарман жок
    Кол, бутта кишен шалдырап...

    Айланган тоонун бүркүтү
    Ак жерден торго чалындым.
    Комузду күүгө келтирген
10 Колума кишен салындым.
    Ойлонуп түшкө кирбеген
    Көркоолорго багындым.
    "Айланайын тийбе" - деп,
    Айласыздан жалындым.
15 Кысталгандан өлсөм дейм,
    Кымбатын кыйбайм жанымдын.
    Күү чертип эркин сайраган
    Күлүк элем, наалыдым.
    Кужурмөн тынбай чуркаган
20 Күлүк элем, талыдым.
    Кор болбой турган алтын баш
    Күйүттө жүрүп карыдым.
    Көз жашын эстеп ич күйөт
    Сүйүшүп алган жарымдын.
25 Он жашар жалгыз баламды
    Ойлонуп күндө сагындым.
    Зарлантып койгон күнөөсүз
    Заманага таарындым.

The Wheeling Mountain Eagle

1   I lay at the foot of a wall not reached by
      the sun,
   My strength is gone, my faltering will
      fails,
   Dampness streams down under me
   While I lay beseechingly desperate.

5   I've no strength left to move,
   Shackles jingle on my hands and feet...
   A mountain eagle that wheeled round,
   I'm now caught in a snare, although
      innocent.
   Those hands of mine that made the qomuz
      sing

10 Are now clapped in irons.
   To jackals I couldn't even dream of
   I've had to surrender.
   Imploring: "Please, don't touch me!"
   In disarray I pleaded for mercy.

15 I told myself: If I shall die being
      harried
   I won't underrate the worth of my soul.
   I sobbed: 'I was a cuckoo
   Freely warbling, plucking melodies'
   I almost fainted: 'I was a foal

20 Nimbly gambolling, gasping for breath'.
   My golden head that knows no taunt
   Grew gray, trudging in hardships.
   My breast's aflame when I recall
   How she would cry, who shared my love.

25 For my one son who's ten years old
   I languish every day,
   And curse an age
   Which makes me grieve, although guiltless.

COMMENTS

Toktogul Satılgan-uulu was born on the 25th
of October 1864 in the Osh district in Southern
Kirghizia. He died on the 17th of February, 1933,
aged 69.
During the early period of his life many aspects of his biography strikingly resemble various
data from T. Moldo's life: same family and geographical backgrounds, same early influence of his
father, locally known for his literary talent, same
importance of the ethnic way of life (his mother
was considered an expert on folklore matters), same
impact of the same historical events during a critical period of time.
However, and probably under the influence of
his father, these social and political events,
instead of making him momentarily envisage the
'profession' of mullah as a stepping stone to knowledge, prompted him to abandon traditional lyrical
themes which had already brought him local fame
and to switch to socio-political contemporary themes: the multifaceted disruption of everyday life
brought in by the Russian occupation and the 'Time
of Troubles' in Kokand.
His criticism of the new social and political
situation was sharp enough and - what's even more
dangerous - sufficiently personalized to earn him
the reputation of a dangerous trouble-maker, the
bitter hatred of some local VIPs and, thanks to
them, the implacable solicitude of the new Russian
military power.
He is arrested on the 11th of June, 1898 and
imprisoned on charges of 'rebellion': in fact, he
had criticized rather harshly the 'private' akin
of a powerful manap. When his trial begins in
August, the 'Andijan uprising' has so efficiently
aroused passions and fears that he is condemned to
death by a Russian military tribunal.
Some time later this sentence is commuted to
seven years of hard labor. Exile to Siberia and
the House of the Dead were to have a lasting influence on him and proved to be, ideologically
speaking, his 'universities'.
Forcefully mingling with the 'politicals'

from all over the Empire, he discovers a social
stratum of Russians absolutely different from that
of the military or civilian 'pacifiers' of Kirghizia. Later on, he was to write that he had been
overwhelmed with gratitude by the way they greeted
him and opened up for him a whole world of unheard
of knowledge, new ideas, new social and personal
relationships.

Intellectual and personal friendship between
idealists eager to educate the colonized 'men'shoi
brat' (younger brother) and the rebellious provincial discovering that his own intuitions and hopes
were shared and systematized by prestigious intellectuals from the capital was undoubtedly sincere
and strong.

In 1903, i.e. four years after being convic-
ted, his new Russian friends even succeeded in
helping him escape:

Aydalıp jürüp tutkunda
Bir tuugang taptım orustan
Atalash taptım orustan...*

He comes back to Kirghizia, as rebellious as
before:

Ayildan chıkkan zulumdar
Arı ekendigi donguzdan...

where he was to live, apparently unbothered by the
Tsarist police until the Revolution of February
1917.

Such a fate, hardly conceivable for modern
Kirghiz readers, is presented by his biographers
without appropriate comments. Neither are we told
what were his reactions during the 1916 drama, or
during the first shady years of the revolution.
All we are informed about is his ardent russophilia -
a feeling which for being certainly deeper in his
own case, was nevertheless shared by all those intellectuals who claimed to draw their inspiration
from Chokan Valikhanov and, more widely, the jadíd
school of thought, but which was mainly directed,
as ultimately shown by a later evolution, toward
the KD or SR tendencies.

In any case, his past sufferings at the hands
of the representatives of the old régime and the
collaborationists naturally placed him in the fellow-
travelers' camp. Contemporary Soviet critics insist
on his anti-Basmachi (from his viewpoint: anti-
kadymist and 'anticlerical') poems, on his innumerable verses to the glory of Lenin, Stalin, the

Party. Even much more than T. Moldo, he became,
until his death, the epitome of the official poet
whose favorite and undoubtedly sincere themes - the
condemnation of social injustice, of scholasticism,
the exhaltation of inter-ethnic friendship, of
modernization - corresponded to those of the official propaganda.

But precisely because he was made an official
symbol, we know nothing of his own, intimate feelings and especially of his own attitude toward
the thorny problem of how to maintain, to what
degree and in which field, national particularism.

He died just one year before the 1934 purge
which saw the liquidation of so many people with a
biography similar to his own.

'Farewell, Mother' was written after his
arrest and 'The Wheeling Mountain Eagle' in exile.
At least in this pedagogical edition, no non-
literary features can be detected. Linguistic comments can thus be limited to the illustration of
'classical' grammatical points:

Text III-A:
          1. 1: K-1771   1.27: K-1778,2228
          1. 8: K-1895   1.28: K-1892
          1.12: K-1820   1.30: K-1337
                    1.33: K-1820
                    1.34: K-1772
1.34: Kerimbay: lit.: 'the arrogant lord': a local
       manap and not the Tsar himself as sometimes
       anachronically stated, nor an abstract, 'feu-
       dal' lord: the author's wrath is personal:
       "Ushundan kelsem kutulup
       Kerimbay, oyormun senin közündü
       Aman kelsem aylanıp
       Alarmın senden öchümdü"*

Text III-B:
          1. 1: K-1311   1. 15: K-1337
          1. 1-4: K-1801, Y-257   1. 18-20: K-1994
          1. 5: Y-392. kozgo is a noun; cf. kozgolo-
          1. 13: K-1892   1. 21: K-1565
          1. 16,23-24: K-2448   1. 25: Y-966
                    1.28: K-1778

Note the complex rhythmic scheme used in text III-A

Toktogul was a musician as much as a poet and com-
posed music for his verses as much as he wrote
verses for his music.

*: cf. M.I.Bogdanova: "O nekotorykh voprosakh
istorii Kirgizskoi literatury 19-ogo i nachala
20-ogo vekov", Trudy Instituta iazyka i literatury
Kirgizskogo filiala AN SSSR, 1952, v. 3, pp. 103-
137.

d) FROM TRADITION TO MODERNITY TEXTS IV

Süyünbay Eraliev:

- Jashtık (in San Toolor, Kırgızstan Basması,
  Frunze 1971)

                                        Text IV-A

- Jayloodogu Tün (in Uyang Jıldızdar, Kırgız
  Mamlekettik Basması, Frunze 1962)

                                        Text IV-B

ЖАШТЫК

С. Эратиев

I   Кайда суулар
    Ошондогу биз кечкен?
    Кайда көздөр,
    Көрбөсө жок издешкен?
5   Ал сууларды кайра да бир кечсем дейм,
    Ал көздөрдү канбас элем тиктештен.

    Турат дале,
    Турат жашыл жылгалар,
10 Турбай бирок жылып кеткен жылдар ал,
    Анткен менен ал жылдардын ордунда
    Ошондогу биз ырдаган ырлар бар.

    Түндөр келчү жылдыздарын жетелеп,
    Чөптөр окшоп
15 Азыркыдан өтө көк,
    Мезгилдин да ашуулары көп эле,
    Биз эңсеген,
    Бирок али жете элек.

    Мен аларды кайра да бир ашкым бар,
20 Мейли ошондой,
    Шыгырасын таш-кумдар.
    Муну минтип айтып жаткан себебим,
    Мени такыр таштай элек жаш кумар.

Y O U T H

1   Where are the streams
    We used to ford?
    Where are the eyes
    Which looked for what they lacked even when
        they didn't see it

5   How I would like to ford those streams
        again,
    And never be satiated with fixing my gaze
        on these eyes!
    Still there, and green
    Forever stand the riversides -

10 But no more there are all these years which
        smoothly flowed away,
    Although, instead of them,
    Still there are all the songs we would sing
        in those days.
    Nights came, dragging along their stars,
    The leaves looked

15 Much more verdant than now,
    More infinite the mountain passes of Time
    Towards which we strove
    But which as yet we didn't cross.
    I still crave for traversing them once more

20 If only as before
    Sands and boulders crunch under my feet.
    If I still sing as then it is because
    Hotheadness of youth has not left me at
        all.

ЖАЙЛООДОГУ ТҮН

С. Эралиев

I Мына, мына кеч кабагы бүркөлүп,
   Барган сайын коюу тартты айлана.
   Анда "жарк" деп учкан жылдыз мүрт өлүп,
   Ай асманда каңгып барат жай гана.

5 Короо-короо койлор жуушап мындагы,
   Жаңырыктайт сайдын жаагы ачылып.
   Ар-ар жерден агыш тартса кумдары,
   Ай талаада туз жаткансыйт чачылып.

   Билбейм, билбейм асман кайда сугунат,
10 Агып өткөн жылдыздары түндөгү?
   Алтындагы апай беттен угулат,
   Кулун, тайдын кишенешкен үндөрү.

   Дөбөт үрсө кокту жакты акмалап,
   Кыз селейип, кулак түрөт дабышка
15 Ит-куш менен жигиттерден шек санап,
   "Чо-ойт!" деп коёт аз уйкулуу абышка.

142

NIGHT ON A HIGH MOUNTAIN PASTURE

1   Lo, lo, the dusk has already knitted its
      brows
   Darkness keeps spreading all around;
   A shooting star sparkles, flickers and dies
   The moon glides calmly in the sky.

5   Sheep in folds lie there in peace
   The furrowed banks send back echoes;
   Sands here and there show white in the
      distance
   Like salt spattered about the steppe.
   I don't know, I don't know how deep the sky
      is sinking,

10 Nor whither flow the nightly stars?
   From the hill sides' golden shelves are
      heard
   Foals and fillies neighing to each other.
   Staring at the ravine, if a dog barks,
   Girls in a trance prick up their ears;

15 And suspecting alike suitors or wolfes,
   The sleepy elder hushes and tuts.

TEXTS IV

COMMENTS

'Youth' and 'Night on the Mountain Pasture'
by Süyünbay Eraliev (cf. Texts VIII 1. 40) quite
vividly illustrate both the developing revival of
modern Kirghiz poetry with its bold search for new
forms of expression and its faithfulness toward
'classical', philosophical and naturalistic themes.
     The author was born in 1921 in the Talas plain
in Northern Kirghizia and is considered one of the
best contemporary poets. Lyric themes and prosodic
innovations make him as different from T.Satılgan-
uulu and T. Moldo as Esenin is from Nekrasov.
     Abandoning the somewhat droning 7 or 8-syllable
rhythm, he introduces a more subtle and complex
scheme based, in 'Youth', on a triple tempo of 4,7
or 11-syllable verses.
     This probably prepared him to systematize
another radical breakthrough: the use of an entirely new prosodic scheme which combines Russian influence (the Pushkin-inspired iambic meter based
on tonic syllables) and the traditional syllabic
accent, typical for languages with a fixed, final
stress.
     All verses have final rhymes and 11 syllables
with a caesura after the fourth one, but all can
be scanned at the same time as a series of iambs
with a final anapaest. Some pyrrhics here and there
bring variety to the second 'hemistich':
     1 : u-u-//uuu-uu-
     2 : u-u-//u-u-uu-
Eraliev's tongue is strictly literary. When
difficulties arise, they stem mostly, and especially in 'Youth', from the 'dismantled', non classical
syntax (IV-A 1. 1,3,etc.).

IV-A: Youth

1. 5:	K-1851	1. 22:	K-1734
1. 13:	K-1811	1. 18,23:	K-1243
			(jetc clek,tashtay elek)

IV-B: Night on a High Mountain Pasture

1. 7:	K-1855	1. 9: K-1799	1. 16: K-1741

1. 4: kangıp: from kanggı-/kangkı-. Not in Y,
but related to kanggıma: Y-341: wanderer and to
kanggır-: to wander (same in Kazakh).

B - THE SOVIET NORMATIVE LITERARY LANGUAGE

a) THE (SOVIET) NORMATIVE LITERARY LANGUAGE

LITERATURE

- Chıngıs Aytmatov: Birinchi mugalim
  (in Samanchı jolu - Povestter jana anggemeler,
  Kırgızstan Mamlekettik Basması, Frunze 1963,
  pp. 8-15 (Excerpt)
                              Text V

- Chıngıs Aytmatov: Obon, 'Egin tashuu'
  (in Z. Bektenov, J. Temirova: Bizdin Adabiyat,
  Mektep Basması, Frunze 1965, pp. 69-70)
  (Excerpt)
                              Text VI

Ч. Айтматов

I   БИРИНЧИ   МУГАЛИМ
                        /Повесть/

Биздин айыл Ак-Жар тоо этегинде, суулар
шаркырап аккан, чоӊ тектирде орношкон,
андан ылдый-туурасынан суналган Кара-тоого
5   чейин -- түзөӊ өзөн, темир жол кеткен казактын сары талаасы.
    Айылдын үстүндөгү адырда, мен бала чак-
тан бери билген, эки зор терек болор эле.
Бул кош терек азыр да ошол жерде. Качан
карабагын, айылга кайсы туштан келбегин,
элден мурун эле дөбөдө жанаша кыналышкан
ушул бийик теректер көзгө учурайт. Эмне
10 үчүн экенин билбеймин, же балалык таасирдин
күчүбү, же болбосо сүрөтчүлүк кесибине бай-
ланыштуубу, айтоор, станциядан түшүп, кап-
чыгайдан чыгып, айылды көздөй бет алганда,
тээ адырда баягы кош теректер турат болду
бекен деп, чыдамсыздык менен ошол тарапты
акмалап караймын. Ушунчалык алыстыктан бак-
тар канчалык бийик болбосун көрүнөрү шек-
15 түү, бирок мен үчүн алардын сөлөкөтү ар
качан байкалгандай туюлат. Эртерек айлына
жетип барып, эртерек дөбөгө чыгып барып,
кош терекке ийилип салам берип, кулагымдын
моокусу кангыча алардын күүлөнгөн үнүн ук-
сам деп дайым дегдеймин. Көчөдө бак деген
толуп жатат, бирок бул теректердин бир ук-
муштуу касиети -- алар бөтөнчө үндүү, тил
20 бүткөндөй жандуу теректер. Түнү-күнү тынбай
качан болбосун жалбырактар дирилдеп, чайпалган чокулары айкалыша, теректер ар кандай үнгө салып шуулдайт. Бирде -- жээкке
урунган эрке толкундай угулар-угулбас шап-
шынып, бирде -- тымтырс ойлоно калып, са-
гынычтуу санаага толгондой, алда эмнеге
муӊдана үшкүрүп, жулкунган шамал булут ай-
25 дап, бутактарын кайрып тийгенде, теректер
бой тиреше чыӊалып, "бизди жыгалбайсыӊ" --
дегендей, өжөрлөнө күүлөнүшөт.
    Кийин эс тартып чоӊойгондо, мен бул те-
ректердин сырын түшүндүм. Бийикте, туш -

TEXT V

тарабы ачык дөбөдө тургандыктан, булар
дайым шамалдын огуна туура келип, абанын
ар бир кыймылына жооп кайтарып, жанагыдай
30 тынымсыз шуулдап, бөтөнчө үндүү болгон
себеби да ошол. Анткен менен менин бул байкап тапканым балалык кыялымдын алгачкы
таасирин сууталбады. Ошол кездеги сонурка-
ганым азыр да тарабай, мен үчүн бул теректер ушул күнгө чейин кандайдыр тегин эмес-
тей, сырдуу, жандуу сыяктанат. Бул теректердин түбүндө менин өмүрүмдүн эң бир сый-
35 кырдуу чагы калгандай, эстеген сайын кайра
баштан эскергим келет.
    Окуудан таркаган жайкы маалда биз бир
топ балдар болуп, балапан алабыз, деп ушул
жерге келчүбүз. Биздин чуркурашкан үнүбүз-
гө ыраазы болгондой, дөбөдө кериле чайпалган алп теректер дайымкысындай жалбырак-
тарын леп-леп желпилдетип, бизди күндөн кө-
40 лөкөлөп тосуп ала турган. Ошондо биз, чор
таман, чор алакан тентектер, теректерге
мышыкча асылып чыга баштаганда, чуу көтөргөн таранчылар жаны калбай чырылдашар эле.
Анысына болобузбу! Улам бутактан бутакка
өйдөлөп, бир убакытта, куштар учкан бийик-
тиктен дүйнөнүн аймагы ачыла калган көрүнү-
шүнө таң калып, баарыбыз тең үн катпай,
45 бутак-бутакка жармашып, алабыз деген чым-
чыктын балапандарын да унутуп коёр элек.
Биз эң чоң имарат деп эсептеген колхоздун
ат сарайы теректин башынан тепкедей эле
көрүнүп, ал эми айылдан төмөн, алда кайда
мунарыктаган мейкиндиктин ушунчалык зор
экенине, бизден нары дагы нечен кыйыр жер-
лер, биздин суулардан башка дагы нечен
50 күмүштөнгөн суулар бар экенине суктана карап, ааламдын чети ошолбу, же андан нары
да ушундай асман, ушундай булут, ушундай
жер барбы деп ойлоно турганбыз. Ошол учурда көкөлөгөн жел күүсү кулакка угулуп, ага
удаа бир дабыштан шапырттаган жалбырактар,
көз көрбөгөн көгүлтүр алыстыкта нечен сонун-
дар, нечен кызыктар бар дегендей тымызын
55 күү чалып беттен эркелете сылар эле. Жүгө-
рүм жарылып кетчүдөй дикилдеп, кош теректин шуулдаганын кыялга батып тыңшар элем.
Көз алдыма жомоктогудай ар түркүн нерселерди

келтирип, ошондо бир гана нерсени ойлобоп-
турмун. Бул теректерди ким тикти, кандай
тилек, кандай үмүт менен өстүрдү экен деп
оюма алып койбоптурмун.

60   Мына ушул теректер турган жерди айылда-
гылар эмне үчүндүр "Дүйшөндүн мектеби" -
деп койчу. Кокус бир мал издеп калганда:
"Ой, баланча, менин тору кунанымды көрдүң-
бү ?" - десе, анда беркиси токтой калып:
"Тээ жогору Дүйшөндүн мектебинде жылкы жүрөт, ошол жактан чалып көр" - деп, бастырып кете берчү. Чоңдорду туурап, биз дагы:
65 "Жүр кеттик Дүйшөндүн мектебине, терекке
чыгабыз" - дей турганбыз.
    Биз кездерде ошол дөбөнүн үстүндө мектеп
болгон имиш. Биз анын ордун да көрбөй калдык, бирок кош теректүү дөбөнүн аталышы эл
оозунда мурунку бойдон келе жатат. Бул мектептин ордун, бала чакта адырларды кыдырып,
70 бир нече ирет издеп да көрдүм, кийинчерээк:
"Эмне үчүн "Дүйшөндүн мектеби" ? Ал кайсы
Дүйшөн ?" - деп, карыялардан сураштырсам,
алар менин бул суроомо, эч бир кызык жок,
жок иштей, кайдыгер гана жең шилтеп коюшту:
    "Э, ушул эле жүргөн аксак-кой Дүйшөн.
75 Кече уруяттан кийин, тиги дөбөдө бир жаман
там болор эле, Дүйшөн комсомол болдум деп
ошого мектеп ачып, бала окуткан. Мектеп
дегендей да эмес болчу, тимеле бир кеп. О
анда өзүнчө бир кызык заман эмес беле, кудай
салбасын, үзөнгүгө буту илингендин баары
эле бет алдынча чоң, ар ким билгенин кылчу.
Дүйшөн да ошондо оюна келгенин бир иштеп
80 койду да. Андан бери эми ал жаман тамдын
топурагы да калган жок, бир пайдасы - аты
жок дөбө эле, "Дүйшөндүн мектеби" - болуп
калды..."
    Дүйшөн деген кишини мен анча жакшы бил-
ген эмесмин. Бою каркайган, бүркүт кабак,
салабаттуу адам окшоду эле. Анын үйү суунун аркы маңдайында экинчи бригаддын көчө-
сүндө. Мен айылда жүргөн кезде Дүйшөн кол-
85 хоздун мурабы болуп, канжыгасына чоң кет-
менди байланып алып, шатектен чыгып калган
өзүндөй калжайган жээрдени минип, биздин
көчөдөн кээде бастырып өтө турган. Кийин,
карый түшкөндө, почточулукка өтүп кетти

деп уктум. Бирок кеп башкада. Комсомол деген менин аңдагы түшүнүгүмдө - ишке да,
90 сөзгө да курч, жалкоо-жегичтерди газетке
жазып жиберчү айыл жигиттеринин чекке чыккан мыктысы. Ал эми жанагы сакалы бууру-
ала карапайым киши, кашаң атын чү-чүлөгөн
кебетеси менен өз заманында кандайча комсомол болуп, анан калса сабатсыз жатып, бал-
дарды кандайча окутуп, кантип мугалим болуп
жүргөнүн эч бир көз алдыма келтиралбадым.
95 Чынын айтсам, айылдагы көп жомоктун бир
жомогу го деп мен бул сөзгө анча да деле
ишенген жок элем. Көрсө "Дүйшөндүн мектеби"
дегендин өзүнчө тарыхы бар экен, мен аны эч
бир күтпөгөн жерден жакында гана билдим.
Өткөн күздө колхоздон мага телеграмма
келди. Эки жылдан бери биздин колхоз өз
күчү менен жаңы мектеп куруп жаткан болчу.
100 Мектептин имараты эми салынып бүтүп, айыл-
дагылар мени мектептин ачылышына чакырган
экен. Элимдин мындай кубанычтуу күнүндө
бирге болоюн деп, дароо эле жолго чыга турган болдум. Сүрөт тартыш үчүн айылга ал
турсун үч-төрт күн мурунурак бардым. Шаардан чакырылгандардан эми академик Сулайманованы келет деп күтүшүп жатышкан экен. Ал
105 киши мында бир күн - жарым күн туруп, ушундан нары поездге түшүп Москвага кетет экен
дешти. Академик Сулайманованын келерин угуп,
мен абдан кубанып калдым. Бул көпчүлүккө
белгилүү илимпоз аял биздин айылдан экенин,
кыз кезинде шаарга кетип, кийин окумуштуу
болгонун анча-мынча угуп жүргөм. Ал эми өзү
менен шаардан тааныштым. Мен көргөндө Алты-
110 най Сулайманова чачына ак кирип, толмоч
тартып элүүлөргө таяп калган киши экен.
Университетте кафедра башчысы болуп, фило-
софиядан лекция окуп, академияда иштеп, анан
ар кандай коомчулук иштери менен чет өлкө -
лөргө барып келип турган айылдаш эженин жай
отуруп, жай сурашууга чамасы келбей жүрдү,
115 бирок ар бир жолуккан сайын, мейли жыйна-
лышта, мейли кокус көчөдө кездеше калганда,
биздин айылдын жалпы аманчылыгын сурап,
менин чыгармачылыгым жөнүндө кыскача болсо
да пикирин айтпай койчу эмес. Мен бул кишинин жөнөкөйлүгүнө, адамгерчилигине ичим

жылып, бир күнү жашырбай эле өзүнө айттым:

120   - "Эже, айыл жакка барып, эл-журт менен
жолугушуп келсеңиз кантер эле ? Сизди сыр-
тыңыздан баары эле билип сыймыктанышат экен,
бирок көпчүлүгү тааныбайт. Атактуу, окумуштуу кызыбыз айылын теңине албай, чаның
жүрөбү деген сөздөр да бар."

   - "Анын туура, иним, - деп, Алтынай Сулайманова үшкүрүп койду. Барууга өзүм да

125 көптөн дилгирмин. Барбаганыма кылым болду.
Айылда анча деле жакын туугандарым жок.
Бирок эл деген тууган, элден чоң тууган
болбойт. Сөзсүз барам, колум бошой калса
эле барам... Сагындым жеримди..."

   Академик Сулайманова ал күнү кечигибирек

130 келди. Мектептин салтанатуу ачылышына жуп
анын машинеси көчөгө келип токтогондо, жыйналышка чогулган эл бүт эле астынан тосуп
чыгып, тааныган-тааныбаганы да, кары-жашы
дебей тегиз учурашып кол алышты. Алтынай
Сулайманова мындайды күтпөгөн болуу керек,
сүйүнгөнүнөн эмне кыларын билбей, элге кол
куушура ийилип жүрүп отуруп, залдагы прези-

135 диумдан орун алды. Мындай салтанаттуу жыйы-
лыштардын нечен мамлекетте, нечендерин көргөн Алтынай Сулайманова бул жолу көзүнө жаш
алып отурду. Жыйналыштын аягында пионерлер
анын мойнуна кызыл жагоо тагып, гүл берип,
жаңы мектептин ардак китебине анын ысмын
бирден бир биринчи жазышты. Окуучулардын

140 шаң-шөкөттүү оюндарынан кийин, кечке жуук
биз бир топ мугалимдер, айыл активдери болуп мектептин директорунун үйүндө конокто
болдук.

   Мына ал Алтынай Сулаймансванын келгенине
сүйүнүп жетиналбай, аны килемдер төшөлгөн
жасалгалуу төргө отургузуп, колунан кели-
шинче урматтап, сыйлап жатышты. Чоң дастор-

145 кондордун тегерегинде жайнап отургандар күү-
күү сөз сүйлөшүп, тосттор артынан тосттор
айтылып, чай ичилип жаткан кезде, колуна
бир тутам газет-журналдарды кармаган жаш
жигит эшиктен кирип келди да, үй ээсине он
чакты телеграммаларды сунуп, кол коюп бериңиз деп кайрылды. Мурунку окуучулардан келген куттуктоо телеграммалар катардан катар-

150 га өтүп, кимдир бирөө сөз арасында:

- " Ой, муну Дүйшөн абышка алып келдиби ?"
деп, сурап калды.
- "Ооба, - деди жигит - Жыйналышка жеткире
барайын деп жакшы эле чаап келген экен,
кечирип калдым деп жатат."
- "Ой, түш де аны аттан, үйгө кирсин!" -
155 деди үй ээси колун булгап.
Жигит эшикке чыгып кеткенде, жанаша отурган Алтынай Сулайманованын өңү кубара түшүп,
алда эмне эсине келгендей, менден сурап калды:
- "Ай, кайсы Дүйшөн, кимди айтып жатышат?"
160 - "Колхоздун почточусу, эже, - дедим мен.
Дүйшөн деген аксакалды тануучу белениз ?"
Ооба дегендей башын ийкеп, Алтынай Сулайманова бир нерсе айтайын дедиби, ордунан
турууга умтула берди эле, ањгыча терезенин
165 тушунан атчандын караны дүбүртөрүп өтө чыкты да, үйгө кирип келген жигит:
- "Түшүңүз десем тиги киши болбой койду,
агай, - деди. Элге кат таркатам деп, бастырып кетти."
- "Тимгой эмесе кете берсин, - отургандар-
дын ичинен бирөө жактырбагандай колун шил-
теди, - ал абышканын отурар жери башка."
170 - "Ой, Дүйшөн дегенди билбейсиңер, ал закон менен гана жүргөн киши, кызматын аткар-
майын эч жакка кайрылбайт," - деди ага
кошумчалап экинчиси. "Мейли эмесе, эчтеке
эмес" - дегендей үй ээси да башын ийкеп
койду.
Ањгыча болбой, төрдө отурган айыл ара-
175 сындагы кадырман кишилердин бири, вино
куюлган чөйчөгүн колуна алып, сөз баштап
калды:
- "Жолдоштор, бир кездерде биз "а" деген
тамганы тааныбаган Дүйшөндүн мектебине да
окудук элек. - Ал бул сөздү таң калгандай,
күлө сүйлөп, башын чайкады. - Азыр ошол
эсиме түшүп жатат."
180 - " Ой тообо десеңчи!"
- " Ырас, ырас! - дешти башкалар.
- " Ой, Дүйшөндүн жоругу курсун. Ушуну да
мугалим деп, окутуучу деп жүргөн экенбиз
да !"
Каткырган күлкүлөр бастай калганда, жана-
185 гы киши сөзүн уланта түштү:
- " Мына эми алдыбыз өлкөгө даңкы чыккан

академик болуп, артыбыз жогорку, орто билим-
дүү эл болдук. Айлыбызга бүгүн жаңы орто
мектеп ачтык. Башкасын айтпайын, замандын
кандай өзгөрүлгөнү ушундан эле байкалып
190 отурбайбы. Кана эмесе, агайын-туугандар,
биздин айылдын уул-кыздары мындан нары да
илимден илимге жетилип, өз заманынын алдыңкы кишилери болушу үчүн!..."
    Бул сөздөрдү эл жапырт колдоду. Жалгыз
гана Алтынай Сулайманова өтө кыжалат болгондой, эрдин тимтенип кызара түштү.
    Ал чөйчөктүн четин оозуна тийгизди да,
кайра ордуна койду. Анын минтип отурганын
195 сөзгө, күлкүгө берилип алаксыган көпчүлүк
байкаган да жок.
    - "Сиз эмне көңүлсүз отурасыз, эже?" -
дедим мен.
    - "Анчейин эле, иним" - Алтынай Сулайманова
эки-үч кайтара саатын карап коюп, башка
эчтеке айткан жок.
200   Ушуну менен коноктор тышка дем алганы
чыкканда, Алтынай Сулайманованын элден чет-
ке бөлүнүп, тээ жогору, адырда чайпалган
кош теректи тиктеп, ойлуу турганын көрүп,
жанына басып бардым.
    Жашыныга чукулдап, күздөө талаанын сур-
гулт четине чыгып алган күндүн кочкул нур-
лары бийикте турган теректердин чокуларына
205 бирде тийип, бирде тийбей кубулуп турган
экен.
    - "Кайран теректер, жалбырак төгүп турган
кези экен, жазгысын бүрдөгөндө көрсөңөр
болор эле!" - дедим мен.
    - "Ооба, мен да ошону ойлоп жатам" - деп,
Алтынай Сулайманова башын ийкеп, шыпшынын
койду. - "Ар бир нерсенин жазы да, күзү да
210 болот тура."
    Анын ажаары өчүп бара жаткан, болпогою-
раак төгөрөк жүзүнө, санаркалуу көлөкө
чалышып, өткүр кара көздөрүнүн тиктеши
өксүй түштү. Бул оокумда ушул далайды билген чоң окумуштуу аялдын түрү, о качанкы
"өтүп кеткен он сегиз кайра келер болсочу"
215 деп, ичтен сызып, кызыл жоолук, кызыл жүз-
дүү чагын эстеген кадимки эле жөпжөнөкөй
кыргыздын аялдарына окшой кетти. Ал дагы
бир нерсе айткысы келгендей, теректерди

тиктеп, унчукпай турду да, бир убакытта
колунда кармалап турган көз айнегин кийип,
сумкасынан папирос алып күйгүздү.
220 - "Москванын поезди биздин станциядан түнкү
он бирде өтөт эмеспи?" - деди.
- "Ооба, эже, он бирде өтөт."
- "Эмесе мен азыр жөнөшүм керек."
- "Эмне үчүн? Сиз бир-эки күн туруп кетмек
225 убадаңыз бар эмес беле? Эл сизди коё бер-
бейт, эже."
- "Жок, менин зарыл жумуштарым бар. Бүгүн
кетпесем болбойт, азыр кетишим керек..."
Айылдаштары жаалап, кетирбейбиз деп таа-
рынып кыйнагандарына болбой, бышып жаткан
тамакка да карабай, айтканынан кайтпай
230 кечирим сурапып, Алтынай Сйлайманова акыры
кетмек болду.
Күн батып калган кечки убакытта, айылдаштар кейип-кепчип жатьгч аны машинага отур-
гузушту. Алтынай Сулайманованы станцияга
узатып, мен да кошо жөнөп калдым.
Бул кишинин эмне үчүн мындай чукул арада,
235 бир топ элдин көңүлүн калтырып, шашылыш
жөнөшүн эч кимибиз түшүнбөй да калдык.
Эки-үч жолу мунун себебин сурайын деп
барып, бирок одоно болуп калбасын деп ий-
мендим. Анын үстүнө ал азыр эч кимге эчтеке
айтпасына да көзүм жетти. Жол катары Алтынай Сулайманова бир ооз сүйлөбөй, өтө катуу
ойлонуп, капа болуп келе жатты.
240 Станцияга келип, поездге түшөрүндө акыры
сурадым:
- "Эже, бир нерсеге кейип, капа болуп кел-
диңиз, таарынган жериңиз барбы?"
- "Жок. Антип ойлобогула. Эмнеге таарынайын.
Таарынсам да өзүмө таарынам, өзүмдүн бил-
бестигиме... Оюңарга эчтеке албагыла - деди.
245 Андан көрө мага нааразы болсоңор жөнү болор."
Ушуну менен Алтынай Сулайманова Москвага жөнөп кетти. Мен шаарга кайтып келгенден кийинки күндөрдүн биринде Алтынай Сулай-
мановадан ойлобогон, күтпөгөн жерден кат
алдым. Өзүнүн илимий иштери боюнча Москва-
да көп убакыт кармаларын жазып, андан нары
250 катында мындай дептир: "Кымбаттуу иним,
канчалык зарыл жумуштарым болбосун, бардыгын жайлаштырып таштап, мен ушул катты

жазууну туура таптым..."

Эгерде ушунда айтылгандар сизди кызыктырса, анда өз чыгармачылыгыӊызга пайдала-
нууну суранам, анткени бул мен үчүн гана
эмес, биздин айылдаштар үчүн гана эмес,
255 биздин жалпы ишке, көпчүлүккө, өзгөчө жаштар үчүн керек го деп эсептеймин. Бул менин
көп ойлордон келип чыккан пикирим. Бул
менин эл алдына жүрөгүмдү сунуп тартуу кылган сырым, андыктан муну канчалык көп адам
билсе, мен ошончолук бактылуу болом, ошончолук эл алдында ыйык парзымды аткарып,
ошончолук менин да кетирген күнөөм кемийт...
260 Эгерде жаза турган болсоӊуз, мени уялат
экен деп тартынбаӊыз, эчтекесин жашырбай,
ачыктан-ачык жазыӊыз..."

Мен ушул каттын негизинде мындан нары
академик Сулайманованын өзүнүн атынан аӊге-
мени уланткым келет.

... Бул иш 1924-жылы болгон. Ооба, мен
265 жакшы билем, так ошол жылы...

1   THE FIRST SCHOOLTEACHER(1)

Our village Ak jar (White Cliff) nestles
at the foot of the mountain, on a wide
shelf through which mountain streams rumble
down; from there on and straight down all
the way to the

5   Kara Too (Black Mountain), the yellowish
Kazakh steppe stretches out into a flat
bassin where the railroad line runs;
On a hill above the village - a familiar
sight since I was a child - stood two huge
poplars. They both still stand there, at
the same place. Whenever you look, from
whatever side you come to the village, even
before seeing anybody, these two high
poplars, closing ranks on the hill, greet
your eyes;
Without even knowing why (is it because
of the strength

10   of recollection from childhood or is it
linked to my being a professional painter?)
in any case, as soon as I descend at the
railroad station and drive out of the
gorge, my face turned toward the village, I
look impatiently in that direction,
wondering whether the two poplars of yester
year still stand on that hill. At such a
distance how big they may be, it is doubt-

15   ful that one can see them, but for me,
their silhouette always seems to be
visible. I always long to reach the
village as quick as possible to go as quick
as possible up the hill in order to greet
them both with a bow and quell my desire to
hear their sweet rustle. There are plenty
of trees in the streets, but these poplars
have a strange peculiarity: they have a
voice of

20   their own, they are living beings endowed
with speech. Endlessly night and day,
continuously rocking their foliage,

intertwining their swaying tops, these
poplars rustle in two voices. Then lapping
in a barely audible murmur like a lazy wave
on the beach, then still and thoughtful, as
if immersed in forlorn thoughts, they sigh
and grieve for something unknown; and when
a gust of

25 wind drives away the clouds and the rain,
lifting up their branches, they stand firm,
holding their heads up high, as if saying:
"You won't be able to break us" and they
face up stubbornly to the storm.
      Later, when I grew up and became
conscious, I understood the secret of these
poplars. Towering up there on a bare hill
open to the four winds, always directly
exposed to the battering winds, responding
to the slightest puff of air, they

30 keep on rustling as before and this is why
they have such a special voice.
Discovering this after keeping watch on
them didn't tarnish however the primeval
memory of my childhood dream. The
wonderful amazement of that time didn't
fade and for me, up to this day, they are
not just trees, but mysterious beings with
a soul... As if the most enchanted time in
my life had

35 remained under these poplars, the more I
recall them, the more I feel like conjuring
them up again.
      In summer, when the school was over, we
- a bunch of children - used to go running
there to take young birds out of their
nests. As if rejoicing from our whooping
voices, the giant poplars smartly swaying
on the hill would spread as always their
fluttering leaves, thus protecting us from
the sun, and

40 making us cosy in their shade. The all of
us, scallywags with horny hands and feet,
would begin to move into the attack,
climbing the poplars like cats while panic-
stricken sparrows in an uproar would go on

squawking and screeching. But we didn't
care! Climbing higher and higher from one
branch to another, bewitched by the sudden
discovery of a portion of the world from a
bird's eyes view, unable to utter a word,
each one

45   clinging to his branch, we would soon
forget about catching any fledgeling. The
kolkhoz stable which we considered to be
the highest building looked minute seen
from the top of the poplars and we would
gaze eagerly at the endless hazy immensity
down there, far away, beyond the village,
wondering whether beyond us there were
other places like ours, other

50   silvery glittering rivers beyond ours,
whether this was the end of the world or
whether farther on there were the same sky,
the same clouds, the same land. Meanwhile,
the swish of a gentle breeze would reach
our ears while the leaves, rustling one
after the other in a single voice, would
caress our faces and gently modulate the
melody of all the wonders and marvels that
exist, invisible to our eyes, in the bluish

55   distance. My heart pounded as if ready to
burst and, immersed in my dream, I listened
to the swoosh of the twin trees. Whilst
all kinds of fairy-tale-like images flashed
before my eyes, one thing didn't even cross
my mind. It didn't occur to me who had
planted these poplars, who had nursed them,
with what aim and hopes.

60   For some unknown reason, the villagers
used to call the place where these poplars
stood "Düyshön's school". If by chance one
was looking for an animal, asking "Say, So-
and-so, have you seen my bay foal?", then
the one standing near would answer:
"There's a horse up there near Düyshön's
school; have a look in that direction" and
go on his way. Imitating adults, we too
used to say: "Let's go to Düyshön's school
and

65 climb the poplars!".
    In our time, people said there had been,
allegedly, a school on that hill. We
couldn't even find the place, but among the
people this way of calling the poplar's
hill dated back from long ago. During my
childhood, walking through the hills, I
went looking more than once for traces of
this

70 school. A little later, I inquired from
old people: "Why is it called 'Düyshön's
school'? Which Düyshön was it?" But
without paying any attention to my
uninteresting and trifling question, they
merely waved their sleeves: "Pooh! that's
just that Düyshön of the Lame Ewe clan.
Earlier, after

75 Freedom(2), there was a shoddy shack on
that hill. Düyshön who had proclaimed
himself a komsomol, opened a school there
and began teaching children. It was not
worth calling it a school, it had only the
name of it. Oh, it was a queer period of
time indeed, Heaven forbid, anyone able to
put his feet in the stirrup was a big shot
by himself, everyone did exactly as one
pleased. Düyshön too stuck then to what he
had put

80 into his head." Since then, even the clay
from that shoddy shack has disappeared...
there was no other point in giving this
name: "Düyshön's hill' to a nameless
knoll...
    I didn't know the man who was called
Düyshön that well. It was a tall, imposing
man with hawk-like eyelids. His house was
on the opposite side of the irrigation
canal, on the

85 Second Brigade street. When I was still
living in the village he was the mirab(3)
of the kolkhoz; with a long spade tied to
the pommel of his saddle, riding a beanpole like reddish brown nag which looked
much like him, he would ride from time to

time along our street. Later, when he grew
old, I was told he was made a postman. But
that's not the point. A komsomol as I
understood it at that time, was supposed to
be

90   one of the most dynamic, hard-working young
tigers in the village, with a sharp tongue
ready to expose lazybones and embezzlers in
the newspaper. But such an ordinary man,
with his pepper-and-salt beard, whom I
vividly remember gee-ing up his broken-
winded horse - I simply couldn't imagine
him being at the same time a komsomol and
almost illiterate, teaching children,

95   being a schoolteacher. To say the truth, I
didn't believe much what people said,
considering it another village legend among
others. In fact, that phrase - 'Düyshön's
school' - had its own story which I was
soon to discover quite unexpectedly.
        Last autumn, a telegram came from the
kolkhoz for me. During the past two years,
our kolkhoz had been building a

100   new school with its own resources. Now
that the roofing had been finished, the
villagers were inviting me to the opening
ceremony. Having decided to be among my
fellow countrymen on such a merry day, I
rapidly got under way. In order to paint
some pictures, I even started off to the
village two or three days beforehand.
Among those invited from the big town, they
were expecting Academician Sulaymenova who
had said she would

105   come. People said she would stay one day,
one day and a half and then take the train
to Moscow. When I heard that Academician
Sulaymenova was to come, I greatly
rejoiced. This woman, now a renowned
scholar, was a native of our village; she
had gone to town when she was a young girl
and I somehow got wind of her becoming a
scholar. But I actually met her only in
the

110   town. When I saw her, Altınay Sulaymenova
was a woman over fifty, already stout with
greying hair. As the chairwoman of a
university department, she taught
philosophy(4), worked for the Academy of
Sciences, fulfilling all sorts of official
missions, frequently travelling abroad.
Although this fellow-villager of ours never
had time to sit and chat quietly,

115   nevertheless each time we met at some
meeting or ran into one another by chance
in the street, she would never omit to ask
how things were going at the village and
give me however briefly her opinion on my
works. Attracted by her simplicity and

120   humanity, one day I told her openly:
"Eje(5), why don't you come to the village
and meet your fellow-countrymen? Everyone
around has heard about you, is proud of
you, but most people don't know you.
Rumour even has it that our famous and
learned fellow-villager shuns the village
and plays the fine lady." - "You're right,
inim(5), said Altınay Sulaymenova with a
sigh. I myself

125   have been longing to go there for a long
time. I haven't been there for a century.
I really don't have near relatives there
anymore. But the villagers are my
relatives, there are no closer relatives.
I'll go without fail, I'll go as soon as I
free myself. I'm homesick...".
    On that day, Academician Sulaymenova
came a little

130   late. When her car came to a stop in the
street just in time for the solemn
inauguration of the school, all the people
who were there for the meeting rushed
towards her, all - young and old, friends
and strangers - shook her hand and welcomed
her. Altınay Sulaymenova who obviously
didn't expect anything similar, overwhelmed
with pleasure and not knowing what to do,
walked towards the crowd with her hands

crossed on her breast and took a seat in
the hall among the officials. Altınay
Sulaymenova

135   who had seen so many similar solemn
meetings in so many countries, this time
sat on the verge of tears. At the end of
the meeting, pioneers knotted a red tie
around her neck, offered her flowers and
her name was inscribed among the very first
ones in the new visitors' book of the
school. After the children's splendid,
magnificent performances, we - a group of

140   teachers and village activists - were
invited towards the evening to the
Director's house.
    There, overwhelmed with joy by her
presence, having seated her in the place of
honor decorated with carpets, each one
greeted her in turn and treated her with
the utmost respect. Just when the loudly
chattering guests, seated around a big low
table covered with a tablecloth, having had
tea, were

145   drinking toast after toast, in came a young
boy holding in his hands a whole stack of
newspapers and reviews, and handed to the
master of the house ten telegrams or so,
asking him to sign, and went out. After
these telegrams of congratulations from
former pupils had passed from one row to
another, somebody asked in passing: "Well,
I suppose it's that old man Düyshön who

150   brought them?" - "Yes, said the young boy,
he said he had put his horse into a gallop
in order to come in time for the meeting,
but was a little late". The master of the
house made a sign with his hand: "Hey, get
him off his horse and tell him

155   to come in!".
    After the young boy had left, Altınay
Sulaymenova who was seated near me suddenly
turned pale as if something had crossed her

mind; she asked: "Which Düyshön are they talking

160 about?" - "The kolkhoz's postman, eje, I said. Do you happen to know old Düyshön?". Nodding her head as to say 'yes', Altınay Sulaymenova was about to say something and almost jerked to stand up but at that very moment the shadow of a horseman passed under the window and the young boy came back into the

165 house: "When I told him to dismount, this man just didn't want to listen, agay(5)", said the young boy. "I have mail to deliver, he said. He's gone". - "All right, leave him alone, let him go, said one of the guests with a gesture of rebuke, let him sit with the old!" - "Oh, you don't know that Düyshön,

170 he is very hot on the rules; as long as he hasn't done his duty, he won't go anywhere", said a neighbor of the first. The master of the house nodded as if to say: "If he doesn't want to, that's just too bad".
    Just then, one of the powerful villagers who was seated at the place of honor, lifting a glass full of vodka

175 began to speak: "Comrades, there was a time when we studied at school with Düyshön who didn't even know the letter 'a'. And as if surprised by his own words, he began to laugh, nodding

180 his head. I just remembered this". - "Well, how strange!" "He's right, he's right", said the others. - "Come on, let's forget about Düyshön's feats. And we swallowed it when he said he was a schoolteacher, a master!".
    When the roars of laughter calmed down, the above-

185 mentioned official continued: "So, the best among us has now became a worldwide

known academician and the rest of us are
now people with secondary or university
degrees   A new school has been opened
today in our village. I won't add
anything: nothing shows better how times
have changed. So, honored guests and

190   relatives, may in the future the young men
and girls from our village continue further
on the path of Science and become the
avant-garde of our time!". With these
words, the whole assembly burst into
applause. Only Altınay Sulaymenova,
evidently very ill-at-east blushed and bit
her lip.
        She touched her glass to the edge of her
lips and put

195   it down immediately. Most people were busy
chatting and laughing and didn't notice her
state of mind. "Why are you so sad, eje?"
said I. - "It's just nothing, inim," and
looking two or three times at her watch,
she didn't say anything else.

200   Then, when the guests went outside to
freshen up, seeing how Altınay Sulaymenova
was staying away from everybody, looking
fixedly at the two quivering poplars up
there on the hill, lost in thought, I came
up to her.
        The dark-red rays of the hastily sinking
sun were shooting from the grey edge of the
autumn steppe, at times flaring up and at
times fading, shimmering on the very top
of the poplars on the hill.

205   "Poor poplars! They are now shedding
their leaves; you should see them when they
break into leaf in springtime", said I. -
"Yes, that's what I was thinking myself"
Altınay Sulaymenova nodded and smacked her
lips as a sign of regret. "Everything has
its own spring, and its own autumn,
indeed".

210   Over her round, slightly plump face
which was already losing its freshness, a

worried shadow passed, as if draining for a
while her black eyes of their brightness.
During that instant, the face of this woman
- a renowned, experienced scholar - as if
expressing 'If only I could recover the
time, now gone, when I was 18!' harbored a
regret and she resembled

215 one of those plain, simple Kirghiz women
with rosy cheeks and a red scarf. As if
she wanted to say something else, she gazed
at the poplars, but remained silent and
suddenly put on her glasses she had been
holding in her hand, took a cigarette out
of her purse and lit it.

220   "The train to Moscow stops at our
station at 11 p.m., doesn't it?" she said.
- "Yes, eje, at 11 p.m." - "Then I have to
go right away". - "But why? Didn't you
promise to stay

225 one or two days? These people won't let
you go, eje." - "Yes they will. I have
urgent things to do. If I don't leave
today, it won't do; I must go immediately".
     No matter how the villagers besieged
her, pestered her, got upset, saying 'We
won't let you go', neglecting the food
which was going to be served, without going
back over her decision, Altınay Sulaymenova
kept on apologizing and finally

230 left.
     Late in the evening, after the sun had
set, the saddened villagers saw her back to
her car. I accompanied her and saw her off
at the station.
     Nobody among us ever understood why she
left so hastily, after such a short stay
and having saddened so many

235 people. Several times, I was on the verge
of asking her why, but I felt shy and
didn't want to seem rude. What's more, I
gathered she would say nothing to anybody
right now. On the road to the station,
Altınay Sulaymenova said nothing; she was

lost in heavy thought and feeling more and more unhappy.

240   When we came to the station, upon seeing her off, I ultimately asked: "Eje, something upset you, you've become sad: something offended you?" - "No. Don't think that. What could offend me? If I got angry, it's at myself, at my being unobliging. Keep that out of your mind", she said. You should

245   rather be angry with me".
      And so, Altinay Sulaymenova left for Moscow. A few days later, after I went back to town, when I wasn't thinking about her anymore, I received a letter, quite unexpectedly. She wrote she was going to be detained for long in Moscow by her scientific pursuits and added in her letter: "Estimated

250   young friend, not matter how exacting my work may be, I interrupted it to write this letter forthwith... If what I say here is of some interest to you, I'll ask you to please use it in your writings because I consider it useful not only for me,

255   not only for our fellow-villagers, for our common cause, for the society, but especially for young people. This is the idea I ultimately came to after thinking for a long time. This is my secret, which I offer to everyone from the bottom of my heart and the more numerous those who'll know it, the happier I'll feel, the more fully I'll fulfill my sacred duty to the people, the lesser will be my guilt about it...If you narrate

260   this, don't be afraid to inconvenience me, don't hide anything, write openly..."
      Because of this letter, I feel I must from now on continue this epistle in the name of the academician Sulaymenova.

265   This happened in 1924. Yes, I remember it well, exactly during that year ....

TEXT V

COMMENTS

1. 1: Compare with the Russian version of the
       same novel: Ch. Aytmatov: <u>Povesti</u> (Pervyi
       uchitel'), Izd. Izvestiya, Moscow 1967,
       pp. 6-13.
1. 2: that is after <u>February</u> 1917. Cf. D. Ayt-
       mambetov: <u>Kul'tura kirgizskogo naroda v
       2-oy polovine XIX-ogo veka i nachala
       XX-ogo veka</u>, Izd. Ilim, Frunze 1967, p.
       271, who mentions a demonstration a Nookat
       upon learning about the February Revolution
       in Petrograd, with people demanding
       'Hurriyat!': Liberty.
1. 3: murab: the man in charge of allotting
       water for irrigation. A duty reserved to
       elderly people with a reputation for fair-
       ness.
1. 4: 'philosophy', i.e. (exclusively) marxism-
       leninism.
1. 5: eje: elder sister - a polite way of addres-
       sing a woman of a higher social position.
       inim: my younger brother - a polite way of
       addressing a younger man.
       agay: the masculine equivalent of eje.

TEXT VI

Ч. Айтматов

ЭГИН ТАШУУ
"Жамийла / Обон"

I   Эртеси күн чыкпай, Данияр экөөбүз аттарды кырманга алып келдик. Жамийла жеңем
да орокто жүргөн жеринен келип калган экен,
бизди көрүп, тигинден эле кыйкырды:
- "Ой, кичине бала, менин аттарым кайсы,
5   бери жетеле! Каамыттары кайсы экен?" - деп,
машыккан арабакечтен бетер дөңгөлөктөрдүн
шалкылдаганын буту менен тээп көрүп жатты.
Аттарды коштой жетелеп, биз жакындап келгенде: - "Оо, узундуу-кыскалуу болгон кай-
рандар десе! Издешпей табышкансыңар го!"
10   Ушундан баштап эле ал бизди башкарып ал-
гансып: - "Болгула, урушта туруш жок, эрте-
рээк салкында жөнөй берели!" - деп, аттарды булкулдата кетенчиктетип, арабага кошо
баштады.
     Жамийланын бул чечкиндүүлүгүнөн Данияр
15   апкаарый түшкөндөй болду. Чекесин тырыш-
тырып, ал аны жактырбагандайда, таң калгандай да түктүйө карап, сыртын салды. Тиги
анысын байкаган да жок, болгондо гана Данияр
тараза үстүнөн каптардын бирин кучактап
20   алып, унчукпай арабасына көтөрүп таштаган-
да, Жамийла аны жемелей кетти:
- " Ал эмнеси экен? Ар ким эле өзүнчө
далбастай береби! Келе колуңду, колдошконду
кудай колдойт! Ай, кичине бала, чык арабага,
каптарды жаткыр!"

CARRYING THE CROP

1   On the next day, before daybreak, Daniyar and I led the horses to the threshing floor. My jene, Jamiyla, who was just coming back from the field which was being harvested, upon seeing us, shouted from afar: "Hey, kichine bala, bring along my horses! Which harnesses

5   are theirs?" she said and she began controlling the wheels, kicking them better than an experienced carter, to see whether they were loose. And as we were coming nearer, leading the horses in pairs: "Well, well, my dear ones - a beanpole and a shorty! An odd match, I would say!".

10   From then on, she acted as if commanding us: "Stand there; there's no pause in war. Let's go as early as possible while it's cool!" she said, and pushing back the horses in fits and starts, she began hitching them up to the cart.

15   Daniyar was flabbergasted by Jamiyla's resoluteness. He frowned as if not approving and, looking quite unkindly in full astonishment, he put on a stiff expression. Jamijla didn't take notice and just when Danıyar was taking hold bodily of the sack on the weighing machine and throwing it on the cart without a word, she began to rebuke him: "What's the big idea?! Is each one going to wear one-

20   self out alone? Give your hand, God helps those who help themselves. Come on, kichine bala, climb onto the cart, lay down the sacks!".

a) THE (SOVIET) NORMATIVE LITERARY LANGUAGE

SCHOOLBOOK MATERIAL

Akılduu Diykan (in Z.Bektenov, J.Temirova: Bizdin Adabiyat, Mektep Basması, Frunze 1965, p. 12-15).

Text VII

LITERARY CRITICISM

S.Jumadılov: "Akındın chıgarmachılık izdenüü-lörü", in Izdenüü jolunda, Ilim Basması, Frunze 1970, p. 42).

Text VIII

I

АКЫЛДУУ ДЫЙКАН
Кыргыз элинин жомогу

Бар экен, жок экен, байыркы-байыркы бир
өткөн заманда бир кыйшык ооз эселек хан
болгон экен. Артын ойлобой иштегендиктен,
анын иштеген ишинен, айткан сөзүнөн эч
натыйжа чыкчу эмес экен.

5 Бирок, эси жок болсо да, ханыбыз деп эл
ага баш ийчү экен. Кыргыз элиндеги: "Оозу
кыйшык болсо да, байдын уулу сүйлөсүн", —
деген макал ошондон улам айтылып калган
дешет.

Хан бир күнү иштээрге иши жок, саларга
кушу жок, эсирип отуруп, шашылыш түрдө
жигиттерин чакыртып, эки жигитине:

10 — "Силер азыр баргыла да, мага акмакты таап
алып келгиле" — деп, буйрук берди.

Айла канча, хан буйругу эки эмес, акмакты таап келиш үчүн, ал эки жигит жөнөп
кетишти.

Мындай чыкканда, жигиттердин бирөө:

15 — "Мына эми, бизди мээнет анык чырмабадыбы!
Акмакты эми кайдан таптык? Аны таппай бар-
сак, башыбыз алынат" — деди.

— "Ой, сен да бир жеткен келесоо көрүнөсүң!
Кимди деп киши таңдап отурмак белек. Биринчи эле
жолуккан кишинин жетелеп барабыз да.
Хан чакырат дегенде, барбай турган эрки

20 барбы" — деди экинчи жигит.

Алар келе жатып, карагай сүйрөтүп бара
жаткан бир кишиге жолугушту да:

— "Карагайыңды таштап, ханга жүргүн, сени
хан чакырып жатат" — дешти.

25 Ал кишинин жүрөгү шуу дей түштү да:

— "Токтоңуздар, карагайымды үйүмө жеткизип
койп, анан барайын. Хан мени эмне жумуштап
чакырды экен?" — деп элтеңден калды.

— "Сен да бир кызык киши экенсиң. Эмнеге
чакыргандыгы жөнүндө сенин ишиң эмне? Хан
акмакты таап кел деген. Жүр дегенде жүрбөй-

30 сүңбү" — деп, жигиттер шаштыра баштады.

— "Жок, жигиттер, карагайын атайын тоодон
мээнет кылып алып келе жатып, жолго таштап
баса бергидей, мен акмак эмесмин" — деп,
ал киши кетип калды...

Ошентип, эки жигиттин айласы кетти да:
35 - "Иштин жөнүн айтып отурганда, болбойт
экен. Эми кезиккен эле кишини зордоп алып
кетели" - дешти.
Алар келе жатып, жолдон жер айдап жүргөн бир дыйканга кездешти да:
- "Ой, дыйкан, жүр ханга!" - деди.
40 Анда дыйкан туруп:
- "Минтип эмгек кайнап турган мезгилде,
эмнеге барам" - деди.
- "Көп сүйлөбөй, жүр дегенде, жүргүн. Хан
акмакты таап кел деген. Сен акмак экенсиң."
деди.
Жигиттерге дыйкандын ачуусу келип:
45 - "Силер үчүн акмакты сээп койгон киши жок.
Көзүмө көрүнбөй, жоголгула" - деди.
- "Андай болсо, сен акмакты таап бергин" -
деп, эки жигит дыйканды туткактап коё бербеди.
- "Мени коё бергиле. Күн ысып бара жатат.
50 Жер кургай электе, айдоомду бүтүрүп алайын"
деди дыйкан.
Анда жигиттер:
- "Жок, болбойт. Же өзүң ханга жүргүн, же
бизге акмактын ким экенин айтып бергин.
Баарыңар эле акмак эмеспиз дейсиңер, кими-
ңер акмак экениңерди биз кайдан билебиз" -
деп, дыйканды коё бербеди.
55 Дыйкан анда:
- "Макул эмесе, мен акмакты айтып берейин,
коё бергиле" - деди.
Жигиттер батыраак айт дешип шаштырышты.
Дыйкан ойлонуп туруп:
- "Акмакты таап кел деген ханыңдын өзү
60 акмак, же акмакты издеп жүргөн экөөң акмак-
сың. Мындан артык акмакты дүйнө жүзүнөн
таппайсыңар" - деди.
Жигиттин ачуусу келип:
- "Сен ханга сөзүңдү тийгиздиң, барып айта-
быз" - деди.
Дыйкан анда:
65 - "Бир айтмактан миң айткын, деги ушуну
ханга угузуп айтсаңар экен" - деди.
Эки жигит ханга келип, кабар кылышты.
- "Ошол дыйкандын колу-бутун байлап, мага
алып келгиле" - деп, хан буйрук берди.
70 Дыйкан хандын астына келип отурду. Хан
дыйканды кекетип:

- "Мени акмак экенимди сен билген экенсиӈ,
билгич болсоӈ, кудай кайсы жерде турат,
билип берчи" - деди.
- "Ханым, мен ушул кебетем менен ханга
акыл айткандай болуп, кудайдын кайсы жерде
тарганын айтсам, кусур уруп кетет. Сиз
75 менин кийимимди кийип, кечирим сурап, тизелеп туруӈуз, мен сиздин кийимиӈизди кийип,
тагыӈызга отуруп, хан болуп туруп айтайын.
Болбосо ушу сыягым менен кантип айтам" -
деди.
Хан макул болуп, кийимин чечип берди,
өзү айыптуу киши болуп, тизелеп отурду.
80 Дыйкан хандын кийимин кийип, тагына
отуруп, жигиттерди чакырды.
- "Ушул убакка чейин акмакты таппай жүрө-
сүӈөр. Мындан артык акмак болчу беле, алып
барып, акмактын башын кескиле!" - деди.
85 Көпкөн жигиттер башка сөздү уксунбу,
ханды желкелеп барып, башын кесип, кумар-
дан чыгышты.
"Ойлобой сүйлөгөн оорубай өлөт" - деген
эл макалындагыдай, элдин башын айланткан
эси жок хандын башы кесилип, дыйкан элине
хан болуп, акыл менен журт сурап, өзү да
жыргап, эли да жыргап-куунап жатып калган
экен.

TEXT VII

THE CUNNING COUNTRYMAN

(A Tale of the Kirghiz People)

Once upon a time, a long, long time ago,
in a past age, there was a stupid khan with
a crooked mouth. Since in everything he
would act thoughtlessly, from what he did
and from what he said usually nothing
(sound) resulted.

5   But, though he had no brain, people used
to bow their head before him, saying: "He
is our khan". People say that precisely
since then the saying goes among the
Kirghiz: 'Let the bay's son speak even if
his mouth is crooked'.
One day, the khan who had nothing to do
nor any falcon to launch, became angry and
summoning hastily his two lads

10   (servants), he ordered them: "You two go
immediately, catch an idiot and bring him
to me!".
What can one do? A khan's order is not
given twice: the two servants started out
to find and bring back an idiot. While
they were thus going, one of the servants
said:

15   "Well now, we're in for trouble. Where
shall we find an idiot? If we come back
without him, it'll cost us our heads".
"Oh, but you don't seem to be quite normal!
Are we actually supposed to find someone
designed by name? We'll take along the
first man wel'll

20   come across" said the second servant.
They continued and met a man who was
pulling a fir tree: "Drop your tree and go
to the khan; the khan is summoning you"

25   they said. The man's heart turned to ice:
"Wait, I'll pull my tree to my home and

then I'll come. For which matter does the
khan call me?" said the man, looking around
fearfully. "You're really a strange man.
Is it your business to know what you're
summoned for? The khan told us to catch
and bring an idiot. Aren't you

30   going to go when you are told to go?" said
the servants, and made him hurry. "No,
servants, I took this fir tree purposedly
out of the forest with great pain. I am
not so stupid as to abandon it on the road"
said the man and went away.
      In the same way, the two servants' trick
fell through.

35   "If we speak about the heart of the matter,
things won't go right. Now let's take
along by force the first man we meet" said
the servants.
      While they were going, they met on the
way a countryman who was ploughing a field:
"O, countryman, go the khan!"

40   they said. The countryman remained on the
spot: "Why should I go at a time when
there is so much work?" "Don't speak much,
go when you are told to go. The khan told
us to bring an idiot. You must be one".
      The countryman became angry with the
servants:

45   "Nobody sows idiots for you. Get out of
my sight, clear off!" "In that case, you
find and bring us an idiot" said the two
servants, caught the countryman and didn't
let him go. "Let me go. The sun is
becoming hot. Let me finish ploughing my
field while the ground

50   still hasn't dried", said the countryman.
      Then the servants said: "No. It
doesn't work. Either you go to the khan or
you tell us who's an idiot. You all tell
us you're not idiots, how can we know who
among you is?" - and they didn't let him
go.

55   Then the countryman said: "All right
then, I'll tell you who is an idiot. Let
me go". The servants made him hurry,
saying: "Tell us quicker!". The
countryman didn't move and said: "Your
khan who said 'go and fetch an idiot' is an
idiot himself or

60   you both who started off looking for an
idiot on the face of the earth!". The
servants became angry: "You made fun of
the khan. Let's go and tell him!" The
countryman then said: "If you tell that to

65   the khan, don't tell him once but a
thousand times".
     The servants came to the khan, made
their report. The khan ordered them: "Tie
up the hands and feet of that countryman
and bring him to me!"

70   The countryman appeared before the khan.
The khan reproached him: "Apparently you
knew I was a fool. So, if you are so
clever, tell me please where God lives"
"My khan, if I look like counseling the
khan in such a state, if I tell him where
God

75   is, he will curse me. You put on my dress,
beg my pardon, fall on your knees (while) I
don your dress, sit on your throne and
speak as a khan. Otherwise how can I speak
with such a look?"

80   The khan accepted, took off his dress,
made himself a culprit, fell on his knees.
The countryman donned the khan's dress, sat
on his throne, summoned the servants: "Up
to now you haven't found an idiot. Can
there be a worse idiot than this one? Take
the fool and cut off his head!" he said.
     Could the presumptuous servants listen
to anything

85   else? Manhandling the khan, they cut off
his head, appeasing thus their desire.

As the saying goes: 'He who speaks
without thinking dies without suffering'.
Having cut off the head of the brainless
khan who turned the people's head, the
countryman became khan over the people,
governing with intelligence, enjoying it
himself while his people lived in
happiness.

I АКЫНДЫН ЧЫГАРМАЧЫЛЫК ИЗДЕНҮҮЛӨРҮ

Ар бир көркөм сөз чебери турмуштук ар
кыл көрүнүштө сүрөттөөдө өзүнө жаккан жана
өзү каалаган стилдик ыкманы колдоно тургандыгы белгилүү. Ар бир жазуучунун бири-бири-
никине окшобогон стилдик бөтөнчөлүктөрү да

5 мына ушундан улам келип чыгат. Демек, ар
кандай адабий чыгарманын идеялык-көркөмдүгү
жазуучунун стилдик өзгөчөлүгү менен аныкта-
лууга тийиш. Бирок стиль өзгөрбөй токтоп
туруучу нерсе эмес. Ал жазуучу адеп колуна
калем кармаганда эле өзүнөн-өзү пайда боло
да калбайт. Стиль жазуучунун ойлонуу ыгына,

10 чеберчилигине карай өсүп, өнүгүп отурат.
Өзүнчө стилге ээ болууга умтулган жазуучу дайыма изденүүдө болот. Изденүү дегени-
биз -- бул кокустук көрүнүш эмес. Изденүү -
доордун талабына баш иет, б.а. турмуштан
туулган тема ошол темага жооп бере турган
ыкманы табууга жазуучуну аргасыз кылат.

15 Ошондой болсо да чыгармачылык изденүүнүн
багыты, алдыга коюлган милдетти конкретүү,
практикалык жол менен чегүү -- жазуучунун
терең ойлонуусун, өзүнүн предметине үңүлө
кирүүнү, аны кадаланып изилдөөнү жана үйрө-
нүүнү талап кылат.
Азыр күндөгү кыргыз поэзиясы адамдын жан

20 сезимин, келечекке карата болгон көз кара-
шын мурдагыдан да ачыгыраак чагылдыра баштады. Ошол эле учурда поэзия жанрындагы чы-
гармаларда жаңыны изденүү, турмуштук ар кыл
көрүнүштөрдү жаңыча сүрөттөө кеңири орун
алууда. Бирок изденүүнүн гана үстүндө болуп,
өткөндөгүнүн бай тажрыйбаларын этибарга албай коюуга да жарабайт. Анткени өткөн тра-
дицияларга таянуу, аларды жаңы табылгалар

25 менен айкалыштыра билүү жазуучунун чыгармачылык өсүү жолундагы эң сонун негиз болуп
саналат. Буга кыргыздын таланттуу акыны
маркум Алыкул Осмоновдун өмүрүнүн акыркы
жылдарындагы канаттуу поэзиясы ачык далил
боло алат.

Алыкул дайыма изденүүчү, тынымсыз эмгек-
30 тенүүчү акын эле. Ага дүйнөлүк жана орус
классиктеринин тийгизген таасири зор болгон. Ошол дүйнөлүк жана орус классиктеринин адабий тажрыйбаларын чыгармачылык менен
өздөштүрүүсүнүн натыйжасында А. Осмонов
өзүнчө поэтикалык жаңы формаларды тапкан.
Акын кыргыз поэзиясындагы традициялык ыр
түзүлүш системасын жаңы форма менен айкалыштыра отуруп, ырларынын новаторлук мүнөз-
35 гө ээ болуусуна жетишкен. Мына ушул себептен Алыкул Осмонов жалаң гана окуучулардын
эмес, жаш авторлордун да сүйүктүү акыны
болду. Көп убактарда колуна жаңыдан калем
кармай баштаган жаштар Алыкулду туурап жа-
зышат. Алыкулду туурап, анын стилдик ыкма-
ларын чыгармачылык эргүү менен пайдаланууга
40 аракет кылып жүргөн акындарыбыздын бири —
дал ушул Сүйүнбай Эралиев. Эгерде аны А.
Твардовскийдин мүнөз түзүү чеберчилиги,
көркөм ойлонуу ыгы кызыктырса, А. Осмоновдун образдуу сүрөттөөсү, сөздөрүнүн экс-
прессивдүүлүгү жана "сөзгө сараң, ойго март-
тыгы" С. Эралиевди таң калтырат. "Алыкул
менин дүйнөм эле. Мен анын ырларын азыр да
зор сүйүү менен окуйм, ошондуктан Алыкул-
45 дун ырларынын бир далайын жатка да айта
алам" - дейт, акын.
    Көрүнүктүү жазуучулардын стилдик ыкма-
ларын пайдалануу чыгармачылык процесстеги
закондуу көрүнүш. Бул жөнүндө дүйнөлүк ада-
бияттан көптөгөн мисалдарды келтирүүгө
болот. Мисалы, Байрон Пушкинге зор таасирин
50 тийгизген. Ал Түштүктө сүргүндө жүрүп, Бай-
рондун романтикалык стилин, чыгармаларын-
дагы саясий эркиндикти сүйүүчүлүк идеясын
ал гана эмес, анын мүнөздөрүнүн, сюжеттик
ситуацияларынын көбүн пайдаланган. Ал эми
Пушкиндин баяндоо манерасы Лев Толстойдун
"Анна Каренинасын" жазууда чыгармачылык
импульстун ролун ойногон. Же болбосо, мын-
55 дай бир фактыны алалы: Некрасов Л. Толстойдун Кавказ аңгемелерин окуп чыгып, И. Тур-
геневге мындай деп жазган экен: "Бул очерк-
тердин формасы дээрлик сеники, ал гана эмес,
"Охотниктин запискасын" эске түшүрүүчү сүй-
лөмдөр, салыштыруулар да бар. Ал эми офицер

болсо, Щигровский уездиндеги аскер мундир-
чен Гамлеттин өзү." Адабий процессте мындай
60 учурлар кездеше берет. Бирок бул - ошол
жазуучунун чыгармачылык манерасын туроо,
же ошонун стилинде жазуу дегендикке жат-
пайт.

Канча кылган менен ар бир жазуучунун
стили ар башка болот эмеспи. Стилдин бирдиги тематикалык жана идеялык жакындыкта,
65 образ түзүү ыкмаларында, сюжет куруу чебер-
чилигинде, ритм менен рифмада, ырдын традициялык өлчөмүндө ж.б. болушу мүмкүн.
Бирок, бирин экинчиси туурап жазышкан эки
жазуучунуну техникалык чеберчиликтеринде
стилдин бирдиги болууга мүмкүн эмес. Мисалы,
С. Эралиевдин айрым лирикалары Алыкулдун
чыгармаларына өтө жакын келип, тематикалык
70 жактан Алыкулдун кээ бир ырлары менен үндө-
шүп турат. Ошондой эле С. Эралиевдин чыгар-
маларында каармандардын образын психология-
лык жол менен ачууга кылган аракетинде,
окуяны, тигил же бул көрүнүштү элестүү жана
картиналуу кылып так сүреттөөсүндө да стилдик окшоштуктардын айрым бир белгилеринин
бар экендиги байкалат. Бирок, буга карабас-
75 тан ал экөөнүн стили такыр эки башка.

С. Жумадылов

NB! This text has been earmarked for self parsing.
Cf. below text XII-E.

ТВОРЧЕСКИЕ ПОИСКИ ПОЭТА

I   Известно, что каждый мастер художествен-
ного слова в изображении различных жизнен-
ных явлений пользуется понравившимся ему,
излюбленным стилевым приемом. Своеобразие
непохожих один на другой стилей каждого
писателя часто вытекает из этого.

5   Следовательно, идейно-художественное со-
держание любого произведения должно опреде-
ляться особенностями писательского стиля.
Однако, стиль не может остановиться в своём
развитии и оставаться на месте, не изменяясь.
Он не может возникнуть сам по себе, сколько
бы писатель не держал в руке перо.

IO   Стиль развивается по замыслу писателя,
по мере роста его мастерства. Писатель, стре-
мящийся овладеть собственным стилем, всегда
находится в поиске. Упомянутый поиск - это
не случайное явление. Поиск подчиняется тре-
бованию века, т.е. тема, рождённая жизнью,
понуждает писателя искать способы ответа на
неё.

I5   Несмотря на это, направление творческого
поиска, решение поставленной задачи конкрет-
ным, практическим методом требует от писателя глубоких размышлений, глубокого проник-
новения в тему, её ревностного изучения и
освоения. Современная киргизская поэзия
лучше, чем прежде начала отражать человече-
20 ские чувства, взгляды на будущее. Именно
поэтому поиски в произведении поэтического
жанра, по-новому изображенные жизненные
явления занимают более широкое место, чем
прежде. Однако, занимаясь поиском нового,
нельзя не обращать внимания на богатый опыт
прошлого. Таким образом, опора на традиции
25 прошлого, умение сочетать их с новыми от-
крытиями считается прекрасной основой на
пути творческого роста писателей. Ярким до-
казательством этого является крылатая поэзия последних лет жизни покойного талантли-
вого киргизского поэта Алыкул Осмонова.
    Алыкул был всегда ищущим, работающим без

устали поэтом. Влияние на него мировой и
30 русской классики было велико. В результате
овладения творческим опытом мировых и рус-
ских классиков, Алыкул Осмонов нашёл соб-
ственные новые поэтические формы. Киргиз-
ский акын, сочетая систему традиционного
стихосложения в своей поэзии с новыми фор-
мами пришёл к новаторству в своих стихах.
35 По этой причине А. Осмонов стал любимым
поэтом не только читателей, но и молодых
авторов. Долгое время молодёжь, впервые
взявшая в руки перо, писала подражая Алыкулу. Подражая Алыкулу, один из таких поэтов, а именно Суйунбай Эралиев, старается
40 использовать с творческим вдохновением его
стилевые приёмы. Если его привлекает в
Твардовском мастерство создания характеров,
образность мышления, то образные выражения
А. Осмонова, экспрессивность его слова, его
"скупость на слова и щедрость на мысль"
поражают С. Эралиева. "Алыкул моё счастье.
Я и сейчас с огромной любовью читаю его
стихи, поэтому многие его стихи могу про-
45 честь наизусть" - говорит поэт.
Использование стилевых приемов известных
писателей в творческом процессе - законное
явление. По этому поводу можно привести
много примеров из мировой литературы. Например, Байрон сильно повлиял на Пушкина.
50 Находясь на юге в ссылке, он использовал
не только романтический стиль Байрона, идею
любви к политической свободе в его произведениях, но и его характеры, его сложные
ситуации. А затем манера повествования
Пушкина сыграла роль творческого импульса
при создании Л. Толстым "Анны Карениной".
55 Или возьмём такой факт: Некрасов, про-
читав "Кавказские рассказы" Л. Толстого,
написал Тургеневу так: "Форма этого очерка
почти твоя, но не только это - встречаются
такие предложения и сравнения, которые на-
поминают "Записки охотника". А что касает-
ся офицера, то это сам Гамлет Щигровского
уезда в военном мундире."
60 В литературном процессе такие случаи
могут встретиться. Однако, это не считается подражанием творческой манере

данного писателя или писанию в его стиле.
Единство стилей возможно при тематической
и идейной близости приемов создания образа,
65 мастерства построения сюжета, ритма и рифмы,
традиционного размера стихов и.т.п. Но не-
возможно единство стиля в техническом мас-
терстве двух писателей, один из которых по-
дражает другому. Например, отдельные стихо-
творения С. Эралиева очень приближаются к
70 произведениям Алыкула,в тематическом отношении перекликаются с некоторыми стихами
Алыкула. Также в произведениях С.Эралиева
наблюдается наличие отдельных следов схо-
жести в попытке психологического раскрытия
75 образа героев, событий, в точном, живом и
образном отображении того или иного явления.
Однако, несмотря на это, стиль этих двух
поэтов совершенно различный.

С. Джумадылов

THE POET'S CREATIVE SEARCH

It is well known that each expert in literature in depicting the various aspects of life resorts to the stylistic means which he likes and which suit him best. The stylistic pecculia-

5   rities of each writer, distinguishing each one from all others, most often stem precisely from that. That is to say that the ideological-artistic value of each type of work must be determined according to the stylistic peculiarities of the writer. But style is not something which remains unchanged and static. It does not reveal itself spontaneously simply because the writer takes up his

10   pen. It develops itself, evolves in accordance with the writer's craftsmanship and way of thinking.

The writer who strives to control his own style is always searching. What we call 'search' is not a random phenomenon. This search is subjected to the demands of the century, which is to say that the theme procreated by life forces the writer to find an appropriate way to satisfy the demands of this very theme.

15   However, the direction of this creative search, the practical, concrete solution to the commitment thus made, demand from the writer a deep reflexion, an osmosis with his theme, the cautious analysis, study and assimilation of it.

Contemporary Kirghiz poetry already began to reflect, more precisely than earlier, man's intimate feelings and his views

20   on the future. Nowadays, in those works which are within the province of the poetical genre, the search for novelty, for

a new representation of the different
aspects of life, are very important.
Nevertheless, precisely in the field of
search, it would be unwise to neglect the
rich experience of the past. In this way,
one must consider the writer's skillfulness
in learning from past traditions and
interweaving them with new findings, an
excellent

25   basis on the way towards his creative
development. A clear illustration of this
is provided by the winged poetry of Alikul
Osmonov, the late talented Kirghiz poet,
during the last years of his life.
      Alikul was a poet always in search (of
something

30   new), who worked tirelessly. The influence
exerted on him by worldwide and Russian
classical authors is tremendous. The
result of this intimate assimilation of the
creative experience of the worldwide and
Russian literary classical authors was that
A. Osmonov found himself new poetical
forms. The poet, welding the traditional
in Kirghiz poetry metrical system with new
forms,

35   succeeded in mastering novelty in his
poems. This is why Alikul Osmonov is not
only the reader's, but also the young
writers' favorite poet. For a long time,
young people who were taking up their pen
for the first time, imitated him.
Imitating Alikul, one

40   of our poets - more exactly Süyünbay
Eraliev - constantly takes advantage, with
creative inspiration, of his stylistic
methods. If he is attracted by A.
Tvardovskiy's skill at creating characters,
by the imaginative strength of his thought,
S. Eraliev is deeply struck by A. Osmonov's
ability to depict in a picturesque way, by
the expressiveness of his words, by his
'conciseness in

45   words and munificence in thought'. He
says: "Alikul is my world. I always read
his poems with much love and this is why I
can recite by heart a great number of
Alikul's poems".
    Resorting to stylistic techniques of
well-known writers is a legitimate
phenomenon in the creative process. On
that subject one can quote numerous
examples taken from world

50   literature. For example, Byron exerted a
great influence on Pushkin. While he was
in exile in the South, Pushkin resorted not
only to Byron's romantic style and to the
idea of love for political freedom, which
can be found in (the latter's) works, but
also to his characters and many of his
thematical situations. Later on, Pushkin's
narrative style played a role of creative
impulsion in the writing of Lev Tolstoy's
'Anna Karenina'. Again: let's take

55   the following fact: Nekrassov, after
reading L. Tolstoy's 'Caucasian Tales',
wrote to I. Turgenev: "The form of this
novel practically is yours; more than that,
there are comparisons, sentences which
bring to mind the 'Hunter's Diary" Let's
take this officer: it is the very Hamlet
from the Shchigrov district, in uniform".

60   Such examples can inevitably be found in
the literary process. However, this is not
to say writing in such and such writer's
style or imitating his manner.
    Be that as it may, each writer's style
is different from all others. Stylistic
unity is possible in the case of thema-

65   tical and ideological similarity, in the
technique of image building, in the
skillfulness for elaborating one's theme,
in rhythm and rime, in traditional poetical
meter. But stylistic unity is impossible
in the technical skill of two writers, one
of which imitates the other. For example,
some lyric poems by S. Eraliev come very

close to Alikul's works and from the
thematical point

70   of view echo various poems by Alikul.   In
the same way, in S. Eraliev's works, one
can note the presence of certain features
of stylistic similarity in the exact, vivid
and picturesque representation of such and
such phenomenon or event, in the tendency
to divulge by way of psychology the image
of the heroes.   And yet

75   in spite of this, the styles of these two
poets are absolutely different.

S. Jumadılov.

a) THE (SOVIET) NORMATIVE LITERARY LANGUAGE

THEATER

Toktobolot Abumomunov: 'Abiyir kechirbeyt' (in
Süyüü jana Ümüt, Kırgızstan Basması, Frunze) 1966.
Text IX

b) THE SCIENTIFIC LANGUAGE

A.V. Peryshkin: Fizika kursu, 3 bölük, Mektep
Basması, Frunze 1971, pp. 352-354.
Text X

I

АБИЙИР КЕЧИРБЕЙТ
Экинчи көшүгө Жетинчи сүрөт

Шайыргүлдүн квартирасынын тамак ичүүчү
бөлмөсү. Пианиного жанаша Шайыргүлдүн
портрети станокто турат. Терезенин
5 түбүндөгү жумшак креслого Омор газета
окуп отурат. Эртерек толуп кеткен жыл-
дуздуу адам. Үстүндө пижама. Коңгуроо
угулат. Омор коридорго чыгып, Нурдинди
ээрчитип кирет.

Нурдин. /Босогодо токтоп/ Кечиресиз.
10 Артистка Шайыргүл Сулайманова ушунда турат
дешкен эле, мен башка үйгө кирип калган
окшойм.
Омор. /Майдары күлүмсүрөп/ Ошол үйдүн
так өзүнө кирдиңиз. Бир гана айыбы...
Шайыргүл үйдө жок.../Нурдин кетмекчи болгонун байкап/ Күтө туруңуз. Жакында келет.
/Нурдинге орундук коюп/ Азыр эле кайра
15 келем. Айып көрбөңүз. /Чыгат/

/Нурдин пианиного барып, адегенде бир
колу менен, андан кийин эки колдоп
"Эсимденин" обонун ойнойт. Костюмун
кийип Омор кирет. Нурдин ойногонду лып
токтолот./

Омор. Ойной бериңиз, жолдош уялбаңыз.
20 "Эсимдени" Шайыргүл дайыма ырдайт. Менде
үн жок. Кээде обонун ойношум болот. Бирок,
Шайыргүлдүн ойногуна санаа менен жетпесем,
мындайынча теңелүү кыйын. Ал пианинодо
ойноп ырдаганда, был ырдан... кандай деп
айтсам экен?... Жүрөктү мыжыккан кайгыны
... аткарылбай калган тилектин муңун
угам... Сиз ойногондо да ошондой үгүлду.
25 Музыкант болсоңуз керек.
Нурдин. Жок!... кайдагы музыкант...
жен эле...

Омор. Сиз ойногондо кадимки музыкант
ойногондой... /Жылдыздуу жылмайып/ Шайыргүлдү улам мактай берчү болдум... Бирок,
именип коюцуз... Аны кандай мактасац да
30   бардыгында арзый турган киши. /Нурдинди
муцайып тиктеп/ Сиз ойногондо, Шайыргүлдүн
өзү ойногондой угулду... Келип калдыбы деген
элем... Азырынча портрети гана турат...
/Болор-болбос күрсүнүп/ Ал ойной да албайт,
ырдай да албайт... /портретке жакындап/ Жаш
художник жазып жатат. Башкаларга кандай
35   экенин билбейм, мага жагат... ийгиликтүү
чыгып калды. /Уялыцкы күлүмсүрөй/ Шайыргүл
үйдө жокто менин эрмегим көбүнчө ушул...
кайра-кайра карап, Шайыргүлгө окшоштурганды
жакшы көрөм...
    Нурдин. /Омордун сөзүнө кулак салбастан
портретти тигиле карап, акырын жана ойлуу/
Менимче, портрет жок... мында татынакай
40   аялдын татынакай гана көчүрмөсү турат...
    Омор. Сиз художниксиз го?
    Нурдин. /Күлүмсүрөй/ Эмненин художниги?
Жөн гана живописти жакшы көргөн ышкыбоздор-
дун биримин. /Портреттен көзүн алып, Оморду
45   тиктеп, акырын/ Тоо көлдөрүн далай эле көргөн чыгарсыз... Түндөсү караганыцызда тып-
тынч... бир нерсеге жаны кейигенсип кайгылуу
... жана ойлуу. Ал эми тац маалында кара-
сацыз, күндү алпарып алардын түбүнө катып
койгон шекилдүү, суунун терецинен жибек та-
рамдалып чыккан нурлар өйдө карай атыла
50   баштайт... Бул учурда тоо көлдөрүнүн суусу
алтынга буулангансып не бир кубанычтуу, не
бир жароокер... Менимче, Шайыргүлдүн көзү
ошондой болууга тийиш... Ал эми портретте
болсо, андан өчтеме жок... Кирпиги кооз,
бирок көздүн өзү жансыз... муздак!...
55   Омор. /Ойлуу/ Сиз туура айттыцыз көрү-
нөт... Ооба, ооба, айтканыцыздын калети жок!
/Өз ичинен/ Бүгүнгө чейин ушунун бирин байкай албапмын!.../ Болор-болбос күрсүнүп/
Кызы-ык! /Нурдинге кайрылып/ Кечиресиз,
Шайыргүл туурасында көрүп-билип жүргөндөй
сүйлөдүцүз... /уялыцкы күлүмсүрөй/ болгондо,
60   таанышсыздар го дейм...
    Нурдин. /Делөөрүй түшүп/ Менби?! Эмне-
нин таанышы?... Шайыргүлдү өмүрүмдө көргөн

эмесмин... Үнүн гана уккам... радиодон...

65 Омор. Тоо көлдөрүн кандай билсеңиз,
Шайыргүлдү да ошондой билгенсип, бардыгын
туура байкап сүйлөдүңүз. Шайыргүл чынында
эле сиз сүрөттөгөндөй. /Нурдин саатына кара-
ганын байкап/ Шашып турасызбы?

Нурдин. Шашылганым деле жок. Сизди убара
70 кылып, убактыңызды алып койдум окшойт...

Омор. Ага кейибеңиз... Иштен кийин эс
алып отурам... Сиз менен аңгемелешкенде,
ишенсеңиз, рахаттанып калдым... Мына, көр-
дүңүзбү, аңгемеге ушунчалык берилип кеткен
экем!... Таанышканга да чамам келбей калыптыр... Фамилиям Акматов. Атым Омор. /Күлүм-
сүрөй/ Кааласаңыз, нары жагында Батырович да
бар.

75 Нурдин. /Колун сунуп/ Шайыргүлгө тууган
болосуз го дейм?

Омор. /Күлүп/ Менби? Албетте. Болгондо
да эң жакын тууганымын... Күйөө деле тууган-
га кирет да, ушундай эмеспи...

Нурдин. /Башка чапкан немедей кеңгирей
80 түшүп, таңдана/ Шайыргүл - аялыңызбы?!

Омор. Билип турам, таң калып жатасыз...
Чынын айтсам, Шайыргүлдүн мага чыкканына
мен өзүм да таң калам... /Портретти көрсө-
түп/ Ал ким... мен ким... /Болор-болбос күр-
сүнө/ Түшүнбөйт десизби!...

85 Нурдин. /Эмне кыларын билбей/ Жок. Жок.
Антпеңиз!... Кеп анда эмес... мен ойлогон
элем... А-а... мага айтышкан эле...

Омор. Билип жатам. Уккан кулакта жазык
жок дейт. Шайыргүл бир доктор жигит менен
турмуш курмакчы болгондо... анысы бандиттик
кылып түрмөгө түшкөн дешет... Бирок бул туу-
90 расында Шайыргүлдөн эч качан сураган эмесмин.
Сурагым да келбейт. Чын болсо аны берүү
Шайыргүлгө кыйын... Жарат козголуп, жан
кейит... эгер ал ушак болсо - мен үчүн да,
ал үчүн да укканга оор... /Папирос чегип/
Менин баардык ырыс-таалайым Шайыргүлүм менен
уулум экөө... Аларсыз күнүм жок... Өмүрүм
95 тайкы, супсак болуп калаар эле... Ошондуктан
кайдагы өткөн-кеткен икир-чикирди козгоп,
Шайыргүлүмдүн көңүлүн ооруткум келбейт!
/Нурдиндин орундуктун кырыша сүйөнө, оор дем
алганын көрүп/ Сизге эмне болду?

Нурдин. Эчтеме эмес... Ысыктан болуу
100 керек... Көңүлүм карангылай түштү... Бук
тартып турат.
       Омор. Бук тартып дейсизби? Бүгүнкүдөй
салкын кайда болсун... Көрүңүзчү терезеден
кирген желди.
       Нурдин. Узак жол жүрүп келдим эле...
Чарчап калган окшойм... /Саатына карап/
Абага чыгайын... Кошуңуз...
105   Омор. Кечиресиз. Абалыңыз бул... Анан
дагы кетмекчи болсоңуз... Жарабаган кеп...
Бул бойдон эч кайда кетире албайм. Отуруңуз.
/Нурдинди креслого отургузат/ Суудан ичиңиз!
       Нурдин. /Суудан ууртап/ Рахмат. Эс алып
калдым. /Турмакчы болот/
110   Омор. Отура туруңуз... Күйпөлөктөн
жүрүп эсимде да жок. Айып көрбөнүз, жөнүңүз-
дү айтыңыз...
       Нурдин. Фамилиям Болотов...
       Омор. Абдан жакшы. Атыңыз ким?
       Нурдин. Атымбы? Кечирип коюңуз.../Тур-
115 макчы болот/
       Омор. /Креслого кайрадан отургузуп/
Ата-энелер көп учурда баа беришпейт... Оюна
келген атты коё беришет... Мен мугалиммин
да... Башкаларга болбосо да мага белгилүү...
Адеп паровоз келгенде, көпчүлүгү Паровозбек
120 коюп жиберишти... Андан кийин Тракторбек,
Комбайнбек, Патефон, Колхоз, Совхоз... Жакында бир аял эгиз төрөсө бирин Атомбек, экин-
чисин Спутник жоюптур... Ушул дагы ат бол-
дубу?
       Нурдин. /Саатына карап/ Мен эми кай-
тайын. /Ордунан турат/
125   Омор. Мынча эмне шашылдыңыз? Шайыргүлдүн келер маалы болуп калды... Отура тур-
саңыз...
       Нурдин. Зарыл жумуштарым бар эле,
бүгүн бүтүрбөсөм болбойт. Убакыт тар...
Анын үстүнө, менин мында келгенимдин себеби... айтууга ооз барбайт... таптакыр ар-
130 зыбай турган нерсе... Ошол үчүн аялыңыздын
тынчын алганым уят болор...
       Омор. Концертке чакырып келгенсиз го
дейм?... Шайыргүл эч качан кыйыктанбайт...
Анын шефке алган жерлери көп... дайыма барат.
       Нурдин. Жок, жок... Масадыктын кайда

135 турганын билбей, окусунан кире калган элем.
Омор. Доктор Кемеловду издеп жүргөн
турбайсызбы? Ой, бой, анан бая эле ошентип
айтпайсызбы!... Доктор Кемелов азыр өзүнүн
клиникасында болууга тийиш... Москва көчө-
сүндө... Сиз аны сөзсүз ошол жерде табасыз.
140 Нурдин. Чоӊ рахмат. /Омордун колун
кысып/ Көрүшкөнчө.
Омор. Көрүшкөнчө!/Бир нерсени эсине
түшүргөндөй, Нурдинди босогодон токтолуп/
Кечиресиз, жолдош Болотов!... Паркта чоӊ
сайран болот имиш... анан кечке жуук...
Элдин суроосо боюнча менин Шайыргүлүм ырда-
145 макчы болуп жатат... Анын мүнөзүн туура
тапканыӊызды өз көзүӊүз менен көрөсүз,
келалсаӊыз дурус болот эле... келесизби?
Нурдин. /Ыргылжыӊыраак/ Келүүгө аракет кылайын.
Омор. Куттуу үйдөн кур чыгарганым уят
болор. Эч болбогондо нан ооз тийиӊиз.
150 Нурдин. /Нандан ооз тийип/ Рахмат.
Омор. /Нурдинди жандай басып/ Биринчи
жүз көрүшсөк да көптөн бери таанышай болуп.
/Муӊайым күлүп/ Эл айткандай, жылдызыбыз
табыша түштүбү, айтор...
Нурдин. /Ойлоно калып/ Асмандан боор-
155 сок жааган күнү туулгансыӊ, жакшы адамдар-
га калганда жолдуусуӊ деп ар ким – ар ким
айтып калар эле... /Жеӊил күрсүнө/ Бул дүйнө-
нө жакшы адамдардын дүйнөсү болгондо, кандай жакшы болор эле!... /Оморго тигиле ка-
рап/ Сабыр этиӊизчи... сол көзүӊүздүн
астында берч бар өндөнөт... /Колу менен
көрүп/ Ооба, ооба. Ошондой. Берч пайда
160 болуп келатыптыр... Операциясы ийне сайган-
дай да сезилбейт. Алдырып таштаӊыз... Ар
нерсенин алдын алган жакшы... Узакка соз-
боӊуз...
Омор. Оорутпаган соӊ... этибар албай
жүрдүм эле... көрсө...
165 Нурдин. Турмуш көрсөтүп жатайбы,
Омор Батырович! Оорутпаган жараттын залалы
көп... Себеби, көп учурда байкабай калабыз!
Омор. Демек, врач экенсиз да?
Нурдин. Ооба, хирургмун.
170 Омор. Кеӊешиӊизге рахмат...ыраазымын
... келип туруӊуз...

TEXT IX

Нурдин. Чамам болсо, сөзсүз, келип
турам... Көрүшкөнчө саламат туруңуз.
175 Омор. Жакшы адам үчүн эшигибиз дайыма
ачылуу... /Нурдиндин соңунан/ күтөбүз...

/Омор кайра келип оор күрсүнөт да, аялы-
нын портретин кейиштүү тиктейт./

ACT 2, SCENE 7

1   (Dining-room in Shayirgül's ('Gay Flower')
     apartment. Near the piano, Shayírgül's
     portrait on an easel. Omor, seated in an
     armchair

5   is reading a newspaper. He is a charming
     man who grew stout at an early age. He
     wears pajamas. The doorbell rings. Omor
     goes out into the corridor, then ushers
     Nurdin in.)

     NURDIN: (stopping onto the threshold)
     Excuse me. I was told artist Shayırgül
     Sulaymonova lived here. I think I probably
     entered

10   the wrong house.
     OMOR: (affably smiling) You have come
     precisely to her house. It's simply her
     fault. Shayırgül is not home. (Noticing
     that Nurdin is about to leave) Please wait
     for her. She'll come soon (offering

15   a seat to Nurdin). I'll be back in a
     minute. If you don't mind... (exit)
     (Nurdin goes to the piano and immediately,
     first with one hand and then with both,
     plays the melody 'In my memory'. Omor
     comes back. He has dressed. Nurdin
     abruptly stops playing)

     OMOR: Please go on, don't feel
     uncomfortable. Shayırgül sings 'In my
     memory' very often. I have no voice.
     Sometimes I try to play the tune. Well, if
     even in thought I cannot play like

20   Shayirgül, it is difficult to equate her
     like that. When she sings and accompanies
     herself on the piano, from this melody
     emanates... how could I say? I hear a
     heart-rending sadness, the sorrow of a
     desire which remained unsatisfied... I felt

the same thing when you were playing... You must be a musician.

25 NURDIN: No, what kind of musician... simply...

OMOR: When you play, it sounds as if a real musician were playing. (smiling charmingly) I'm always praising Shayırgül ... But, believe me, no matter how you praise her, she remains dear to

30 everyone. (looking sadly at Nurdin) When you were playing, it seems as if Shayırgül herself were playing. I told myself: 'She probably has come back'. For the time being, there's just her portrait (sighing faintly) It can neither play, not sing... (getting nearer to the portrait) A young artist is painting it. I don't know what other people think of it. I like it... it

35 has turned out successfully (smiling with embarassment) When Shayırgül is not home, it's my main comfort. I look and look at it, and I appreciate how it looks like Shayırgül.

NURDIN: (does not listen to Omor's words and stares hard, thoughtfully and for a long time at the portrait) According to me,

40 there's no portrait, but only a wonderful copy of a wonderful woman.

OMOR: You're an artist, aren't you?

NURDIN: (smiling) Why, me, an artist? I'm just a connoisseur in love with painting (turning his eyes away from the portrait

45 and looking slowly at Omor) You probably have seen mountain lakes. When you look at them at night, so peaceful... They are sad and thoughtful, as if their soul lamented something... but if you look at them at dawn, they seem to drag down the sun,

hiding it in their depths and then the
sunrays begin to stream out of the water
like fraying silk strands. At that

50 time, the lake water seems to be covered
with gold, it is cheerful, soft... In my
opinion, that's how Shayirgül's eyes must
be. There's nothing of all that on the
portrait. Eyebrows are beautiful, but the
eyes themselves are soulless, icy...

55 OMOR: (thoughtfully) You're probably right.
Yes, yes, no doubt (to himself) And to
think that up to now I didn't notice
anything. (sighing faintly) How strange
(facing Nurdin). Excuse me, you just talked
as if you knew Shayirgül perfectly.
(smiling

60 with embarassment) As it is, you are
certainly one of her acquaintances...

NURDIN: (looking suddenly nervous) Me?
Which acquaintance? I've never seen
Shayirgül in my life. I only hear her
voice...on the radio

OMOR: You spoke as if you had actually
observed and known all that the mountain
lakes as well as Shayirgül. Shayirgül
truly is as you depicted her (noticing that
Nurdin glances at his watch). Are you in a
hurry?

NURDIN: I'm in no hurry at all. But I
disturb you, its seems I'm taking up your
time.

70 OMOR: Don't bother about that. I relax
after my work. You have made me very happy,
believe me, having a chat with me. But as
you see, I have let myself drift into
chatter, I didn't even introduce myself. My
name is Akmatov, my first name Omor
(smiling). After that, if you like, it will
be Batırovich.

75   NURDIN: (holding out his hand) You're probably a relative of Shayırgül?

OMOR: (laughing) Me? Of course and even the closest relative. The husband also is part of the family, isn't he?

NURDIN: (suddenly stunned as if somebody had clubbed him on the

80   head - with surprise) Shayırgül is your wife?

OMOR: I understand; there you are, amazed. To tell you the truth, I am amazed too that Shayırgül married me (pointing to the portrait) Who is she... who am I.... (faintly smiling) Do you think I don't understand?

85   NURDIN: (not knowing what to do) No, no... Don't say that. That's not what I meant... I thought...er...er...I was told...

OMOR: I understand. The ear is not responsible for what it hears. People say Shayırgül was about to marry a young doctor. But he was indicted on a charge of banditism and put into jail. But I

90   never asked Shayırgül about that. I don't feel like asking her. If it's true, it would be difficult for Shayırgül to confess it. The wound still bleeds, she suffers... and if it's a lie, it would be hard for me and for her to hear it (puffing at his cigarette). My whole happiness, my whole joy is Shayırgül and

95   my son. Without them, there's no life for me. My life would be empty, dull. That's why I don't feel like hurting Shayırgül's heart by turning over and over again what happened God knows when (noticing that Nurdin is leaning against the back of his seat and breathing with difficulty). What's the matter with you?

NURDIN: Nothing... it must be the heat. My heart suddenly gave

100 a pang. I felt a cramp.

OMOR: A cramp, you say? It cannot be cooler than today. Do you feel the draft coming from the window?

NURDIN: I made such a long trip...I must be tired (glancing at his watch). I'd better go out into the fresh air. Good bye.

105 OMOR: Excuse me... You're in such a state... if you have to go after that... it's not what I mean... I can't let you go in such a state. Sit down (he makes him sit down in an armchair). Drink some water.

NURDIN: (swallowing some water) Thank you. Now I feel better, I feel revived (ready to get up).

110 OMOR: Please remain seated. I loose my head when I become nervous. Excuse me: what is your name?

NURDIN: My name is Bolotov.

OMOR: Excellent... and your first name?

NURDIN: My first name? Excuse me (ready to get up).

OMOR: (making him sit down again in the armchair) Parents often don't care. They give you the first name that crosses their mind. I am a teacher. If other people don't know, I do. As soon as the locomotive appeared, there comes a majority of

120 Locomotive-bek... After that came Traktor-bek, Combine-bek, Gramophone-bek, Kolkhoz-bek, Sovkhoz-bek... Some time ago a woman gave birth to twins. One she called Atom-bek and the second Sputnik. What kind of names are these?

NURDIN: (looking at his watch) However, I must be going (he stands up).

125 OMOR: Why are you in such a hurry? It's just Shayirgül's time to come. Please sit down.

NURDIN: I have urgent business to do. If I don't settle it today, it won't be good. Time presses... Moreover, ... I just can't tell you what I came for. Something absolutely trifling.

130 I'm ashamed to bother your wife for it.

OMOR: You wanted her to participate in a concert? Shayirgül never makes any difficulties. There are many places where she directs cultural activities. She always goes...

NURDIN: No, no... simply I didn't know where Masadık lives and I just came in.

OMOR: Isn't it doctor Kemelov you were looking for? Well, well, you should have said it right away. Doctor Kemelov must be at his clinic now, in Moscow Street... You'll certainly find him there.

140 NURDIN: Thank you so much (he shakes hands with Omor) Good bye.

OMOR: Good bye (as if suddenly remembering something, he stops Nurdin in the doorway). Excuse me, comrade Bolotov. I heard there will be a garden fête in the park, in the evening. On request of the public, Shayirgül intends to sing there... You'll

145 be able to convince yourself how right you were - it would be nice if you could come. You will, won't you?

NURDIN: (rather hesitatingly) I'll try

OMOR: It would be a shame to let you out of

a happy home without regaling you with
something. Please try a slice of this cake.

150 NURDIN: (tasting the cake) Thank you.

OMOR: (coming closer to Nurdin) We have
met for the first time, but it is as if
we had known one another for a long time
(smiling sadly). As people say, our stars
finally met, so to say.

NURDIN: (suddenly thoughtful) You were born
under a lucky star and you're lucky
remaining among good people, as everyone
says... as everyone continues to say
(sighing slightly). If this world of ours
were full of good people, how nice it would
be! (staring at Omor). A moment, please...
a lipoma is growing under your left eye...
(he touches it with his hand) Yes, yes.
That's

160 it. A lipoma is developing. Upon having it
removed you won't feel more than a needle
prick. Get rid of it. It is good to take
the initiative in everything. Don't linger
for long...

OMOR: It doesn't hurt... I didn't notice
it... but if you look at it...

165 NURDIN: Life shows it to you. Things that
don't hurt bring much harm... Because...
how long have we remained without seeing
it?

OMOR: That is to say that you are a
doctor?

NURDIN: Yes, I am a surgeon.

170 OMOR: Thank you for your advice... Very
glad... Please come back.

NURDIN: If I am strong enough, I'll come
back certainly. Until then, be healthy.

OMOR: Our door is always open for good people (to Nurdin who is

175 leaving). We'll be waiting for you... (Omor comes back, breathing heavily and stares at his wife's portrait).

COMMENTS

This popular play on a then popular theme (a
remake of the never outdated Russian problem
illustrated by Repin in his painting 'Ne Zhdali'-
now adapted to the new conditions of post-1953
Kirghizia) earned its author in 1967 the "honorary
title of Toktogul-prize laureate".
       The unusual 'acuteness' of the subject ('ban-
ditism' - cf. 1. 89- is, in local journalese, the
password for armed nationalist resistance) and of
some pseudo-tolstoyan retorts (1. 103, 166) was,
in accordance with the unwritten rule of 'inoska-
zanie', deftly counterbalanced by an idyllic description of the new intellectuals' thoroughly
Europeanized material life, as it is supposed to
be in accordance with the canons of interethnic
'merging'.
       Sociolinguistically speaking, this text pro-
vides an example of contemporary spoken Soviet Kirghiz as used in the urban, partially Russianized
social layer (cf. C-191-211).
       For parsing, cf.:

1. 2 :	K-2163	1. 22:	K-1597
1. 3 :	K-1223,1281	1. 23:	K-2063
1. 7 :	K-1276	1. 24:	K-1350
1. 9 :	K-1607,1902	1. 25:	K-1850
1. 10:	K-1385,2017	1. 26:	K-1095
1. 12:	K-1607,1778	1. 27:	K-1218, K-1342
1. 14:	K-1799	1. 30:	K-1342
1. 15:	K-1607,1802	1. 31:	K-1778, K-2015
1. 17:	K-1593	1. 32:	K-1304
1. 18:	K-1332,2349	1. 33:	K-1799, K-1802
1. 20:	K-1183	1. 37:	K-1332
1. 38:	K-1307	1. 125:	K-1310
1. 42:	K-1607	1. 126:	K-1851
1. 44:	K-1350,1354	1. 129:	K-1802
1. 46:	K-2153	1. 130:	K-1819
1. 56:	K-1329	1. 131:	K-1789
1. 57:	K-1826	1. 135:	K-2015
1. 62:	K-1382,1786,2019	1. 136:	K-2170

1.	64:	K-1862	1.	138:	K-1270
1.	66:	K-1332	1.	144:	K-1214
1.	72:	K-2052	1.	147:	K-1819
1.	73:	K-1830	1	157:	K-1841,
					K-2041
1.	77:	K-1607	1.	160:	K-1830
1.	79:	K-1786	1.	162:	K-2024
1.	81:	K-1702	1.	170:	K-1877
1.	82:	K-1332	1.	175:	K-1799
1.	83:	K-1304			
1.	86:	K-2105			
1.	87:	K-1702			
1.	88:	K-1220			
1.	93:	K-2842			
1.	95:	K-2041			
1.	102:	K-1900			
1.	103:	K-2024			
1.	104:	K-1889			
1.	105:	K-2174			
1.	107:	K-1802			
1.	109:	K-1214			
1.	118:	K-1593			
1.	121:	K-1857			
1.	122:	K-1830			

I № 196. АТОМ ТЕОРИЯСЫНЫН ӨНҮГҮШҮ
АТОМДУН ЭЛЕКТРОМАГНИТТИК ТОЛКУНДАРДЫ
ЧЫГАРЫШЫ ЖАНА ЖУТУШУ

Атомдун планетардык моделин белгилеген
Резерфорддун тажрыйбасы менен бирге, атом
теориясынын өсүшүндө атомдордун электро-
5   магниттик толкундарды чыгарышы жана жутушу
жөнүндөгү маселени үйрөнүү өтө чоң роль
ойноду.

№ 182-де жарыктын электромагниттик теги
жөнүндө, жарык толкунунун булагы болуп, заттын атому эсептеле тургандыгы жөнүндө
айтылган эле. Атомдор кандай түрдө нур чы-
10   гарат? Бул суроого жооп узак издөөдөн кийин
гана табылган. Эң башталышында ага төмөнкүдөй жооптордү айтышкан.

Атомдо терс зарядцалган электрон оң зарядцалган ядронун тегерегинде ылдамдануу
/борборго умтулуучу/ менен түюк орбита
боюнча айланып жүргөндүктөн, ал өзгөрүлмө
15   электромагниттик талааны түзөт, ошондуктан
атом электромагниттик толкундардын булагы
болуп эсептелет. Бул толкундардын узундугу,
же нур чыгаруу жыштыгы ядронун айланасында
электрондун айлануу жыштыгы менен белгиле-
нет.

Бирок, электрон ядронун айланасында ар
20   кандай жыштыкта айланышы мүмкүн, ошондуктан, берилген заттын атомдорунун чыгаруу
спектринде ар кандай толкун узундугундагы
нурлар болушу мүмкүн.

Бул теорияга ылайык кандайдыр бир газды
- көп сандагы атомдун чогуусун алсак жана
аны жарык берүүгө мажбур кылсак /мисалы,
25   аны кызытсак/, анда бул жаркыроонун спектри
туташ болуу керек, б.а. бир жыштыктын экинчи жыштыкка өтүүсү үзгүлтүксүз түрдө болууга тийиш.

Бирок да, атомдун нур чыгаруу механизми
жөнүндөгү маселеге ушул сыяктуу жооп берүү
30   туура эмес. Тажрыйба таптакыр башканы көр-
сөтөт.

Биринчиден, жарык чыгаруучу сейректел-
ген газдын спектри туташ болбостон, дискреттүү айрым-айрым сызыктардан түзүлгөн
болот. Экинчиден, бул сызыктардын жыштык-
тарын электрондордун ядронун тегерегинде
айлануусунун натыйжасында келип чыккан

35   чыгаруу катары түшүндүрүүгө болбойт.

Андан башка, жогорку жакта баяндалган
түшүнүктөр атомдун туруктуулугу жөнүндөгү
маселени чечүүдө өзүнүн негизсиздигин
толук түрдө көрсөттү.

ХХ кылымдын башында эле окумуштуулар:

40   электромагниттик толкундарды атомдордун
чыгаруу жана жутуу механизми жөнүндөгү жаңы
түшүнүктөр зарыл деген жыйынтыкка келишкен.
Мындай түшүнүктөрдү бардыгынан мурун фото-
эффект кубулушун /биз аны № 183-тө карап
өттүк/ түшүндүрүү иш талап кылган.

Жарыкты кээ бир учурларда hv энергиялуу

45   фотондордун агыны катарында кароо керек
экендигин тажрыйба көрсөттү /рентген жана
γ-нурлары үчүн да ошол эле сыяктуу/. Фотон-
дор кантип пайда болушат?

Бул суроого да ядронун тегерегинде айланып жүргөн электрондун үзгүлтүксүз нур чы-
гаруусу жөнүндөгү түшүнүктү колдонуп, жооп

50   берүүгө мүмкүн эмес.

1913-жылы Даниянын физиги Нильс Б о р
жогору жакта коюлган суроолорго жооп бере
тургандай теорияны чыгарды.

Бор төмөнкүдөй божомолдогон: атом энергияны чыгарбай жана жутпай турган учурунда
стационардуу абалдар деп аталуучу абалдарга

55   болушу мүмкүн. Ушул абалдардын биринде болгон атомдогу электрондор с т а ц и о н а р-
д ы к   о р б и т а боюнча айланышат жана
бул учурда электромагниттик толкундарды
чыгарышпайт.

Энергияны чыгаруу менен жутуу, атомдун
бир стационардык абалынан, мисалы E^1 энергиялуу, абалдан экинчи бир E^2 энергиялуу

60   абалга өтөт дегенди билгизет, бул болсо,
электрондун бир стационардык орбитадан
экинчи орбитага өтүшүнө туура келет.

Ушул түрдөгү өтүү кезинде электромагниттик энергияга ээ болуучу фотон чыгарылат

же жутулат; анын чоңдогу:

$$/I/ \qquad hv = E^1 - E^2$$

65 катышы менен аныкталат, мында v = электромагниттик нур чыгаруунун жыштыгы, h =
Планктын туруктуусу.

Заттардын атомуна жарык менен таасир нур-
лары, α -бөлүкчөлөрдүн агыны же электрондор
менен таасир этип, атомду стационардык бир
абалдан экинчисине өтүүгө мажбур кылууга
70 болот. Атомдун абалынын ушундайча өзгөрүшү
атомдун дүүлүгүүсү деп аталат.

Атом дүүлүккөн абалында узак тура албайт
/секунданын милиард үлүшүнө чейин гана тура
алат/; ал жыштыгы /I/ формула мене аныктала
турган фотонду өзүнөн чыгарат да, натыйжада
75 өзүнүн нормалдуу, дүүлүкпөгөн абалына кайта
кайтып келет.

Атомдордун дискреттүү энергиялык абал-
дарынын бар болушу алардын касиеттеринин
бирден-бир мүнөздүү бөтөнчөлүгү болуп
саналат; ал болсо, көп сандаган тажрыйбалар
менен далилдеңген.

Атом теориясынын андан ары өсүшү азыркы
80 убакта к в а н т м е х а н и к а с ы н а н
орун алган. Квант механикасы атом менен
молекуланын дүйнөсүндө – микродүйнө деп
аталуучу дүйнөдө, макродүйнө деп аталуучу
дүйнөдөгү – бир түздөнтүз байкай алуучу
нерселердин дүйнөсүндөгү закон ченемдүүлүк-
төрдөн башка болгон закон ченемдүүлүктөр
бар экендигин көрсөттү.

1   PAR. 196 - THE DEVELOPMENT OF THE
      THEORY OF THE ATOM:

      Emission and absorption of the
      electromagnetic waves of the atom.

      Together with Rutherford's experience
      which revealed the planetary model of the
      atom, the study of the question of

5   absorption and emission of electromagnetic
      waves of the atom played a very important
      role in the development of the atomic
      theory.

      In Par. 182 about the electromagnetic
      origin of light, it has been said that the
      atom of matter was considered to constitute
      the source of the light wave. How does the
      atom emit light? The

10   answer to this question was discovered only
      after a long search. Here below are the
      answers which were given at the very
      beginning.

      Since inside the atom a negatively
      charged electron makes, around a positively
      charged nucleus, a constant rotary movement
      along a closed orbit with acceleration
      (centripetal force), it

15   creates a variable electromagnetic field;
      therefore, the atom is considered to be the
      source of electromagnetic waves. The length
      of these waves, or frequency of light
      emission, is determined by the rotation
      speed of the electron around the nucleus.
      But since the electron can rotate around
      the nucleus at any speed, it will

20   be possible (to find) in the emitted
      spectrum of the atoms of a given matter
      radiations of various wave lengths.

According to this theory, if we take a gas (a set of very numerous atoms) and if we force it to emit light (for example, if

25   we heat it), then the spectrum of this luminescence should be continuous, i.e. the shift from one frequency to the next one should be uninterrumpted.

Neverless, giving such an answer to the question of the mechanism of light emission of the atom is not right. Experience

30   shows precisely something else.

Firstly, the spectrum of the discharged light-emitting gas is not continuous, but constituted of isolated, discrete stripes. Second, it is impossible to explain the frequencies of these stripes on the basis of a radiation due to the rotation of electrons around the nucleus.

35   Moreover, the above given explanations revealed in an absolute manner their own groundlessness for the solution of the problem of the stability of the atom.

At the very beginning of the XX century, scholars came to

40   the conclusion that new explanations were necessary concerning the mechanism of absorption and radiation of the electromagnetic waves of the atoms.

Thus, the explanations were to concern above all the reappraisal of the concept of the photo-electric effect (alluded to in Par. 183).

45   Experience showed that in certain cases it was necessary to consider light to be a flow of photons with a hv energy (the same thing for X- and Gamma-rays). How do photons appear?

If we resort to the explanation of an emission of a continuous ray of electrons rotating around the nucleus, it is impossible to

50 give an answer to this question.

In 1913, the Danish physicist Niels Bohr proposed a theory which seemed to give an answer to the above-stated questions.

Bohr made the following supposition: when the atom doesn't

55 emit and doesn't absorb energy, it must find itself in one of those conditions called a 'stationary condition'. The electrons of the atom which find themselves in one of these conditions rotate along a stationary orbit and during that time emit no electromagnetic waves.

The radiation and absorption of energy indicates the transition from one stationary condition of the atom with, for example,

60 an E^1 energy, to a second condition, with an E^2 energy, which means that an electron shifts from one stationary orbit to a second orbit.

During such a shift, photons charged with electromagnetic energy are emitted and absorbed; its magnitude is determined by the ratio

(1) $h v = E^1 - E^2$

65 where v = frequency of the electromagnetic radiation, and h = Planck's constant.

By acting on the atoms of matter with the aid of light, of a flow of alpha particles or electrons, it is possible to make an atom shift from one stationary condition to another. Such

70   transformation in the condition of an atom
      is called 'stimulation'.

      An atom doesn't stay for a long time in
      a state of stimulation (no more than one
      billionth of a second); it emits a photon,
      the frequency of which is given by the
      above mentioned formula (1)

75   and finally comes back to its normal, non-
      stimulated conditon.

      The existence for the atom of discrete
      energetical conditions is considered to be
      one of their most characteristic
      peculiarities; it is a fact which has been
      proven by numerous experiences.

80   Today, the further development of the
      atom theory depends on quantum mechanics.
      Quantum mechanics revealed that in the
      world of the atom and of the molecule - the
      microcosm - laws different from those of
      the macrocosm, i.e. of the world of bodies
      that we can observe directly, were at work.

TEXT X

COMMENTS

This text - an excerpt from a high-school
handbook (University-level courses of Physics are
taught in Russian) - gives an insight into the
capacity of a language recently put into writing
to express modern scientific concepts.
Note the numerous Russian loanwords and
calques:
- tolkun: rus.: волна : wave
- borborgo umtuluuchu: literally= striving for the
  center: rus.:центростремительный : centripetal
- jıshtık: literally= thickness, density : rus.:
  частота : frequency, from rus.:частый : thick,
  frequent

For parsing cf.:

1. 1: K-1256,2493
1. 2-6: K-2678
1. 8: K-995,1336
1. 9: K-2015
1. 11:K-1786

1. 14:K-1197,2225
1. 16:K-1589,1799,2678
1. 18:K-1799
1. 20:K-1256
1. 21:K-1096
1. 25:K-1280,1863,1866
1. 26:K-1266,1283
1. 27:K-1256
1. 31:K-1347
1. 32:K-1336
1. 33:K-1945

1. 40: K-2450
1. 44: K-99
1. 45: K-1336
1. 48-50: K-2505
1. 52,54: K-1280,
          K-1349
1. 57: K-1799
1. 58: K-1266
1. 63,65: K-1799
1. 80: K-1786

Summary

        Texts V-X and XII have been chosen as repre-
sentative of the contemporary Soviet literary norm.
This is the official language of the Federal Republic of Kirghizia with all its alphabetical, orthographical (K-547, C-160), morphological and lexical peculiarities.
        A comparison with texts XVI which illustrate
the Kirghiz official norm in Chinese Xinjiang re-
veals minute differences as far as morphology is
concerned, but relatively important discrepancies
in the lexical field, not to speak of the alphabetical system.
        Text V in particular, by the contemporary,
internationally known writer Chingis Aytmatov, can
be considered the modern reference linguistic
standard. Paraphrasing Boileau on Malherbe, one
could say: "At last Aytmatov came...". Personal
literary talent, minimum traces of 'Socialist rea-
lism', but also half a century of use in its new
written form are responsible for both the complexity and the strict rationality of the syntax - a
capital development in comparison with texts 1-B,
1-C, 1-E and 1-G.
        Within this modern Soviet framework, the con-
trast - at the lexical and idiomatic levels -
between texts V, VI, VII, IX on the one hand and
texts VIII and XII on the other hand is striking.
        It illustrates two opposite ways of integra-
ting Russian influence and adapting to the demands
of modernity: through an "activation of internal,
autochtonous linguistic resources", or through blind
aping and linguistic denationalization.
        Aytmatov's tongue is, from the viewpoint of
its 'kirghizity', perfectly pure from gratuitious
Russian lexical and idiomatic 'zasorenie' (litter-
ing), in spite of the fact that the author probably
wrote the first version of this text in Russian,
'translating'it himself afterwards into Kirghiz (he
now writes mostly in Russian).
        Globally speaking therefore, these two groups
of texts highlight the opposition, inside the 'Literary Kirghiz Norm' between what has been called
the 'Autochtonous Standard' and the 'Soviet Standard'
(C-166-188, 195-202).

Other distinctions can be made within each group.In the first one, the language of texts V and VI can be termed 'written norm of the intellectuals' as opposed to the 'spoken intellectual norm' (text IX) and to the 'written non-intellectual norm' (text VII).

In the second group, Text VIII illustrates both the russianized and russified (C-160, 183) intellectual written norm as opposed to non-intellectual (text XII-D), while texts XII-A,B,C,E provide examples of Kirghiz ideological journalese.

Text X (and, for an earlier period, text XI-F) gives an insight into the still-born scientific style which, with Russian being now increasingly used in this field, seems bound to play an extremely secondary role.

Because of their 'classical' character, texts V, VI, and VII have been selected for systematic parsing.

C - THE "LATINIZATION" STAGE

(1926 - 1941)

KIRGHIZ   TEXTS   IN   LATIN   SCRIPT

1926 - 1941

a)THE ALPHABETICAL / ORTHOGRAPHICAL REFORM

- The first version of the new Latin script as
  published in the newspaper 'Erkin Too' (cf.
  Kh. Karasaev: Turmush Küzgüsü,Kırgızstan Bas-
  masɪ, Frunze 1966, p. 82.

  Text XI-A

- Parallel samples of short Kirghiz texts in
  the 'Reformed' Arabic script and in the newly
  introduced 'Latinized' script (cf. Nash No-
  vyy Alfavit (Our New Alphabet), Kirggosizdat,
  Frunze 1927 (ed. by the Committee for the
  New Alphabet)

  Text XI-B

- Second version of the 'Latinized' alphabet
  (cf. K.Tynystanov: Proèkt novoy orfografii
  kirgizskogo yazyka, Kirggosizdat, Frunze
  1934, p. 25., Trudy Kirgizskogo nauchno-
  issledovatel'skogo Instituta Kul'turnogo
  Stroitel'stva.

  Text XI-C(a)

- Cover page (and pp. 29-30) of the first
  Primer in Latin script (second version):
  E. Arabay-uulu, Q.Qarasay-uulu: Canьlьq
  (Jangɪlɪk: Novelty), Pьrunza şaarь 1928,
  2nd edition, 10,000 copies)

  Text XI-C(b)

 b)   EXCERPTS FROM SCHOOLBOOKS

- Internacanal (The 'Internationale')

  Text XI-D(a)

- Lenindin emyry (Lenin's life)

  Text XI-D(b)

- Badьşa zamanьnda qьrσjьz eli (The Kirghiz
  people in Tsarist times)

  Text XI-D(c)

- 1916 -ҷы1 (The Year 1916)

  Text XI-D(d)
- Çer-suu teꞑkeryşy (The Land/Water Reform)

  Text XI-D(e)
- Badьşa zamanьnda aoꞑartuu işteri (Educational works in Tsarist times)

  Text XI-D(f)

c)   THE   ADMINISTRATIVE   TONGUE

- Qьroҗbzьstan Respuвlikesinin Borвorduq Atqaruu Kemijtetinin II-sessьjasьnьn cьoꞑaroꞑan Toqtom-doru (Decisions of the 2nd Session of the Central Executive Committee of the Republic of Kirghizstan), 20-26 th January 1932 - Excerpts

  Text XI-E

d)   LINGUISTIC / GRAMMAR

- Baqtьвajev Ysej: "Çardamcь etişter" (Auxiliary verbs), in Kızıl Kırgızstan, 1940, Jan. 5, n° 4.

  Text XI-F

e)   THE   'CYRILLIZATION'

- Jangı Alfavittin Dolbooru (Preliminary Draft for the New Alphabet), Kh. Karasaev: Turmush Küzgüsü, Kirgizstan Basmasi, Frunze 1966, p. 84.

  Text XI-G

قیرعیزدین جاڭی الیب - بەەسی.

НОВЫЙ КИРГИЗСКИЙ АЛФАВИТ

(a) ا	(б) ب	(n) پ	(m) ت	(дж) چ
a	*в*	*p*	*t*	*c*
(o) و	(ч) چ	(g) د	(л) ر	(з) ز
o	*ч*	*d*	*r*	*z.*
(y) ۇ	(c) س	(ш) ش	(-) ع	(-) ق
u	*s*	*z*	*ᶜ*	*q*
(ы) ى	(к) ك	(ъ) گ	(-) ڭ	(л) ل
ə	*k*	*g*	*ŋ*	*l*
(э,е) ە	(м) م	(н) ن	(й) ي	(ь) ـ
e	*m*	*n*	*ц*	ЗНАК СМЯГЧЕНИЯ

TEXT XI-B

eskə taməanə araetəqə eken dcə ıana taətaəayəəz, anən teknəke caıənan kemʋə-ləktərə əolıonduqtan taətayəəz.

الیپ‌بەەەل يچينە مادانىيات تاراتا تۇرعان قۇرال.

aləp̄-ɛee-rl əʋəne madanəyat larala turıan qural.

جاكى الیپ‌بەەنى ۇيبرونۇۇ ۇجونۇندە قيزيل مۇعالىمدار، وقۇيۇچۇ جاشتار جانا سانالۇۇ ەمگەدكچيلەر باشقالارعا ۇلگۇلۇۇ جولباشچى بولۇۇزلارى كەرەك!

canə aləp—ɛecuə ʿayrannu ʿconundo qəzəl muraləmdar, oquuuu caśtar cana sanaaluu emgekuəler əaəqularıa ulguluu coloaзʋə əoluularə kerek!

TEXT XI-B

TRANSLATION

    - We do not abandon the old letters merely because they are Arab, we abandon them because of their technical shortcomings.

    - The alphabet is a cultural weapon put at the disposal of the people.

    - As far as the study of the new alphabet is concerned, the red teachers, the student youth and the conscious workers must be exemplary scouts for all others.

(Note that the 'kıbachı' is lacking before ulguluu: ülgülüü!)

Imlanьn ereçeleri

I. ADABIJ TILDEGI FONEMALARDЬN SASTABЬ ÇANA ALIPPENIN TARTIBI

1. Adaвij tilde 37 fonema qoldonulat da, eularӧьn Icinen 31 fonema ajrьm tamqalar manen вelgilenct, qalqan 6. yndÿy fonema imlada qoş tamqalar menen вelgilenip, alardьn syrettery alippenin qatar tartiьində kərsətylвajt.

a) alippenin tartibi, alardьn вasma çana çazma tyrlery.

Basma		Çazma		Oqulьştarь	Basma		Çazma		Oqulьştarь
Bas tamqalar	Kicine tamqalar	Bas tamqalar	Kicine tamqalar		Bas tamqalar	Kicine tamqalar	Bas tamqalar	Kicine tamqalar	
A	a	*A*	*a*	a	O	o	*O*	*o*	q
B	в	*B*	*в*	вь	Θ	ө	*Θ*	*ө*	ө
C	c	*C*	*ç*	cь	P	p	*P*	*p*	pь
Ç	ç	*Ç*	*ç*	çь	Q	q	*Q*	*q*	qь
D	d	*D*	*d*	dь	R	r	*R*	*r*	ьr
E	e	*E*	*e*	e	S	s	*S*	*s*	ьs 1)
G	g	*G*	*g*	gi	Ş	ş	*Ş*	*ş*	ьş 2)
Qı	q	*Qı*	*qı*	qь	T	t	*T*	*t*	tь
I	i	*I*	*i*	i	U	u	*U*	*u*	u
J	j	*J*	*j*	ij	Y	y	*Y*	*y*	y
K	k	*K*	*k*	ki	Z	z	*Z*	*z*	ьz 3)
L	l	*L*	*l*	lь	Ь	ь	*Ь*	*ь*	ь
M	m	*M*	*m*	mь	F	f	*F*	*f*	fь
N	n	*N*	*n*	nь	X	x	*X*	*x*	xь 4)
Ŋ	ŋ	*Ŋ*	*ŋ*	ьŋ	V	v	*V*	*v*	ьv
					H	h	*H*	*h*	he

1) S tamqa V çana R tamqalardьn aidьnda SЬ вolup, qalqan yьsyz tamqalardьn aldьnda ЬS вolup oqulat.

2, Ş tamqa V aldьnda çana ŞЬ вolup oqulat.

3) Z tamqa R tamqaanьn aldьnda ZЬ вolup, qalqan ynsyzderdyn aldьnda ЬZ вolup oqulat.

4) V tamqa z, l, n, r, s tamqalardьn aldьnda VЬ вolup, qalqan ynsyzderdyn aidьnda ЬV вolup oqulat.

25

TEXT XI-C(a)

TRANSLATION

ORTHOGRAPHICAL RULES

I. Phonematic composition of the literary language
   and alphabetical order.

1- 37 phonemes are used in the literary language,
   among which 31 are marked by a special letter,
   the remaining six vocalic phonemes being indicated by coupled letters; the form of these is not
   given in the alphabetical list.

a) Alphabetical order, printed and cursive aspects
   of the letters:
Printed / Written (form):Capital/Small/Name upon
                                          reading

1) The letter S in front of V and R is to be read
   as Sь, but ьS in front of other consonants.
2) The letter Ş in front of V (alone) is to be
   read as Şь.
3) The letter Z in front of R is to be read as Zь ,
   but ьZ in front of other consonants.
4) The letter V in front z,l,n,r,s is to be read
   Vь , but ьV in front of other consonants.

aɣaʙaj uulu
q. qaɣaʙaj uulu

çaɳьlьq

(coɳdoɣ ycyn aliʙ-ʙee).

ekinci iʁet tyzetylyʙ ʙasьlьşь

———✶———

pьʁınʒa çoɣь
1928-çьl.

— 30 —

qьrqьz tilinde tamş tamqalarь çьjьr‑ma çetь (27)

alardьn segizi (8) ındyyi

a, o, ө, u, y, e, ь, i

qalqandarь (19) ınsyz:

в, p, t, ç, c, d, r, z, s,

ş, q, q, k, g, n, l, m, n, j.

— 29 —

qьrqьz tilindegi tamş tamqalar ıreti menen çьzьlqanda mьna mьnav:

a	aь
в	вaь
p	apa
t	taв
ç	çan
c	зaj
d	dawь
r	rьaj
z	zalьm
s	saz
ş	şьrь
q	aqa
q	qьj
k	kelim
g	iveje
n	on
l	çol
m	mon
n	naь
o	to
ө	te
u	uruq
y	yıkyn
ь	tьrьa
i	icik
e	el
j	ojeo

TEXT XI-C(b)

TRANSLATION

- Cover page:

Arabay-uulu (cf. Texts I-E(a),I-G(a)
Q.Qarabay-uulu (=X.Karasaev, the author
    of 'Turmush Küzgüsü')

NOVELTY (A Primer for Adults)

Second edition
Frunze 1928

- pp. 29-30:

p. 29: Here is, in writing and in (normative)
        order, the pronunciation of the letters
        in the Kirghiz language.

p. 30: There are 27 letters in Kirghiz, among
        them 8 are vowels and the remaining ones
        consonants.

internatsanal

tuɪ, qɑɪqɨş menen tamqalanqan
ʙytyn dynyjesy, ɑɔquldɑɪ
qajnaʙ, ʙizdin, eqɨl ɛɛɪɴqɑn,
majɟanqa qɑʙdɑɪɪ dɑɪ-dɑjoɪ.

eʙki dynyjeny qulɑtɑʙьz,
tyʙyneн tyɪe ʙiz ʙuzuʙ;
ɛzilqeн eldi ҫьɪqɑtɑʙьz.
ҫɑnьdɑn dynyje tuɪquzuʙ.
ʙul ʙizdin eн ɑqьɪqь
ҫenişeɪ ɛoн majdan.
inteɪnɑtsɑnɑl menen
kөɟeɪeɪ ʙɑɪ adam!
eɪkindik ʙizɟe eɛkiɪɪ qьjʙɑs.
ʙɑdьşɑ dɑ, ʙɑɑtьɪ, ʙɑjɟɑmʙɑɪ.
eɪkindik, teнdik, kekteн ҫɑaʙɑs
qoɪqʙoɟɑɪ ʙizdin qol ɑlɑɪ.
oɔdoɪmoq ojloson qulduqtu,
ҫɑɟɑmɑq ʙolson keniɪi.-
ьldamdat yjlet ʙɑs keeɪykty,
muzdɑtʙaj uɪqun temiɪdi!
ʙul ʙizdin eн ɑqьɪqь
ҫenişeɪ ɛoн majdan.
inteɪnɑtsɑnɑl menen
kөɟeɪeɪ ʙɑɪ adam!
ʙytkyl dynyjenyn qьzmɑtkeɪi,
ҫeɪɟe ҫɑlqьz ʙiz ɟɑna ee
eseʙsiz emɟek ʙiz askeɪi;
miteɟe qɑlʙɑs ecteme!
eɟeɪde ɛɑqьlqɑn cɑɪtьldɑʙ,
nьqɑcь kөɥyn ʙɑsщɑ dɑ
ʙiz ycyn, ҫɑɪьq kyn ҫɑɪqьldɑʙ
tyşyɪeɪ ҫɑqşь nuɪ şoola.
ʙul ʙizdьn eн ɑqьɪqь
ҫenişeɪ ɛoн majdan.
inteɪnɑtsɑnɑl menen
kөɟeɪeɪ ʙɑɪ adam.

———

THE 'INTERNATIONALE'

1   Stand up, you malediction-branded,
Starving slaves from the whole world!
Our mind satiated with humiliation is
    boiling
And quite ready for the bloody battle.

5   We shall topple the old world,
We'll destroy it from top to bottom
We'll appease the oppressed people,
We'll rebuild the world anew.
    This is our very last

10   Great victorious struggle
    With the 'Internationale'
    Mankind will thrive.
Nobody will bring us liberty,
No emperor, no prophet, no hero.

15   Liberty, Equality do not fall from heaven,
Our dauntless arm will win them.
If you think that slavery must be
    suppressed
And that the masses should thrive,
Then hurry up, stoke the forge

20   Strike while the iron is hot
    (Refrain)

25   Toilers from the whole world,
We are the sole masters on earth;
The innumerable soldiers of labor,
Nothing will be left for blood-suckers!

If the thunderstorm rumbles,

30   If it crushes the stubborn exploiter,
For us the bright dazzling sun
Will shoot its rays of light.
    (Refrain)

TEXT XI-D(b)

lenin

çeʼı çyzynyn çumuşçulaʼınʼın çol вąçсʼʼ lenin (ʼilją uʼulu)
1870-çьь 23-apiʼelde tuuldu. 1924-çьь 21-çanʼ·aʼıdą oldy.

lenindin өmyʼıy.

1 вьlademiʼı ilija uulu· leniṅ 1870-çьь, apiʼeldьn 23-kyny
simBiʼı qalasьndą tuulqan. lenindin aqasь aliкsandьʼdь вądьşą
өкyməty өltyʼıqən aqasьnьn qazą вoluu çąş leninqe eʼı qьjьn
tijqen.

5 lenin qemnazьjąnь вytyʼıqənden кijin 1887-çьь qazan unu-
вeʼıstetine кiʼıqen. lenin unuвeʼıstette oquв çyʼıqen кezde өzqөʼıyş
qьzmatьnı qattaşą вąştąjt. oşol uвąqtąn mundaj вьlademiʼı ilija

uulu leniu вʼıdьş өmyʼıyʼıı eɪɪqeкeɪleʼıdl qьʼıiɪmcʼьʼıqtan qʼıtąą.
ʼıuuqą çumşąʼıąʼı.

10 1895-çьь çąş leniu ąjtiʼıвoʼıdo çumuʼı̧ qьʼıtə çalcьlʼıʼı oʼıąʼıą.
du ujumdaʼı aʼıqan; anьʼıtь вiɪɪnɪʼ̃ qalьв вądьşą өкyməty leniɪɪdɪ
qaʼıтąв nвąątьʼıqą çąuв. 1897-çьь sɪвiʼıqe ąjdąв çiвeʼıqen sʼ̧ʼıʼıde
уе çьl ąjdooʼo çyʼıqen. oʼ̧ondo çyʼıqende lenin teʼıen ɪɪ̃iɪɪ кiteʼ̧ɪɪ
çazʼ̧ąʼı.

15 вądьşąnьn sąʼ̧cьʼluʼıı leninqe oʼıusują dą qьʼınąt qьlʼınąʼ̧
mymкyndyк вeʼıвeʼ̧en. andan кijin lenin eet ɪɪɪemleкette (sʼ̧вʼ̧ʼ̧ʼ̧-
sąʼıьjąʼ̧ą) кetкen. cetкe кetyʼıde lenindi oʼıusujądą вoluв çʼ̧tʼ̧ʼ̧ą
өzqөʼıyş çolunąn вʼıąaqtątвądь, вąjlаnьʼ̧ьn yzвedy. cette çyʼıʼ̧ʼ̧
lenin oʼıusujądąʼ̧ь өzqөʼıyş кyʼıeʼ̧yne çen şiɪteв. çol кʼ̧ʼ̧ʼ̧ty̧ʼ̧
20 ʼıuʼıqąn. вąlşąвeк кemunus pаʼıtьjąsьnьn çol вąçсьʼь вoluв oɪʼ̧ʼ̧ʼ̧-
ʼıuв, uʼıuu өzqөʼıyʼ̧tьn çolun сąвą ·вeʼıdi.
1917-çьь өкtөвʼıʼı ąjьndąʼ̧ь çumuʼ̧cu, dьjqąn coʼ̧ʼ̧alouʼ̧ʼ̧ʼ̧
вąjlʼ̧ʼı өкymətyne qąʼıʼ̧ь çąsąʼıąn өzqөʼıyʼ̧yne lenin çol вąçʼ̧ʼ̧ʼ̧ą
qьʼ̧ьв кeldi.
25 çumuʼ̧çulaʼıı вąjlʼ̧ʼı өкymətyʼ̧yn tąʼ̧ tąlqąnьn cьʼ̧qььв, çeʼ̧-
qenden кijin, çoldoʼ̧ lenindi el кemijseʼıдeʼıinin кeneʼ̧ine teʼ̧ ąqʼ̧ʼ̧-
ьʼ̧qqą ʼ̧ąjląʼ̧qąn.
lenin 1924-çьь 21-çanьвąʼıdą eldy; вiʼıoq ezy quʼıuв кetкʼ̧ʼ̧ʼ̧
кemunus pąʼıtьjąsь qąldь. кemunus pаʼıtьjąsь lenin osuʼ̧ątʼ̧ʼ̧
oʼıundąв ıenin tuusun qoldon tyʼ̧ʼıʼ̧ej ɪɪ̃qeʼıi çyʼımeк

LENIN'S LIFE

1   Vladimir, Ilyas' son, Lenin was born on April 23, 1870 in the town of Simbirsk. The Tsarist government executed Lenin's elder brother Alexander; the death of his elder brother deeply hurt the young Lenin.

5   Lenin, after graduating from high school, entered the University at Kazan' in 1887. While studying at the university, Lenin began his revolutionary activities. From then on, Vladimir, Ilyas' son, devoted his entire life to freeing workers from oppression.

10   In 1895, the young Lenin settles in St. Petersburg and organized cells among the proletarians; having learned about that, the Tsarist government, after arresting Lenin and putting him in jail, sent him in 1897 to Siberia where he lived in exile for three years. During that time, Lenin wrote a deeply scientific book.

15   The Tsar's warders didn't give Lenin the possibility of working in Russia.

After that, Lenin left for a foreign country (Switzerland). While he was abroad, the revolution which was developing in Russia did not remove Lenin from his path, did not sever his links.

From abroad, giving a strong impetus to

20   the revolutionary struggle in Russia, he incessantly shows the way to be followed. After becoming the leader of the Bolshevist Communist Party, he kept on orienting the revolution.

Lenin came back to take the lead of the revolution carried out against the power of the rich by the rural toilers and the workers in October 1917.

25   The workers, having succeeded in totally
        annihilating the power of the rich, after
        their victory, elected Comrade Lenin
        president of the council of the people's
        commissars.

        Lenin died on January 21, 1924 but the
        Communist Party he had built is still
        there. The Communist Party, fulfilling
        Lenin's last will, must march forward
        without dropping his standard.

вadьşa zamanьnda qьʼqjьz eli.

1   вadьşa təʼələʼy qьʼqjьz eline keleʼi menen ele mansaвqa
qьzьqqan вuzuqtaʼdь kəвəjtə вaştadь. mansaвtьn вaaʼь muʼunqu вajlaʼ menen вekteʼdin qoluna ətty. qalьq вuqaʼanь eq овol
вajlaʼdьn ajaq astьna salьь веʼdi. qьʼqjьz elinin muʼunqudaj
5 qajʼatь əcə вaştadь.

    qьnq etken çandь вadьşa təʼələʼy menen вekteʼi aвaqqa
salьв, sіве ʼqe ajdaв, atьв-asьв aвdan ezdi. uşul sajasatь aʼqasьnda, вadьşa əкуmətу qьʼqjьzdь çeʼinen suusunan, ata qonuşunan, açьʼata вaştadь. qьʼqjьz çeʼine вadьşa təʼələʼy əz adamʼaʼьn otuʼquzʼu. qьʼqjьz eli кedej вoluв, çeʼ-suusunan açьʼa-
10 qandan кijin, aʼ вiʼ вajdьn, aʼ вiʼ təʼənyn qolunda 15-teв,
30-daв qul вoluв qala веʼdi.

THE KIRGHIZ PEOPLE IN THE DAYS OF THE PADYSHAH

1   As soon as the padyshah's (Tsar's)
chieftains came to the Kirghiz people, the
greedy go-getters began to multiply. All
influential positions came into the hands
of former bays and beks. The masses first
of all threw themselves at the bays' and
beks' feet. The former steadfastness of the
Kirghiz people

5   began to wane.

Those who grumbled, the padyshah's
chieftains and the beks threw into jail,
chased out to Siberia, shot and hung them,
oppressed them heavily. Thanks to that
policy, the Tsarist government began
dispossessing the Kirghiz of their land and
water and of their native encampments. The

padyshah's chieftains settled

10   their own people on Kirghiz soil. After
the Kirghiz people had become miserable
and been deprived of its land and water,
it turned out that each bay, each
chieftain had in his hands (between)
fifteen and thirty slaves.

1916-çьl.

1   1916-çьl *aвdɑn* qoʼqunuctuu çьl. al çьldɑɋь təqylqən ça-zьɋsьz kedej qɑnь, вul kynɋə cejin eldin esinen da ketken çoq. oʼ?ol kezdəqi kedej qɑnьna suɋaʼьloɋan вadьşa təʼələʼynyn qь-lьcь вul kyndə da eldin kɵz aldьnda tuʼat.

5   1916-çьldьn oqujasь, qeʼɯmen sooɋuşu menen вajlanьştuu. qeʼɯmen sooɋuşu eki çьlɋa sozuldu. askeʼleʼdin **sanь** azajdь. uʼuş ʼɯajdɑnьnda qaʼa qьzɯat qьluu ycyn çalcь вeʼilsin deв 25-ьjunda вujʼuq cьoɋaʼьldь, eldin yʼəjy qactь.

10   вujʼuq *aвdɑn* qatuu cьqtь. 18 çaş menen 50 çaş ekəənyn oʼtosundaɋь eʼʼkek teqiz alьnsьn, çyk taşьj tuʼɋan unaa, aʼɋan, çiв, teʼi-teʼsek, qaltьʼвaj вeʼilsin, deв вujuʼuloɋan, çana вizdin ʼquʼoɋьz sьjaqtuu kecɯməndyy elqe вujʼuq ɵzɋəce вoldu: 18 çaş-tan 42 çaşqa dejʼe qaltььlвaj ʼalьnsьn delinqen.

15   вaj вaldaʼь вaʼвasa da вolot, anьn oʼduna kedej çaldaв çiвcʼeвiz, deв təʼələʼ, ʼɯanaвtaʼ вiʼ çaoɋьnan вaʼaɋa tojo вaştaştь.

    kedejleʼ emine qьluu keʼek?

    uʼuş вolso вajlaʼdьn вajdasь ycyn вoluв çatat, al emi вaj-lɑʼ вolso aɋca menen qutuldu, ələ tuʼɋan ele çalɋьz kedejвi? вiz вaʼвajвьz, eʼte ɵlɋən kişi, вadьşaoɋada, вajıaʼoɋa da qaʼsь 20 ʼ???oвuz, deв kedejleʼ kətəʼylyş çasadь.

    вizdin qьʼoɋьz çeʼindəqi oʼustaʼdьn kɵвy вajlaʼ ele, oşon-duqtan alaʼ çalpь вajlaʼdьn вadьşanьn вajdasьn kezdəşty da, kedejleʼqe təʼələʼ ʼɯenen вiʼdəşiʼ, qaʼsь cьqtь.

25   вul iş seвeв вoluв, qьʼoɋьz, oʼus aʼıasьnda ulut duşɯandь-ɋь ʼtuuв ketti da, qьʼoɋьzdьn вaj-ʼɯanaвtaʼьnьn kɵвy da qalьn elqe qoşuluв ketti. al mından da qan təqʼlyş вaştaldь.

    qolunda quʼʼal ʒɵɋ, çaɋьş ujumdaşa ʼalɨaɋan kedejleʼ, вa-dьşanьn çaвdьqtuu askeʼine cьdaɯdьq вeʼe aʼɨadь. qьʼoɋьnoɋa 30 tyştу. aɋьʼ cʼdaj ʼalвaj, ɵlqəndən- qaloɋanь qьtaj çeʼine ɵtə qacьştь.

    al çьldaɋь kɵtəʼylyskə ʼɯıqtьlaв qaʼьşqandaʼ puunza qь-ʼaıʼzdaʼь menen qaʼaqol qьʼʼɋьzdaʼь вoluştu. çazьqsʼz adam-daʼdьn qanь suudaj aɋtь. ilqeʼten вeʼi ʼɯekən qьlьв, kindik 35 kesiв kiʼ çuuʼɋan ɵz çeʼi qaldь.

1916

1 1916 was a terrible year. The poor innocents' blood shed during that year remained until now in the memory of the people. The Tsarist henchmen's swords, soaked then in the blood of the poor, remains until now in front of the eyes of the people.

5 The events of 1916 are linked with the German War. The German War was in its second year. The number of soldiers was diminishing. On June 25th, the order was given to send labourers to carry out heavy tasks on the battlefield: the people were afraid and fled.

The order was very harsh: "Let also be called up one out of two among all men between 18 and 30, draft animals, lassoes,

10 ropes, hides" - the order was to hand them over to the very last one and a special order concerned nomads such as our Kirghiz. It was said: "Let all men between 18 and 42 be called up to the very last".

The bureaucrats said: "If bay children don't go, we'll hire

15 and send poor people in place of them" and manaps began to fatten just from bribes. What could poor people do?

As far as war (is concerned), it was advantageous for the bays; as far as bays (are concerned), they pulled through with

20 money - (so) only the poor were to die? Saying: "We won't go, we shall die tomorrow against the Tsar and the bays", the poor organized a revolution.

The majority of Russians on our Kirghiz land were bays and because of this,

supported all the bays' and the Tsar's
interests and, uniting with the
bureaucrats, marched against the poor.

25   This is why national hostility broke out
between Kirghiz and Russians and the
majority of Kirghiz bay-manaps suddenly
united with the popular masses.
Consequently, blood began to flow.

The poor who had no weapons and could
not organize themselves well, could not
resist the Tsar's armed soldiers. They were

30   slaughtered. Unable to endure the end, the
survivors fled to Chinese territory.

Those who had thouroughly participated
in the revolution of that year were the
Kirghiz from Frunze and Karakol. Innocent

35   people's blood flowed in streams. The
native soil which had become since long
their motherland remained uninhabited.

çeı suu teŋkө̇ıyşy.

1   qьıɪ̧ьzьstandьn tyştyk qantonдoıunda çeı, suu teŋkө̇ıyşy
çyıΥв, çaqьnda вytty; mьndan tyştyk qantonдoıdooıu вatьıaq,
kedejleı aвdan soŋ вajdalanьşьв qalьştь. çeıi çoq вatьıaq, kedejleı çeı, suuoıa ee вoluştu. köв çeıdyıleıdyn əzdəıynə вiı
5 enci oıana çeıı taştav, qaloıan aıtьq çeıleıi, çeısiz, suuzuz вatьıaqtaıoıa alьв вeıildi.

   uşundaj вoluв 17500 kedej вatьıaqtaı
çeıgə oınoştuıuldu. mьndan вaşqa daoıь ça-
ıьdan suu cьoıaıoıan çeıieıgə 716 kedej caı-

10 вasь çeıgə oınoştuıuldu. çeıgə oınoştuıuloıan
kedej caıвasь вaıdьoıь 18216. вaj manaвtaı-
dьn qolunan alьnьв, kedej вatьıaqtaıoıa вeıil-
gen suulu çeı 10184 gektoı, qaııaq 9978
gektoı.

çol. istaliɪ

в. k. ç. k. p.(в)
niɪ вaş qatcьsь.

THE LAND / WATER REFORM

1   In the districts of Southern Kirghizia, the land-water reform, once started, was promptly completed. This is why farm-hands and poor people from those Southern districts gained great advantage from it. Landless farm-hands and poor people become masters of the land and of the water. Only a plot was left to those who had large stretches of land, the other good

5   plots having been given over to the landless and waterless laborers.

    Thus, 17,500 poor laborers were settled on (such) plots and 716 other poor households on newly irrigated land. All in all, 18,216 poor households were settled on these lands. 10,184 hectares of irrigated land and 9,978 hectares of non-irrigated land, confiscated from bays and manaps, were handed over to poor laborers.

вadьşa zamanьnda aqaʁtuu işteʁi.

1 вadьşa ǝkymǝty qьɪqьzqa mekteв acьв веʁqen çoq. qьʁ-
qьzdьn ǝz ene tilinde alaqandaj qaqaz cijyyqǝ uʁuqsat qьlqan
çoq. вiʁin-seʁin mekteв acьlьв, вaj-manaв вaldaɪьn çьjʁaв, alaʁ-
dь oʁusca oqutuв. eldi eze tuʁqan вuźuqu tilmecteʁ dajaʁdoo-
5 qo tьʁьştь. qalьn вuqaʁaqa quʁan oquuqa qana uʁuqsat qьldь.
вytkyl aq seldeʁy moldoloʁdu aqcaqa satьв alьв, alaʁdьn çaʁ-
damь menen da eldi ezdi. çanьca oquqan qapьʁ вolot, „вadьşa
qudaj emes, qudajdan kem da emes“ dediʁiв şaʁьjat ujtqьzьв
qojdu. mьna oşonun kesepetinen eldin вaaʁь qat taanьвaj, sa-
10 вatsьz qalьв, ǝneʁ-вilimqe çetişe alqan çoq. ǝneʁsyz, saвatsьz
qalqan kim? al da вolso, qaʁa вuqaʁa, qalьn kedej.

EDUCATIONAL WORKS IN TSARIST TIMES

1   The Tsarist government has opened no
schools for the Kirghiz. It gave no
permission to write on paper or whatsoever
in the Kirghiz' own mother tongue. Having
opened a few schools, assembling bays' and
manaps' sons, teaching them in Russian, it
strove to train rascal interpreters who
oppressed the people. It allowed

5   only the Qoran to be taught to the
destitute masses. Bribing the white turban
mollahs, it oppressed the people with their
help. Whoever has studied according to the
new (jadid) way, was a kafir, it had the
shariat proclaim that "The Tsar is not God,
but he is no less than God". Because of
this infamy, the whole people didn't know
how to write, remained illiterate and was
unable to gain

10   access to knowledge. Who remained without
skill, without knowledge? Always the
(same): the villeins, the poor.

Rytyn dynyjə prol.tarlarь, eirikkile!

Qьrqьzьstan Respublikesinin
Boʁvonduq Atqaʁuu Kemijtetinin
II-sessьjasьnьn cьqaʁqan
TOQTOMDORU

20—26 çanьʙar 193?-çь?

Prunza   QЬRMEMBAS   1932-ç

QьRQЬZ̦STANDьN BӦRBORDUQ ATQARUU KEMIJTETININ 2-SESSЬJASЬNЬN

TOQTOMU

„Qьrqьzьstandьn 1932-çьlqь вudçetinin qantьrol sandarь tuuralu

Воↆвоↄduq atqaↄuu kemijtetinin Sessьjasь 1931-çьl-qa tyzylqən вudçettin atqaↄьlьşь çaпа 1932-çьldьн qaп-tьↄоl sandaↄь tuuralu Atq. Kemijseↄijetiпiп вajaпdama-sьп uqup, təmeпkyleↄdy ajtьp ketet:

1. 1931-çьldьn вudçetinen el саↄваsьпьп таↄmaqta-ↄьп aqcalandьↄuu çumuşu teqizsiz çaпa таↄtipsiz atqa-ↄьlqaп Bul: a) Çeↄqiliktyy Atqaↄuu Kemijtetteↄi çaпа keпↄşteↄdiп, dolвoↄlonqon kiↄeşeleↄdi oↄundoo ycyn kyↄe-şyyleↄy воşоↄ волqonduqtan; в) Aqca pьlanьn оↄuпdoo çumuşuna kөpcylyk çetişince таↄtьlваqandьqtan.

2. 1932-çьlqь вudçettin вekityy ycyn tapşьrьlqan qautьↄol sandaↄь yztyвyzdəqy çьldьn el-саↄва pьlanьпa ьlajьq tyzylyp, Ɍespuвlikeвizdin madanьjat çaпa саↄва-sьn keleↄkiↄe kөteↄyy çaпa веş çьldьq pьlandь 4 çьlda оↄuпdoo çaqьпan paↄьja meпеп өkyмөtyвyzdyn ваↄdьq пeqizqi deↄektiptcↄin ez icine alьp oltuↄat.

Açьↄatьp ajtqanda, Sessьja qautьↄol sandaↄdьп tə-мепky саↄaluↄdь ez icine alqandьqьn ajtьp ketet:

a) Өпeↄ çajlaↄь çaqьпaп-çeↄqiliktyy cijki maldaↄ-dь iştep cↄqaↄa tuↄqan iş оↄuпdaↄьп (teↄi zoottoↄun) kөвejtyy, çeↄqiliktyy quↄuluş matьↄьjaldaↄьп iştep cↄ-qaↄa tuↄqan iş оↄuпdaↄьп (kiↄpiç zoottoↄun) quↄuuпↄ kyↄetyy, toqoj өпeↄ çↄjlaↄь çaпa ваşqalaↄ;

(...)

Eki majda coŋ qoɩqunuctuq qatarьnda „solcul-
ijmeleeleɩqe, çana al qьjşajuulaɩqa kөnyycylyk
mamilelerinde вoluularqa qarşь, Lenindin ulut saɟasatьn
mьndan orь taɩta—daqь mьqtap işke aşьruu çana coŋ
qoɩqunuctuq qataɩьnda вolqon ulu orustaɩ ulutcu-
luqu çana çeɩqiliktyy ulutculuq menen çanqda
alaɩqa kөnyycyleɩ menen kyɩeşyy neqizinde çyɩqyzyl-
qөn ɩajьmsьz tyrdeqy kyɩeşte, çol. Бstalin вaş вolup
tuɩqan Lenincil BK-nin aввdan sьnalqan вalşeвekoil çol
вaşcьlьqь astьnda, paɩtьja menen өkymөt вeş çьldьqtьn
ajaqqь teɩtyncy çьlьnda вeɩqen tapşьrɩmalaɩьn orunda-
tuunun natьjçanьn, Qьɩqьzьstan, satsьjaldьqtь quruunun
çanь вolqon cecyycy çeniltɩrine kelet.

Qьɩqьzьstan вorвoɩduq atqaɩuu kemijtetinin
teɩ aqasь: *Orozвek uulu.*

Qьɩqьzьstan вorвoɩduq atqaɩuu kemijtetinin
çooptuu qatcьtь: *Şamurzin*

26-çanьварг 1932-çьl prunza şaɩɩь.

TEXT XI - E

D E C I S I O N

1 OF THE 2ND SESSION OF THE CENTRAL EXECUTIVE
COMMITTEE OF KIRGHIZSTAN
5 "ON THE SCHEDULED FIGURES OF KIRGHIZSTAN
FOR THE 1932 BUDGETARY YEAR"

Having heard the report of the Executive
Committee concerning the fulfillment of the
budget planned for 1931 and the scheduled
figures for 1932, the Session of the
Central Executive Committee has ordered as
follows:
10   1. The handling of the financial
evaluation of the (different) sectors of
the economy on the basis of the 1931 budget
has been dispatched in an uneven and
disorderly fashion. This is due to

a) the weakness of the struggles
(=efforts) of the local Executive
Committees and Soviets to collect the
planned revenues,

b) the non-completion, in most cases,
in a satisfactory

15 manner of the fulfillment of the financial
plan

2. Having reconsidered the scheduled
figures which had been provided to settle
the 1932 budget in order to make them fit
with the economical plan of the current
year, our Party and Government took the
following measures concerning the
fulfillment in 4

20 years of the Five-Year Plan and the
improvement in the future of the economy
and culture of our Republic.

In particular, the Session ordered the
adopting of the following measures enclosed
here below concerning the scheduled
figures:

a) on the matter of industries, to
increase the number of local factories
producing raw cattle breeding goods (fur
dressing plants); to strengthen the
construction of local factories producing
building material (brick plants) and to
develop lumbering, etc.

30   In the throes of a terrible danger on
two fronts in the struggle against leftist
deviationnists and against those elbow-
rubbing with the deviationnists of the
other side, implementing Lenin's
nationality policy, putting into practice
ever more fundamentally this policy and
struggling against the terrible danger
coming from great-Russian nationalism,
local nationalism and those who

35   lean toward them, under the expert
bolshevist direction of the leninist
Central Committee with comrade STALIN at
its head and thanks to the implementation
of commitments made by the Party and the
Government at the end of the fourth year of
the Five-Year Plan,

40   Kirghizstan will achieve new decisive
victories in the edification of socialism.

The President of the Central Executive
Committee of Kirghizstan - Orozbek-uulu
The Executive Secretary of the Central
Executive Committee of Kirghizstan

Shamuzin

Purunza, January 26, 1932.

BAQTЬBAJEV YSEJ.

ÇARDAMCЬ ETIŞTER

§ 1. Kiriş sez.

Qьrqьz tilindegi вardьq etiş sezderdyn tyzylysy çana tЬsqь tyry çaqьna qaraj taldoo çasaqan ucurda, anь eki qana negizgi gruppaqa вolyp qatьştьruuqa mymkyn:

1. Çenekej etişter. 2. Tataal etişter.

I. ÇENEKEJ ETIŞTER. Qajsь вir etiş sezder tyzylysy çana tЬsqь tyry çaqьnan вir qana sez dy kersetet da, вir qana aсьq maanige ee вolo alьşat. Mekteptik taçrijвada mьndaj etiş sezderdy aсьratuu ancalьq qьmвat emes. Maselen: çaz, çazьş, qamcьla degen etiş sezderdy ala turqan вoлoq, tyzylysy çana maanisi çaqьnan da aсьraqьs вir taq maanini kersetyp turuşaт.

Çalqьz qana вir sezden turup, aсьraqьs вir maanini kersetyycy etiş sezderdy çenekej etiş sezder dejвiz. Qьrqьz tilinde çenekej etişter kep aлar negizinen ye tyrlyy вolup kezdeşet:

1. Unqu etişter. 2. Ulama etişter. 3. Qurama etişter.

2. TATAAL ETIŞTER. Qьrqьz tilinde qajsь вir etiş sezder eki sezden qoş ajtьlat da, aсьraqьs taq вir maanini kersetyşet. Mьndaj etişter en ele kep kezdeşet. Mьndaj etiş sezderdyn tЬsq formasьna qaraj qoş maanini kersetet dep talquuloo en ele вьcaqtьn mizindej nerse. Oşonduqtan grammatikaльq faktьlardь tekşergen ucurda, anьn tЬsqь formasьna qaraвaj, icki maanisine qarap taldoo çasoo en вir ьntajluu вolot. Bul maselenin cьbьqь aльqtьqьna kez çetkizyy ycyn, temenky dalikderge toqtoluuqa вolot. Bara çatat, aльp çatat degen etiş sezder, tЬsqь formasь çaqьnan eki sez qatarьnda велek çazьльp turqanь menen da, icki maanisi çaqьnan aсьraqьs taq вir maanini kersetyp, вir qana sez вolup mildet atqarat.

TEXT XI - F

AUXILIARY VERBS

1   Foreword.

    Upon conducting an analysis of all
Kirghiz verbal forms according to their
structure and external aspect, one can
divide

5   them into two basic groups:

        1. Simple verbs 2. Complex verbs

        1- SIMPLE VERBS. Certain verbs,
    according to their structure

10 and external aspect look like a single
    word and can have only one, clearly
    determined meaning. In pedagogical
    practice it is not difficult to single out
    such verbs. For example, if we take such

15 verbal forms as 'to write', 'to write
    together', 'to whip', they reveal through
    their structure and meaning only one
    global, clear

20 meaning. We shall call 'simple verbs'
    those verbal forms which reveal only one
    global meaning and are made up of only one
    word. Simple verbs are numerous in
    Kirghiz; they are found under

25 three basic forms: root verbs, derived
    verbs, composed verbs.

        2- COMPLEX VERBS

30   In Kirghiz, some verbs, although made
    up of two words coupled together, display
    but one global, precise meaning. Such verbs
    are

35 quite numerous. To consider that these
    verbs, in accordance with their external
    aspect, display a double meaning is

something similar to a knife blade (=
debatable). Because of this, upon

40   analyzing grammatical facts without taking
into account their external form, it is
much more convenient to describe them in
accordance with their internal meaning. In
order to secure the

45   accuracy of this, one should consider the
following examples. Although verbs like 'he
is going', 'he is taking' are written from
the viewpoint of their external form as a
series of two

50   distinct words, they play the role of a
single one, displaying through their
internal meaning only one global, precise
meaning.

Çань alfavittin dolbooru

(Qarqas tiulein çasa çazmasuana fiun izliáeo laoffitain tyzgsa)

№	Çань ийорй		мий ийорй		Sonsp kordsof sóipna
	basoin houmoqular	оrd сыгчэ tamagalar	mosion tamoqulaa	mid sanmoi tamoqulor	
1	Аа	*Aa*	Aa	*Aa*	а
2	Бб	*бб*	Bb	*Bb*	бе
3	Вв	*Вв*	Vv	*Vv*	ве
4	Гг	*Гг*	G g	*Gg*	ге
5	Ғғ	*Ғғ*	Oq oq	*Gg*	га
6	Дд	*Dg*	Dd	*Dd*	дэ
7	Ее	*Ее*	Ee	*e*	е(и)
8	Ёё	*Ёё*	Jоjо	*Jo*	и(о)
9	Жж	*Жж*	Zz	*Zz*	жэ
10	Җҗ	*Җҗ*	Cc	*Cc*	жа
11	Зз	*Зз*	Zz	*Zz*	зэ
12	Ии	*Ии*	J j	*Jj*	и
13	Кк	*Кк*	Kk	*Kk*	ка
14	Ққ	*Ққ*	Qq	*Qq*	қа
15	Лл	*Лл*	Ll	*Ll*	эль
16	Мм	*Мм*	Mm	*Mm*	эм
17	Нн	*Нн*	Nn	*Nn*	эн
18	Ңң	*Ңң*	Ŋ ŋ	*Nŋ*	эн
19	Оо	*Оо*	Oo	*Oo*	о
20	Өө	*Өө*	Ѳѳ	*Өө*	ө
21	Пп	*Пп*	Pp	*Pp*	пе
22	Рр	*Рр*	Rr	*Rr*	эр
23	Сс	*Сс*	Ss	*Ss*	эс
24	Тт	*Тт*	Tt	*Tt*	тэ
25	Уу	*Уу*	Uu	*Uu*	у
26	Үү	*Үү*	Уу	*Уу*	ү
27	Фф	*Фф*	Ff	*Ff*	эф
28	Хх	*Хх*	Xx	*Xx*	ха
29	Цц	*Цц*	Tsts	*Tsts*	це
30	Чч	*Чч*	Cc	*Cc*	че
31	Шш	*Шш*	Şş	*Şş*	ша
32	Щщ	*Щщ*	Scsc	*Scsc*	ша
33	ъ	ъ	–	–	ер
34	ыы	*ыы*	b	*bб*	еры
35	ь	ь	–	–	еро
36	Ээ	*Ээ*	Ee	*Ee*	э
37	Юю	*Юю*	Juju	*Juju*	ю(ю)
38	Яя	*Яя*	Jaja	*Jaja*	я(я)

TEXTS XI

COMMENTS

The documents and texts presented here illustrate a key phase in the sociolinguistic evolution
of Kirghiz during the so-called 'latinization'
period which extended from 1925 until 1941. (For
a more complete survey of this movement, cf. C-155-
159 and G. Imart: "Développement et Planification
des Vernaculaires: l'expérience soviétique et le
Tiers-Monde", Language Reform, ed. by I. Fodor and
cl. Hagège, vol. 2, pp. 211-240, and Yu.D.Desheriev:
"Iz sovetskogo opyta planirovaniia nacional'nykh
iazykov", id., vol. 1, pp. 401-448, Buske Verlag,
Hamburg 1983).
Beginning in the early 1920s, the implementation of an official 'linguistic policy' in Kirghizstan suddenly tended to greatly widen the specter
of the 'social functions' performed by the national
languages. This in turn implied:
A) An Alphabetical Reform
The systematic use of Kirghiz as the basic
means of teaching in newly opened primary schools
and courses for illiterate adults is generally presented as the main reason, and justification, for
the sudden implementation of the Latin script in
1926.
In fact, other, non linguistic and often more
pressing motives played here a key role. But, once
the decision was taken, it is true that its main
field of implementation was, together with the new
press in the national language, the rapidly developing web of schools.
In 1926, the 'Erkin Too' newspaper gave its
readers a brief survey (Text XI-A) of the 'New Alphabet'. It is easy to note that it was a simple
transliteration of the 'Reformed Arabic Alphabet'
used in Kirghizia since about 1924.
As made evident by the samples proposed from
a 1927 schoolbook (Text XI-B), the 'kabachi' system
had been kept: written in front of a word, it indicated that u and o were to be read as ü and ö. But
this did not extent to a/e, or i/ı. The alphabetical order (Text XI-Cb), basically, was that of the

Arabic script (alif, ba, ta, etc.) and, as in the
latter, the q/k, g/ ɥ distinction remained.

From a typographical viewpoint, one can note
the introduction of some cyrillic graphemes: ɥ for
ch, ɜ for sh, Γ for ɥ. Only ɳ had a diacritic
mark. There is no doubt that this solution was
motivated first by pedagogical reasons (these graphemes were easy to learn), but also had more practical motives. War-torn Kirghizia lacked everything,
including printing material and had to rely on what
was available on the spot, in particular in the
Russian printing houses.

This last reason most probably accounted for
the choice of y for rendering ü and especially of
ө for ö: the main influence here was not that of
the International Phonetic Alphabet or of the
Danish ø, but the existence of 'fita's: ө, then
useless in Russian after the 1918 orthographical
reform.

Some years later, this first Latin system
was modified so as to allow Kirghiz to conform itself to the new, panturkic (in all sense of the
word...) alphabet, designed by the Central Committee of the New Alphabet for all Turkic languages.

Besides the use of j for yod and ɔ (curious-
ly borrowed from the now abandoned German 'Gothic'
handwriting), the removal of ɥ caused the introduction of ç. This in turn triggered off a change
in value, c being now ch and ç: j.

Cyrillic ь (the Russian 'soft sign') can be
considered a more satisfactory solution for ı than
Turkey Turkish ı which is difficult to identify,
particularly in handwriting in such (frequent)
endings as mın, ın, etc.

Capital letters were not used in pedagogical
material - a solution which made possible the use
of в (i.e. cyrillic v!) for b.

This system, presented in 1928 in a new primer: çaɳьlьq (Text XI-Cb) by E. Arabay-uulu and Q.
Qarasay-uulu (first editor of 'Erkin Too', cf.
also text 1-G) is the one used in schoolbooks and
newspapers from which texts XI-D,E and F have been
taken.

K. Tınıstanov, First Secretary of the CP in
Kirghizstan (he was shot in 1937) published in 1934
ɥ 'Draft for a New Orthography of the Kirghiz Language' (Text XI-Ca). A copy of this book (classifi-
cation mark M 222/1772, Lenin Library, Moscow)

bears two superposed rubber stamps on its cover:
one reading, in Russian, 'Specotdel' (special collection) and, on top of it, a second one: 'Pogashe-
no': rescinded - a late testimony to the bloody
ideological struggle for which the Latinization was
a lame excuse between 1934 and 1941.

Kirghiz was 'cyrillized' by a decree dated
September 12, 1941 (at the height of the Nazi pressure on almost besieged Moscow!), the Latin system
having been 'critized' as early as 1939, i.e. immediately after the physical liquidation of its supporters.

Document XI-G gives the new Cyrillic alphabet (note the ironic use of this then extremely
prestigious term) which is the present day official
one. It is also nothing less than a transliteration
of the former, Latin script - with the addition of
a certain number of incongruities.
(For the use of the Latin script in China, cf.
Text XVII, Comments).

B) Lexical Updating
We already noted in texts 1-E and 1-G the
reformers' eagerness to secure for Kirghiz the best
possible lexical appropriateness in accordance with
the new needs and fields of communication. This
tendency to "activate the inner resources" of the
ethnic language, expresses itself in two ways:
- through semantic specialization:
tamga+la-: initially= to brand animals with the
stamp of the tribe → XI-Da: karkısh menen tam-
galagan = rus. prokliat'em zakleimënnyi: male-
diction branded
ayda-: to drive a herd, an animal in front of
oneself → to send into exile
sakchılar: guards → policemen
kengesh: council → a soviet
kürösh: struggle → political struggle
özgörüsh: transformation → revolution
tör aga: elder brother on the seat of honor
          (facing the 'door' of the yurt) →
          president
ezilgen: crushed → oppressed, exploited
kedey: the needy → poor peasant = rus. bedniak
This spontaneous method had been used long
before 1917 by Kazakh review editors and by the
intellectuals. As suggested by text XI-E, this did

not prevent the ethnic language from evolving in
some cases into a petrified politico-bureaucratic
jargon. Often, the calque, as used within the framework of the ethnic language, acquired a new meaning,
different from that of the original.
   - through lexical loans:
   One must note however that in texts XI-E and D
the numerous Russian loanwords all appear to have
been phonetically adapted to the Kirghiz norm (cf.
K-526-546, C-167-176):
   ьstalin, kemijtet, qantьrol, pьlan, kemünüs par-
tijasь, unuвerstet (university), Bitiвor (Petersburg!), Siвetsarija (rus. Shvecariia): Switzerland,
Balsaвet (bolshevist), jaŋьвar (rus. ianvar'): January, etc.
   All these forms are now considered obsolete -
and philistine. They allow us, however, to imagine
what in fact was the <u>autonomous</u> evolution of the
language prior to State intervention. A systematic
comparison between texts XI-E and XVI-G or XIII
(Chinese or 'Western' Kirghiz, where many of these
early Russian loanwords have kept their Kirghiz
form: aptonom, komandır, gezit, pirogram (program),
noyabır (november, etc.) suggests that many of them,
even if excluded from written texts, are most probably used in oral communication (cf. the 'double
norm' phenomenon in literary kirghiz: C- 190-200).
   The recurrent and particularly acute character
of these pseudo-linguistic discussions on Russian
loanwords, their form and number that have been
endlessly cropping up (in the 1920s, in 1934, 1941,
1966, 1977, etc.) is due to the fact that these
debates revolve in fact around the problem of how
to maintain - or how to erase - ethnic specificity.
Very recently, the question was raised anew by
Ch. Aytmatov in an interview to 'Literaturnaia Gazeta' (n° 33, August 13, 1986, p. 4).

PARSING

XI-C(a)

imla: ar.:orthography
sastab: rus.: **состав:** composition
ereje: decision of a biy, rule

XI-D(a) Internacanal

1. 14: bajgambar ~pajgambar: the Prophet
1. 25: qь,zmatker: from kızmat: duty; in the
        1920s, one among several new words for
        'proletarian'; in contemporary lit.
        kirg.: civil servant
1. 28: mite: pest, parasite, sponger
1. 30: mьqась: lit. kirg.: mıkaachı: a man-
        eater, an ogre
1. 32: şoola: ar.: a ray

       The Kirghiz text has obviously been
translated from the Russian version, not from
the French original:

> Вставай, проклятьем заклеймённый,
> Весь мир голодных и рабов,
> Кипит наш разум возмущённый
> И в смертный бой вести готов...

       Stand up, malediction-branded,
       You, whole world of famished and slaves!
       Our stirred-up reason boils
       Ready to lead (us) to a fatal fight

XI-D(b) Lenindin ömürü

1. 1: Bьlademir: Vladimir
       apirel: rus.: апрель : April
1. 2: qala ~kalaa: ar.: town
1. 3: qaza bol-: ar.: to die

l. 5:   gemnazija: rus.: гимназия : high-school
l. 6:   unuвerstet: rus.:университет :university
l. 9:   çumşa: here, to devote (one's life to)
l. 10: çalcь: (casual) laborer => proletarian
         now obsolete
l. 12: abaq: rus.: гауптвахта, from German
         Hauptwache: jail
         çaap: Gerund of jap-: to cover, to clo-
         se, K-359
l. 13: ajdoo: exile Y-30
l. 15: Orusuja: Russia
l. 19: çən şilte: to show the way
l. 20: çol başcьsь: scout → leader (rus. вождь)
l. 21: caвa вer-: or jol chap-: to open the
         way K-1729
l. 25: taş talqanь cьɔjar-: to annihilate

XI-D(c)

l. 1: törö: lord (in epic poems) → Tsarist
        officials
        mansa : ar.: position, career
l. 3: qalьɲ buqara: the 'deep simple folk'
l. 6: qьɲq et-: Y-491: to grumble
l. 7: Siвer: Siberia

XI-D(d)

l. 5: germen sɔɔjuş: rus. германская война :
        World War I
l. 7: qara qьzmat: rus.: чёрная работа : heavy
        works
l. 15: bara : bribe; bara je-: to 'eat' bribes,
        to take brihes, hence: to fatten on
        bribes
l. 23: bajda: lit. kirg.: payda: advantage
l. 30: qьtaj: China (cf. XVI: Junggo); literally
        the country of the Khitay - who were
        not Hans
l. 32: P(ь)runza: Kirghiz pronunciation for
        Frunze
l. 34-35: Y-387: kindik kesip, kir juugan jer:
        the place where one's umbilical cord has
        been cut (and) dirt washed: the native
        soil

XI-D(e)

teŋkyryş: Y-758, from töngkör-: to turn upside down → revolution, reform (now obsolete)

1. 2:   batьraq: rus.: батрак : farm hand
1. 13: gektor: rus.: гектар : hectare (about two acres)

XI-D(f)

1. 3:   birin-serin: Y-136: some, here and there

XI-E

Most of the then official Russian loan-words and idiomatic calques are now considered obsolete.

1. 1:   atkaruu: rus.: исполнительный: executive
1. 4-5: qantьrol sandarь : rus.: контрольные цифры scheduled figures for a given period in a given branch allowing to draft a mathematical model in a planned economy
1. 8:   bajandarma: report
1. 10: el carbasь : rus.: народное хозяйство economy
1. 15: çumuşuna... tartьl: now turmushka/ishke ashır-: rus.: проводить в жизнь : to put into practice, to carry out
1. 20: partьja menen ekymet: rus.: Партия и Правительсто : the Party and the Government
1. 21: direktip: rus.: директива : instructions
1. 23: algandьq: rus.: принятие : the 'taking'/ adoption (of measures)
1. 25: zoot: rus.: завод : factory
1. 27: kirpic: rus.: кирпич : brick
1. 31: ulu orustar ulutculuq: rus.: Великорусский национализм : Great-Russian chauvinism
1. 36: rajьmsьz: lit. kirg.: ırayımsız: pityless; here: implacable
1. 46: çooptuu qatcьsь : rus.: ответственный секретарь

XI-F

1. 1:   çardamcь: rus.: вспомогательный (глагол) auxiliary (verb)
1. 15: taçrijba: experience

D - THE CONTEMPORARY SOVIET PRESS

SOVETTİK KIRGIZSTAN
April 8, 1969

LENİNCHİL JASH
October 7, 1971

SOVETTİK KIRGIZSTAN
September 4, 1983

БАРДЫК ӨЛКӨЛӨРДҮН ПРОЛЕТАРЛАРЫ, БИРИККИЛЕ!

СОВЕТТИК КЫРГЫЗСТАН

ГАЗЕТА 1924-ЖЫЛДЫН
7-НОЯБРЫНАН БАШТАП
ЧЫГЫП КЕЛАТАТ

Кыргызстан Коммунисттик партиясынын Борбордук Комитетинин,
Кыргыз ССР Жогорку Советинин жана Министрлер Советинин органы

№ 82 (13225) ◆ Шейшемби, 8-апрель 1969-жыл ◆ Баасы 2 тыйын

TEXT XII-A

Түштүк Вьетнамдагы согуштар

Боштондук басма сөз агентствосу (АПО) Түштүк Вьетнамдан мындай деп билдирет: боштондукка чыгаруучу армиянын отряддары 18-мартта америкалык — сайгондук аскерлердин Дананг шаарынын районунда жайгашкан согуштук бир нече аэродромун бир мезгилдин өзүндө аткылашты. Ошонун натыйжасында кыркка жакын самолёт жок кылынган, согуштук объектилер кыйратылган.

Март айындагы согуштарда номер он тогузунчу жолдун боюнда түштүк вьетнамдык патриоттор душмандын 500гө жакын солдатын катардан чыгарышкан, 194 бронемашинаны, ошонун ичинде 87 танкени жана бронетранспортёрду жок кылышкан. Беш самолёт атып түшүрүлгөн.

Контум провинциясында 29-мартта боштондукка чыгаруучу армиянын жоокерлери америкалык аскерлердин позицияларын артиллерия менен аткылашып, бир нече замбиректи жок кылышкан.

(ТАСС).

TEXT XII-A

TRANSLATION

Fights in South Vietnam

The Liberation Press Agency communicates from South Vietnam: on the 18th of March, detachments of the Liberation Army simultaneously machine-gunned various military airfields of the American-Saigonese troops situated near the town of Danang. As a consequence, about 40 planes were destroyed and military objectives annihilated. During fights in March along highway n° 19, South Vietnamese patriots put out of the fight about 500 enemy soldiers, 194 armored vehicles, among them 87 tanks and armored transports. Five planes were shot down.

In the Kontum Province, on the 29 of March, soldiers of the Liberation Army machine-gunned positions of the American army and annihilated various batteries of artillery. (Tass)

ORIGINAL TEXT IN RUSSIAN

Бои в Южном Вьетнаме

Агенство Печати Освобождение сообщает из Южного Вьетнама: 18-ого марта отряды освободительной армии одновременно обстреляли разные военные аэродромы американских-сайгонских войск в районе города Дананг. В результате было уничтожено около 40 самолётов и разгромлены военные объекты.

Во время боев в марте на дороге № 19 южновьетнамские патриоты вывели из строя около 500 солдат противника и уничтожили 194 бронемашины, в том числе 87 танков и бронетранспортеров. Сбито пять самолётов.

29-ого марта в провинции Контум воины освободительной армии обстреляли позиции американских войск и уничтожили несколько орудий.

Канадалык коммунисттердин съездинде.

ТОРОНТО, 5-апрель. (ТАСС). Кечээ Канаданын Коммунисттик партиясынын ХХ съездинде делегаттар генеральный секретарь Уильям Каштандын докладын жана саясий резолюциянын долбоорун талкуулашты. Делегаттар Канаданын жумушчу табынын аң-сезиминин өскөндүгүн, эмгекчилердин өз укуктарына монополиялардын чабуул жасашына каршы күрөшүнүн күчөгөндүгүн белгилешти.

Съезддин трибунасынан АКШнын Вьетнамдагы агрессиясын токтотуу үчүн күрөштү активдештирүүгө жана баатыр вьетнам эли менен бир туугандык тилектештикти чыңдоого чакырыктар айтылды.

Кечээ талкуулоонун жүрүшүндө чыгып сүйлөгөн бардык делегаттар социализмдин жеңип алгандарын коргоо ишинде чехословак элине жардам көрсөтүү боюнча Варшава договоруна катышкан өлкөлөрдүн аракеттерин колдогон Канаданын Компартиясынын Борбордук Комитетинин билдирүүсүн жактырып, бул актыны пролетардык интернационализмдин эң жогорку көрүнүшү катары баалашты.

Эл аралык коммунисттик жана жумушчу кыймылын бөлүп-жарууга багытталган Маонун группировкасынын авантюристтик саясаты канадалык коммунисттерди тынчсыздандырып жатат. Чыгып сүйлөгөн делегаттар маочулардын анти марк系тик, антилениндик линиясын айыпташты.

АБА ЫРАЙЫ

Фрунзедеги аба ырайы бюросунун берген маалыматына карагаңда 8—11-апрелде Кыргызстандын территориясында күн бүрколүп, мезгил-мезгили менен күн жаайт. Фергана, Чаткал, Талас кыркаларында жамгыр көбүрөөк жаайт. Сыдырым жел жүрөт. Айрым жерлерде шамал болот. Абанын температурасы түнкүсүн 2—7, күндүз 13—18 градус жылуу, тоолуу райондордо түнкүсүн 8—13 градус суук, күндүз 0—5 градус жылуу болот.

TEXT XII - B

1   At the Canadian Communists' Congress
                Toronto, April 5 (Tass)

        Yesterday, during the 20th Congress of
     the Communist Party of Canada, the
     delegates reviewed Williams Cashtan's (the
     General Secretary) report and the
     preliminary draft of the political
     resolution.

5   The delegates underscored the growing
     awareness of the working class of Canada
     and the intensification of the struggle in
     the face of attacks at the hands of
     monopolies against the workers' rights.

        Appeals were issued from the tribune of
     the congress to activate the struggle for
     putting an end to the US appression in Viet
     Nam

10   and for intensifying solidarity with the
     heroical brotherly people of Viet Nam.

15   In the course of yesterday's debates,
     all the delegates who addressed the meeting
     approved the declaration of the Central
     Committee of the Canadian Communist Party
     on the action of the members of the Warsaw
     Pact, concerning the help brought to the
     Czecoslovak people in the defense of the
     conquests of socialism and rated this
     action as a high proof of proletarian
     internationalism.

20   The adventurist policy of the Maoist
     fraction which tends to divide the
     international communist and workers'
     movement bothers the Canadian communists.
     The delegates who took the floor condemned
     the Maoists' antimarxist, antileninist
     line.

W E A T H E R   R E P O R T

According to information conveyed by the meteorological station in Frunze, from April 8 to April 11, the weather on the territory of Kirghizstan will be cloudy, with occasional showers. Rain will be more important in the Ferghana, Chatkal and Talas ranges.

Winds will be light, locally strong; temperatures from 2 to 7 degrees at night, from 13 to 18 in daytime and from -8 to -13 at night, from 0 to 5 in daytime in the mountains.

267

TEXT XII-D

АЛДЫДА АЛТЫ ОЮН БАР

ФУТБОЛ

«Алганын» күйөрмандары турнирдик таблицага дыкаттык менен көз салып турушат. Кемеровонун «Кузбасс» командасын жеңгенден кийин фрунзелик футболисттер 18-орундан дароо 15-оруига көтөрүлүшкөн болучу.

— Быйылкы сезондо бул орун жердештерибиз үчүн жаман орун эмес. Эми үч оюнду катары менен өз талаапарында өткөрүшөт. Буюрса, үч команданы тең намыска жыкса, 6 очко кошулат. Ошондо «Алга» 11—13-орундарга бекийт. Калганы өзүнөн-өзү белгилүү болуп калат,—деген кептерди айтышкан күйөрмандар. Чындыгына келгенде не болду! Алгалыктар бул саамда күйөрмандардын үмүт-тилектерин актай алышпады. Программа максимум оюнчуларда да, тренерлерде да бар эмеспи. Өткөн үч оюнда ушул программа аткарылган жок. Ал эми азыркы кырдаал бир кадам да артка жылбоону талап кылып олтурбайбы.

Өткөн дүйшөмбү күнү фрунзенин «Алга» командасы Ленинграддын «Динамосун» кабыл алды. Алдын-ала айта кетели, быйылкы футболдук сезондун биринчи айланмасында жердештерибиз баатыр шаардын футболисттерин 1:0 эсебинде жеңип кайтышкан. Демек, фрунзеликтер мейман-

дарга караганда дагы техникалуу жана максаттуу оюндарын көрсөтүүлөрү керек. Анткени, өз талаасы. Балтика жээгинин командалары менен беттешүүдө нечендеген ыңгайлуу учурлар пайдаланылбай, эки командага эки очко алдырышты алгалыктар. Ленинграддыктар менен беттешүүдө максат орундала турган болсо, ал-абал ончоло түшмөк. Мына ушул себептен күйөрмандардын күткөнү жеңиш эле.

Бүткүл союздук категориядагы судья М. Черданцов оюнду баштады. Жышаана жакшы, алгалыктар алгачкы минуталарда дөмилгени колго алышты. Жарым коргоочулар Орешин менен Тентимишов ишенимдүү эле алдыңкы линняга чейин келишип, чабуулчуларга активдүү жардам берүүдө. Активдүүлүктүн белгиси ушунда, бир аз убакыттын ичинде 2 жолу бурчтан топ берилди. Бурчтан топ берүүнүн опуртапы көп

268

эмеспи, бирок «Динамонун» коргонуучулары коркунучтуу кырдаалдын абалын өзгөртө алышты. Тентимишовдун алыстан тепкен тобу дарбазадан кыйгач кетти.

Алгалыктардын ушул темпи көпкө узабады. «Алганын» айрым оюнчулары адатынча демилгелүүлүктү .көрсөтүүнүн ордуна, баамыбызда көнүлсүздөй, «Алдыма топ келбесе, не кылам» деген сымал. Бул эмнеси! Азыр ушундай учурбу! Ар бир оюн, ар бир минута кымбат го. Алгалык коргонуучулар эмнегедир жашыл талаада иретсиз.

Ленинграддын футболистери жооп кайтаруу чабуулуна өтүшкөн эле. Эч кандай коркунучтуу кырдаал деле түзүлгөн эмес. Анткени менен топту Переудин өз дарбазасынан алып чыкса болобу! Кандайча болуп кетти бул учур! «Динамонун» чабуулчусу Кондрашев сол канаттан алгалыктардын коргонуучуларынын каталыктарынан пайдаланып, борбордук аянтты карай бет алды. Алгалыктар аны топту дарбаза тарапка багыттайт, — деп ойлошкон жок. Переудинге не болду! Ар дайым сак туруу керек го. Кондрашев чечкиндүүлүк менен дароо дарбага тепти. Гол! Переудин топту көз кыры менен гана узатып туруп калды. Кандай өкүнүчтүү.

Экинчи бөлүк башталар замат эсеп теңелмек. Чокморов бир-нече коргонуучудан өтүп барып, топту Орешкинге жылдыра койду. Аттиң ла, топ кекөлөп кетпеспи. Чабуулчулар Канцуров, Стрельцов, Шубин, жарым коргоочу Подкорытов меймандардын коргонуучуларынын шаштысын кетирди. Штрафтык аянтчада ленинграддыктар оюндун эрежесин да бузушту. 11 метрлик штарфтык топ белгиленди. Щевченко аны эң сонун аткарды. Эсеп теңелди —1:1. Ошентип, алгалыктар кезектеги үч оюнду тең чыгуу менен аякташты.

К. ТИЛЕКОВ,

Фрунзе шаары.

ANOTHER 6 MATCHES TO GO

1   The 'Alga' fans are looking at the
League Championship tables with some
concern. After their club won against
'Kuzbass' of Kemerovo, the Frunze players
had suddenly improved their league position
from 18th to 15th place.

5   It was not a bad position for our fellow
countrymen this season. They had now to
play three consecutives matches on their
home ground. If everything goes well and
Alga win against the three visiting clubs,
they will take six points, therefore
establishing themselves in a solid 11th or
13th position.

10   "Then we will have the time to take a
breather", the supporters said.

But what actually happened?

This time the players were unable to
answer the supporters' dreams.

Everyone knows that both players and
coaches aim at an optimum program. But
during the next three matches they were
not up to it. Now they have to try at all
costs not to take another backward step.

15   Last Monday Alga of Frunze played
against 'Dynamo' of Leningrad. But first
we must remember the beginning of the
season when our fellow countrymen had won
by 1 goal to nil against the players of the
hero city. Which means that our players had
to show a better technique and more
determination in front of their opponents.

20   Now they were playing on their own
ground. During their previous meetings with
their Baltic Coast opponents they had not
been able to take advantage of several

scoring chances and had to concede two points to their opponents.

This game against the Leningrad team would have allowed them to consolidate their position if they had succeeded. Therefore a victory was very much expected by the fans.

25   The referee Cherdancov whistled the start of the match. Good omen: right from the kick-off our players took control of the match. The midfield made up of Oreshin and Tentimishev boldly dashed forward and supported actively their front men. As proof of this activity, in no time at all two corners were won.

30   Everybody knows that corners can be dangerous but the Dynamo defense were able to handle this perillous situation. A long shot by Tentimishev shaved the upright. The Alga players could not maintain for very long their early rhythm.

35   Some players, instead of showing initiative as usual seemed to say with a shrug: "What can I do if the ball isn't played to my feet?".

What an attitude! What timing! When each match and minute counts!

For no known reason, our defense were completely disorganized on the field. The Leningrad team used this opportunity to mount an attack.

40   Not one dangerous situation has been exploited. And then the next thing you know goalkeeper Pereudin was removing the ball from the back of his net. How did this happen? The Dynamo attacker, Kondrashev, took advantage of defensive errors and ran at the defenders from left to the center. It did not occur to our players that he would shoot at goal.

45   And what happened to Pereudin? A
      goalkeeper must always be prepared.
      Kondrashev shot powerfully and accurately.
      Goal. Pereudin stood, rooted to the spot,
      watching the ball enter from the corner of
      his eye.

      It makes you cry.

      Immediately after the restart, our
      players had to get an equalizer. Several
      times Chokmorov dribbled around the defense
      before passing to Oreshin.

50   Unfortunately, the latter ballooned the
      ball. Our forwards Kanchurov, Strel'cov,
      Shubin as well as the midfielder Podkorytov
      began to pressure the opponents defense.

55   The defense then committed a foul in the
      18-yard box. A penalty was awarded. It was
      brilliantly converted by Shevchenko. The
      match was drawn, one goal each.

      So, for the third time running the Alga
      players had conceded a draw.

                                    K. Tilekov - Frunze

ТАССТЫН БИЛДИРҮҮСҮ

1   Мурда билдирилгендей, ушул жылдын 31-августунан 1-сентябрга караган түнү кимге таандык экендиги бел-

5   гисиз самолет Совет мамле-кетинин чек арасын одоно бузуп жана Советтер Сою-зунун аба мейкиндигине те-рендеп кирген. Чек араны

10   бузган самолет белгиленген эл аралык трассадан Совет-тер Союзунун территориясы-нын ичине 500 километрге чейин кирип келип, эки

15   сааттан ашык убакыт Кам-чатка жарым аралынын үс-түндө, Охот деңизинин райо-нунда жана Сахалин аралы-нын үстүндө болгон.

20   Эл аралык эрежени бузуп, самолет аэронавигациялык жарыксыз учкан, советтик диспетчердик кызматтардын радиосигналына көңүл бур-

25   ган эмес жана өзү мындай байланышты түзүүгө эч кан-дай аракет жасаган эмес.

    Чек араны бузган белги-сиз самолет СССРдин аба

30   мейкиндигинде жүргөн учурла абадан кол салуудан коргоо-чу советтик самолеттор аба-га көтөрүлгөндүгү, алар жал-пы колдонулуп жүргөн сиг-

35   налдардын жардамы аркы-луу аны менен байланыш түзүүгө жана аны Советтер Союзунун территориясында-гы жакынкы аэродромго чы-

40   гарууга нечен жолу аракет-тенгендиги табигый иш. Би-рок чек араны бузган само-лет ушунун бардыгын эти-барга алган эмес. Сахалин

45   аралынын үстүндө ал учуп келе жаткан багыт боюнча советтик самолеттор жар-кылдап көрүнүүчү сnaряд-дар менен эскертип атуулар-

50   ды жүргүзгөн.

Ушундан кеп этпей чек
араны бузган самолет советтик аба мейкиндигинин чеги-
нен чыгып, Япон деңизи та-
55 рабына учушун уланткан. Ал
болжол менен он минута
убакыт радиолокациялык ка-
ражаттардын байкоо зона-
сында болгон, ушундан ки-
60 йин, ага байкоо жүргүзүү
үзүлгөн.

Эми АКШда жана кээ бир
башка өлкөлөрдө Нью-Йорк-
тон Сеулга учуп келе жат-
65 кан Түштүк Кореянын само-
летунун жоголушунун айла-
насында чуу көтөрүлдү. Бул
жөнүндөгү биринчи билди-
рүүдө эле АКШнын Борбор-
70 лук чалгындоо башкарма-
сына шылтанкандыгы өзүнө
көнүл бурат. Кошмо Штаттар-
дан чыгып жаткан андан кийинки маалыматтар учуунун,
75 маршруту жана мүнөзү ко-
кусунан болбогон деп, эсеп-
төөгө улам көп негиз берип
жатат. Азыр, өткөн число
менен америкалык тарап бул
80 самолеттун советтик аба
мейкиндигин бузгандыгынын
фактысын официалдуу гана
моюнуна албай, ошондой эле
Американын тийиштүү кыз-
85 маттары ал учкан мезгилдин
ичинде анын учушуна эң
кунт коюп көз салып тур-
гандыгы көрүнүп олтурган
маалыматтарды келтирген-
90 диги мүнөздүү.

Эгерде сөз тынымсыз бай-
коо жүргүзүлгөн граждан-
дык самолеттун демейдеги
учушу жөнүндө болсо, анда
95 эмне үчүн америкалык та-
раптан СССРдин аба мей-
киндигин одоно бузууну токтотуу жана самолетту эл
аралык трассага кайтаруу
100 боюнча эч кандай чаралар
көрүлгөн эмес? — деген суро-
роо туулат.

274

TEXT XII-E

105 Эми СССРге карата ар кандай түрдөгү ыплас ушакка барып жаткан Американын бийликтери эмне үчүн советтик тарап менен байланыш түзүүгө жана бул учуу

110 жөнүндө зарыл маалыматтарды берүүгө аракеттенген эмес? Бул үчүн убакыт абдан жетиштүү болгондугуна карабастан мындай эч аракет жасалган эмес.

115 Американын самолетторунун Советтер Союзунун мамлекеттик чек араларын, анын ичинде Ыраакы Чыгыштагы чек арасын атайын

120 бузуулары ушул эле эмес экендигин эске сала кетүү орундуу. Буга байланыштуу АКШнын өкмөтүнө нааразылыктар нечен жолу билди-

125 рилген.

Ушул фактылардын негизинде жогоруда көрсөтүлгөн самолеттун аба мейкиндигине кирип келишин күн

130 мурунтан пландаштырылган акция катары гана баалоо керек. Граждандык самолетторго жамынын атайын чалгындоо максатын тоскоолсуз

135 ишке ашырууга мүмкүн экендигине болжолдонгондугу ачык көрүнүп турат.

Ал гана тургай, бул провокацияны уюштургандар

Советтер Союзун жаманатты 140 кылууга, ага кастык-сезимди таратууга, тынчтыкты сүйүүчү советтик саясатка көө жабууга аракеттенип, эл аралык кырдаалды, андан 145 ары курчутууга атайын барышты деп айтууга негиз бар.

Бул жөнүндө ошол эле замат АКШнын президенти 150 Рейгандын Советтер Союзунун адресине жасаган уятсыз, ушакчылык билдирүүсү айтып турат.

Советтер Союзунун же- 155 текчи чөйрөлөрүндө адамдардын курман болгондугуна байланыштуу кейигендигин жана ошону менен бирге атайын же 160 кылмыштуу этибарга албоонун натыйжасында адамдардын өлүшүнө жол бергендерди, ал эми азыр болгон окуяларды кара санатай 165 саясий максатта пайдаланууга аракеттенип жаткандарды чечкиндүү айыптагандыгын билдирүүгө ТАССка полномочие берилген. 170

ORIGINAL TEXT IN RUSSIAN   TEXT XII-E

Заявление ТАСС

Как уже сообщалось, в ночь с 31 августа на 1 сентября с. г. самолет неустановленной принадлежности грубо нарушил советскую государственную границу и глубоко вторгся в воздушное пространство Советского Союза. Самолет-нарушитель отклонился от существующей международной трассы в сторону территории Советского Союза до 500 км и более двух часов находился над полуостровом Камчатка, районом Охотского моря и над островом Сахалин.

В нарушение международных правил самолет летел без аэронавигационных огней, на радиосигналы советских диспетчерских служб не реагировал и сам никаких попыток установить такую связь не предпринимал.

Естественно, что во время нахождения неизвестного самолета-нарушителя в воздушном пространстве СССР были подняты советские самолеты ПВО, которые неоднократно пытались установить с ним контакты с помощью общепринятых сигналов и вывести его на ближайший аэродром на территории Советского Союза. Однако самолет-нарушитель все это игнорировал. Над островом Сахалин по курсу его движения советским самолетом были даны предупредительные выстрелы трассирующими снарядами.

Вскоре после этого самолет-нарушитель вышел за пределы советского воздушного пространства и продолжал полет в сторону Японского моря. Примерно десять минут он находился в зоне наблюдения радиолокационными средствами, после чего наблюдение за ним было потеряно.

Теперь в США и некоторых других странах поднята шумиха вокруг исчезновения южнокорейского самолета, совершавшего полет из Нью-Йорка в Сеул. Обращает на себя внимание то, что уже в первом сообщении об этом делалась ссылка на Центральное разведывательное управление США. Дальнейшие сведения, исходящие из Соединенных Штатов, дают все больше оснований считать, что маршрут и характер полета не были случайными. Показательно, что сейчас, задним числом, американская сторона не только официально признает факт нарушения этим самолетом советского воздушного пространства, но и приводит данные, из которых видно, что соответствующие американские службы самым внимательным образом следили за полетом на всем его протяжении.

Спрашивается, если речь шла об обычном полете гражданского самолета, за которым велось непрерывное наблюдение, то почему же с американской стороны не было предпринято никаких мер по прекращению грубого нарушения воздушного пространства СССР и возвращению самолета на международную трассу?

Почему американские власти, которые теперь прибегают к разного рода грязным инсинуациям в отношении СССР, не попытались установить связь с советской стороной и дать необходимые данные об этом полете? Ни того, ни другого сделано не было, хотя времени для этого было более чем достаточно.

Уместно напомнить, что преднамеренные нарушения американскими самолетами государственных границ Советского Союза, в том числе на Дальнем Востоке, далеко не единичны. По этому поводу правительству США неоднократно заявлялись протесты.

В свете этих фактов вторжение в воздушное пространство указанного самолета нельзя расценить иначе, как заранее спланированную акцию. Расчет делался, очевидно, на то, что под прикрытием гражданских самолетов можно беспрепятственно осуществлять специальные разведывательные цели.

Более того, есть основания полагать, что те, кто организовывал эту провокацию, сознательно шли на дальнейшее обострение международной обстановки, стремясь опорочить Советский Союз, посеять чувство враждебности к нему, бросить тень на советскую миролюбивую политику.

ТЕКСТ XII-E

Об этом говорит и беспардонное, клеветническое заявление по адресу Советского Союза, с которым тотчас же выступил президент США Рейган.

ТАСС уполномочен заявить, что в руководящих кругах Советского Союза выражают сожаление в связи с человеческими жертвами и вместе с тем решительно осуждают тех, кто сознательно или в результате преступного пренебрежения допустил гибель людей, а теперь пытается использовать происшедшее в нечистоплотных политических целях.

TEXT XII - E

A PRESS RELEASE FROM TASS

1   As already indicated, during the night
of August 31 to Sept 1 of this year, a
plane of unknown origin blatantly violated

5   the Soviet State border and intruded deeply
into Soviet air space. The violating plane
swerged up to 500 kms from the

10   existing international course in the
direction of the Soviet territory and for
more than two hours flew above the
Kamchatka

15   peninsula, the Sea of Okhotsk and the
island of Sakhalin.

20   In violation of international rules,
the plane was flying without navigation
lights, didn't react to the radio-

25   signals of the Soviet control services and
didn't itself try to establish such a
contact.

        Naturally enough, while the unknown
violating plane found itself inside Soviet
air space, Soviet planes from the

30   Air Border Defense were sent up, trying
several times to contact it by means of
the generally accepted signals and to

35   lead it to the nearest airfield on Soviet
territory. However,

40   the violating plane ignored everything.
Above the island of Sakhalin Soviet planes
fired warning shots with tracer shells

45   along its course.

50   A short time later, the violating plane
left the limits of Soviet air space and

continued its flight toward the Sea of
Japan. For about ten minutes it remained
within the

55 observation zone of our radar installa-
tions, after that contact

60 with it was lost.

Now in the US and various other
countries a loud fuss is raised about the
disappearance of a South Korean plane

65 flying from New York to Seoul. It should be
noted that already in the first report
about this, reference was made to the

70 Central Intelligence Agency of the US.
Further information issued by the US
provides more and more reasons to believe

75 that the route and the character of the
flight were not fortuitous. Significantly,
now, post factum, the American side not
only openly accepts the fact that this
plane violated

80 Soviet air space, but also gives data
which show that the competent American
services followed this flight with the

85 utmost attention all the way along.

90   If the problem concerned the ordinary
flight of a civil airplane under constant
observation, why were no measures taken by
the American side to stop this blatant
violation of

95 Soviet air space and guide the plane back
to the international route? This is the
question that arises.

100   Why didn't the American powers which now
resort to all

105 sorts of dirty insinuations towards the
USSR try to establish contact with the

Soviet side and give (them) the necessary
data concerning this flight? No measures
were taken, although

110   there was ample time for them.

        It should be said that this is not the
only planned

115   violation of Soviet state borders by
American planes, as well

120   as in the Far East. Protests have been
filed several times to the US government in
connection with this.

125   On the basis of these facts, the
intrusion of the above mentioned plane
within (our) air space must be considered

130   a premeditated action. Evidently enough,
the calculation was to fulfill a deliberate
intelligence mission without obstruction

135   under the cover of a civil plane.

        More than that, there is evidence
showing that those who planned this
provocation deliberately intended to

140   aggravate the international situation even
more, to calumniate the Soviet peace-loving
policy, to propagate a feeling of enmity

145   towards the USSR and to defame our country.

        The slanderous, shameless statement
immediately made by Reagan, the President
of the US against the USSR testifies to
this.

155   Tass has been empowered to express the
regrets of the ruling circles of the USSR
in connection with the human victims and
together with that (to stress) a decisive

160   condemnation of those who deliberately or
as the result of criminal carelessness
permitted the death of men and now try to
take

165   advantage of the events (using them) to a
black political end.

COMMENTS

These articles, taken from two well-known
dailies, have been selected as typical, both in
form and content, for the contemporary Kirghiz-
language press. They keep perfectly in tune with
the analysis proposed by Momun Mirza: "The World
According to 'Sovettik Kyrgyzstan'", Central Asian
Survey, vol. 2, n° 4, Dec. 83, pp. 109-126.
They illustrate a series of politico-ideolo-
gical and sociolinguistic phenomena which have been
described and commented in C-160-162 and 176-182.

It is, indeed, in such journalistic texts on
political issues that two sociolinguistic features,
typical for what has been called the 'linguistic
Soviet standard' appear more clearly: an overt
'overdose' of Russian lexical loans and a covert
overdose of Russian phraseological loans (semantic
calques).

These are in fact so numerous (20% in Text
XII-A and 23.5% in Text XII-B) that they constitute
a variety of Kirghiz which is actually unintelli-
gible to any Kirghiz-speaking person (Soviet and
especially non-Soviet) who does not have a good
knowledge of Russian. It is worth noting, by way
of example, that no more than 2.5% of lexical or
idiomatic borrowings from Western languages were
found in articles of equal length and similar content published roughly at the same time by the
'Hurriyet' newspaper in Republican Turkish - a
language which also made extensive borrowings from
French, English, etc.

Besides the relatively new modern layer of
national terminology (for ex. aba ırayı: literally
'the state of the air' = the weather (forecast)-
the evolution of this lexical/idiomatic layer is
precisely what has not been coordinated between the
USSR and China), the following examples, given here
in hierarchical order of 'un-kirghizity', can be
noted:

- justified loanwords such as gradus: degree, the
phonetic structure of which is at odds with the ethnic norm (no initial /g/ and no initial consonant
cluster).

- a gratuitious excess of Russian loanwords. One
wonders whether the pre-1917 Kirghiz were unable
to name such concepts as delegate, pact, district,
territory, temperature, etc. or what new subtle
nuance the Russian words allow to convey that the
corresponding ethnic lexical items could not. The
answer to this puzzling questions becomes clearer
upon noticing that the loanword 'soldat' is reser-
ved for the ideologically positively loaded Viet
Cong fighters, while the old, ethnic term is affec-
ted exclusively to those of the 'American-Saigonese
puppet troops'. Russian loanwords fall thus within
the common province of ideological pedagogy and
'orthoglossy'.
- syntactical/idiomatic calques are nothing
else than an exact reflexion of basically Russian
images and comparisons in the ethnic linguistic
mirror:
. jardım körsöt- = rus. оказать помощь = to
        show help: to help
. katardan chıgar-: = rus. вывести из строя =
        to take out of the formation: to put
        out of action
. chıgıp süylö- = rus. выступить с речью =
        to walk out with a speech: to take the
        floor
The last text (XII-D) about a football game is
interesting for both its modern aspect (the sport
commentator's prose is neither better, nor worse
in Kirghizia than anywhere else) and its authentically national character, in spite of a handful of
perfectly justified Russian loanwords. Sociolinguistically speaking, it corresponds, as an equally
spoken, but non-intellectual variant, to the spoken,
intellectual tongue of text IX.
The contrast between these two series of texts
within the framework of the same kind of dailies
perfectly illustrates the sociolinguistic phenomenon of 'bi-normativity' (double standard) as described for Soviet kirghiz in C-195.
These texts should be compared with their Xinjiang equivalent (Text XVI-H).
For grammatical parsing, cf.:

XII-A : K-1791
    1. 1: K-1101   1. 7: K-2750
    1. 3: K-1223   1. 8: K-1019
    1. 6: K-1022   1. 8: K-2222

XII-B

    l. 1:   K-1101   l. 6:   K-1336,1358

    l. 2,3: K-806   l. 8:   K-1096

    l. 4,5: K-2694   l. 10: K-2915

    l. 13: K-1325   l. 20: K-2225

    l. 19: K-1101

XII-C

    l. 2:   K-2691   l. 3,5:K-1799

XII-D

    l. 1:   K-806   l. 36: K-1866

    l. 14:   K-1286   l. 38: K-999

    l. 20:   K-1278   l. 41: K-1602,1854

    l. 22:   K-2457   l. 51: K-1819,2227

    l. 27-30: K-1602

N B !

For sociolinguistic comments on these two texts, cf. Guy G. Imart: "Dancing in Front of a Mirror: Orthoglossy as a Means of Salvation from the 'Traduttore-Traditore' Deviationism", to be published in Papers from the Fifth Conference on the Non-Slavic Languages of the USSR, (= Folia Slavica) Chicago

These two texts have been earmarked for self-parsing.
This should include, in the following order:
- systematically looking up the exact meaning of every word in the dictionary,
- a precise morphological analysis of each sentence so as to determine the function of every lexical unit (which of them are connected and how, which are not and cannot be connected). In the absence of a native speaker, this analysis is meant to make up for intonation and its structural role,
- a careful syntactical analysis, which should highlight:
. the key functional elements of the sentence: the predicate (at the end), the subject, the direct object, the adverbial phrase(s)
. each complex functional constitutive phrase centered on a last (to the right) key element as morphologically determined in the above mentioned point and preceded (on the left) by determinative and/or objectal constituents. The key element, if formed on the basis of a verbal root, often bears an /(I)p/ or a /GAn/ suffix
- each phrase should be translated separately,
- only then should an attempt be made at connecting the different phrases into a meaningful whole. A rewarding method is to begin with the far right end of the sentence (the main predicate) and wind back one's way from phrase to phrase up to the beginning where one should expect to find the subject (alone or preceded itself by an adverbial element): cf. K-2377, etc.

E - KIRGHIZ IN THE WEST

KIRGHIZ   IN   THE   WEST

- Cili respublikasının azırqı aqıbalı tuurasında
    A Radio Liberty broadcast   TEXT XIII

- Afghan Kirghiz:
    .Kalpötöš   TEXT XIV-A
    .Toy   TEXT XIV -B

- Ioanndan ıyık injil   TEXT XIV-C
    The Gospel according to
    St John

- S. Bet-Alman: Foreword to Manas TEXT XV
    Millij Türkistan Komitetiniŋ
    janında ĭ ədebij-ilimij bölü-
    münin tarapĭnan ciɓjariloɟan,
    Berlin 1943.

1 CİLİ RESPUBLIKASININ AZIRQI AQIBALI TUURASINDA

Qımbattuu radio tıŋşocuular!

Bügünkü kündö Cili respublikasinda, altı ay-
dan beri, emi mar-/ksist president Allende-
5   nin sotsialistterden, kommunisterden / qurulgan koalitsion ökümötü başqarmaqta. Marksist
president Allende çana anın sotsialistterden,
kommunistterden qurulgan koalitsion ökümötü,
Amerika kontinentinde, demokrattiq erkindik-
terden paydanalıp, eriktüü şayloogo tayanıp,
biylik başina birinçi sotsialist ökümöt.
Marksist President Allende çana anın sotsia-
10   listik partiyası, quralduu küc menen, qubat
qoldonu çolu menen biylik başina kelişti artqa qagat, anın maqsatı Cili respublikasında
çaşagan demokratiyadan paydalanıp, tınıc çol
menen şayloolor ötkörüşü arqaluu biylik ba-
şında keliş maqsatına kirişken ele. Marksist
President Allende çana anın sotsialistik par-
15   tiyasi, başqa bardıq sotsialistik partiyalar-
dan dagı soluraq topton turmaqta. Anın maqsatı Cilide aqırındap köŋtörülüşcül reforma-
lar ötkörüp, memlekettin ünömünü, qaraçatını
çana sayası quruluşunu bütündöy almaştıruudan
turmaqta. Dagı da acıgıraq qılımı aytqanda
çekemenciksiz, tapsız qoomculuq quruştu oylo-
20   moqto. Biroq markist Allende, bul maqsatqa
çetişe biliş ücün uzun ubaqtar, kerek bolso
qılimdarda kerek boluşunu köz aldında tutat.
Cili respublikasının carbacılıgında, anın
çaşoo turmuşunda eŋ kerektüü orundu eelegen
çez öndürüşü. Cili eksportunun 80/ti çezden
turat. Cili ünömündö eŋ kerektüü orundu eele-
25   gen çez öndürüşünün çarımı memlekettin, al
emi qalgan çarımı cet memleket firmalarının
uyuşmalarının qolunda. Tekstil öndürüşü da,
bankalar da, öndürüştün başqa türlörü da,
negizinde çekemencik eelerinin qoldorunda,
bolboso ret mamlekettik firmaları menen or-
toqtuqta bolup ömür sürmöktö. Marksist Pre-
30   sident Allende ökümöt azırqı (azırınca ?),
çeke mencik qolundaqı öndürüştü, ayrıqca çez

çana tekstil öndürüştörünü uluttaştıruu pla-
nını turmuşqa aşıruucu, alardı zaŋdaştıruu
işterini baştagan ele.
Eŋ aldında Amerika-Cili çez kompaniyasın
uluttaştıruu köz aldında turmaqta. Al emi iri
35 öndürüştördü uluttaştıruu parlament tarabı-
nan da qabıl qılıngan. Uzaqtan emes, President Allende ökümötü, cet mamlekettik firmaları menen ortoq bolqon cez öndürüşü üstünön
- ökümöttük kontrol ornoşturdu. Çetekcilik
qıluu çana qaraçat işi da ökümöttün qoluna
alındı. Bul bolso çez öndürüşün uluttaştıruuga birinci attalgan adım degen söz. Mına uşun-
40 day ele ubaqtının icinde çekemencik qoldordoqu çe bolboso cet mamlekettik firmaları menen
ortoq bolgon tekstil öndürüşü da çetekcilik-
ti ökümöt qoluna aluu işi baştaldı. Bolboso
qaysı bir tekstil fabrikalarında işciler çe-
tekcilikti öz qoldoruna alışmaqta.
Öndürüş dünüyösündö gana emes, ayıl carbacılı-
45 gindaqı dünüyödö da, uşunday aqılbaldooran
sürmöktö. Qaysı bir aymaqtarda al toptor go,
oşol toptoqu çetekcilerdin egin aydooduları,
iri çer carbasının çerlerini tartıp aluuga
çana da öz aralarında cataqtaşmaqta. Cın marksist president Allende, başalamandıq, tartıp-
sızdıq çolu menen tartıp aluularga çol qoyuş-
50 tu tilebeyt. Cili respublikasında iri çekemencik murastı uluttaştıruuga, attalgan birinci adımdar, albette, ar türlüü oorluqtar tuu-
dura baştadı. Maslen, çez öndürüşünü uluttaştıruu ücün qılıngan birinci adımdardan kiyin
ele 200dön artıq inçinerler, tehnikter öz işterini tartap ketiştiler.
Natıyçada çez öndürüşünün produktsiyası kemiy
55 baştadı. Mına oşol ubaqta öndürüştü uluttaştıruu ücün attalgan adımdar natıyçasında iş-
sizdik da aynıqca köböyö baştadı. Ayrıqca sol-
cular tarbındaqı toptor, çekemencik qoldorun-
daqı çerleri, öndürüştü, cet memleket kapitalın
ec nerse tölöböstön-boşuna tartıp aluunu,
uluttaştıruunu talap qılsolarda, president
60 Allende, boşuna tartıp aluu çolun qaalabayt.
President Alendin pikiri boyunca, cet mamle-
ket kapitalın çe bolboso çekemencik qoldorunda-
qı, iştep cıgaruucu çerlerin tölöböstön - ec
nerse berbesten tartıp aluu, memlekettin car-
barcılıgın qaqşatuuga çana cet memleket aldında,

65 Cilinin daraçasın kemitüügö gana alıp kelmek-
ci. Çıyıntıqtap gana kelip aytqanda, Cili
marksist ökümötü, ünömünün kerektüü dünüyösündö, ullutaştıruu planın turmuşqa aşıra
baştadı. Anın natıyçaları qandayca bolor eken,
sotsialisttik metottor özülörünün baştagan
çolundaqı maqsattarın aqtay alarbı, anı kele-
cek körsötör.

70 Azattıq radiyosunan süylöbüz. Tüştük Amerika-
nın respublikalarının biri Cili tuurasında
berüübüzdü tıŋşadıŋızdar. Qoş saq salamat
boluŋuzdar.

TEXT XIII

Author : Galim
Translated and read by A. Altay

ON THE PRESENT SITUATION IN CHILE

1   Respected radio listeners!

Today in the republic of Chile it's
been six months since the socialist and
communist coalition government of Marxist

5   president Allende has been in power.
Marxist president Allende's coalition
government, formed by socialists and
communists, is, on the American continent,
the first one to come to power through free
elections and thanks to democratic freedom.
Marxist president

10   Allende and his socialist party rejected
the accession to power through violence
and armed struggle and have reached their
goal: coming to power by way of elections,
peacefully and by taking advantage of the
democratic régime which existed in the
republic of Chile. Marxist president
Allende and his socialist

15   party pertain to a group more to the left
than all other socialist parties. His goal
is to make in Chile such progressive
revolutionary reforms as to fundamentally
transform the political structure, the
means of production and the economy of the
country. To define more clearly his action,
he plans to create a classless society with
no private property. But Marxist Allende

20   does not loose sight of the fact that it
will take long years, maybe centuries
before this goal could be reached. The
copper industry plays in the life and
economy of the republic of Chile a very
vital role. 80% of Chile's exports consist
in copper.

25 Half of this industry which plays (such) a
very vital part in Chile's economy is in
the hands of the government, but the
remaining half is in the hands of a
consortium of foreign companies. The
textile industry, the banks, the other
branches of industry are mainly in the
hands of private owners or developing in
tight

30 relation with foreign companies. For the
moment, Marxist president Allende's
government, after activating a plan of
nationalization of the private industry
and in particular of the copper and textile
industries, began working on the
legalization thereof. First of all, he has
in mind the nationalization of the US-Chile
copper

35 company. The nationalization of big
industries has been already accepted by
the Parliament. Recently, president
Allende's government established
governmental control over the copper
industry linked to foreign companies.
Management and investments are in the
hands of the State. This is probably the
first step toward the nationalization of
the copper industry. In the same way and

40 at the same time, the State began taking
into its hands the management of the
textile industry linked to foreign firms
or pertaining to private owners. In any
case (however), in some textile fabrics,
the workers have taken the management into
their own hands. The same situation can be
found not only in the industrial

45 field, but also in the field of
agriculture. In some provinces, such
groups and cereal growers quarrel between
themselves and with the group leaders in
order to take over latifundia lands. As a
true Marxist, president Allende does not
wish to follow the way of anarchy and
disorder. The first measures to

50   nationalize the large hereditary farms of the republic of Chile of course began to trigger various feelings of discomfort. For example, after the first steps were taken to nationalize the copper industry, more than 200 engineers and technicians left duty. As a result, the copper production began to drop. At the

55   same time, as a result of these first measures of nationalization, unemployment began to rise. If leftist oriented groups implement nationalization through appropriation and free (without compensation) expropriation of foreign capital, industry and

60   private estates, president Allende, personnally, does not want to follow this scheme. According to president Allende's opinion, expropriating without giving anything, without compensation for estates exploited by private owners or foreign capital, can only lead to the ruin of the country's economy and to a diminution

65   of Chile's prestige abroad. Briefly, the Marxist government of Chile has begun to implement a plan of nationalization in key sectors of the economy. The future will show what the results are and whether socialist methods justify the goals fixed by them.

    This is Radio Liberty speaking. You have just heard our

70   broadcast on Chile, one of the republics of South America.

    Good bye, keep well!

TEXT XIII

COMMENTS

This is the text of a broadcast in Kirghiz beamed to Kirghizia by Radio Liberty in Munich.

The original text has been translated and read by a Kirghiz native speaker, an émigré, Mr. Azamat Altay. What we know about his life allows us to make some comments on the peculiarities of his tongue.

He was born in 1920 near lake Issık-köl to a very modest family. From 1929 to 1935 he studied at the primary school of his village and then, until 1938, at the Pedagogical Institute. He then became a journalist. A prisoner of war in Germany, he escaped and has been living since in the West (cf. A. Altay: "Kirghizia during the Great Purge", Central Asian Review, vol. XII, 2, 1964 and Momun Mirza: "The World According to 'Sovettyk Kyrgyzstan'", Central Asian Survey, Dec. 83, vol. 2,4, pp. 125).

A) The Alphabetical System:

Like the vast majority of Kirghiz and other Turkestanian émigrés (cf. Text XIV-A), the author uses here the Latin alphabet in such a way as to combine

. the main peculiarities of the 'Kemalist' system in use for Turkey Turkish: ş = sh, ı = ı, y = yod.

. and some of the features of the Latin system used in Kirghizstan until Sept. 1941, i.e. during his youth (cf. Texts XI). In particular, c is ch and ç is j. ŋ and q have been kept, but not ŋ which is rendered through g (in other similar texts, sometimes ğ before back vowels). The result is an orthography perfectly adapted to the phonological/phonetical peculiarities of Kirghiz, easy to use with all typographical means available in the West.

B) The Language:

The author's social and geographical origin guarantees the authenticity of his tongue. The Issıkköl dialect has been chosen as the normative reference for Literary Kirghiz and the author's training as a journalist corroborates this analysis.

Only a few 'turkishisms' reveal the main linguistic influence the author has been exposed to since he left Kirghizia: koalitsion (instead of rus. koaliciia), çetişe biliş ücün, with the bil-, instead of al-, auxiliary verb (K-1726) - although cf. Y-134.

The morphology and the Vocalic Harmony system is in perfect conformity with the official norm. Those few discrepancies that can be noted are frequent in oral usage:

qolundaqı, qoldordoqu for /DAGI/: K-411, 1095 unsteady long vowels: K-190: tıŋşocuular: lit. kirg.: tıngshoochular
soluraq: lit. kirg.: soluraak
acıgıraq lit; kirg.: achıgıraak
some ultra-short vowels: tınıc lit. kirg.: tınch; eriktüü lit. kirg.: erktüü; oorluqtar lit. kirg.: oorуluktar; tarbındaqı lit. kirg.: tarabındagı: maslen lit. kirg.: maselen.

Note also, as in Turkish, the /LAr/ suffix instead of /(I)s/ as a plural verbal marker.

All these features are perceptible only to trained specialists.

And yet this text, upon being submitted to some Soviet Kirghiz speakers, has been said to "sound strange and old-fashioned". Only one morphological feature can account for such an impression: the /mAkDA/ predicative form which is not often used in the Soviet literary norm, but which is considered to be perfectly normal in Xinjiang: cf. Text XVI-F, 1.5: keltirilmekte.

The main reason for such a reaction is therefore to be found at the lexicological level. Without really being a 'purist', the author strives to use mainly autochtonous lexemes instead of Russian loanwords as it is standard practice in the USSR:

uyuş for 'consortium'; aymaq (mong.) for 'province' ünöm for 'economy'.

The author knows and uses the autochtonous post-revolutionary vocabulary: tapsız qoomculuq: a classless society; solcu: leftist; carba: economy; plan: plan. Among the most typical lexemes of this group, one can quote:

uluttaştıruu: nationalization
zaŋdaştıruu: legalization (on zaŋ: law - not in Y.).
öndürüş: industry
köŋtörüş: revolution (cf. 1-G, Erkin Too and texts XVI).

Secondly, the author uses certain words in
such a meaning which is **not** currently accepted in
contemporary Soviet Kirghizia:
  dünüyö: field lit. kirg.: world
  aydoocu: farmer
  iri çer carba: latifundia
These peculiarities, no more than those of
texts XVI, certainly do not point to any 'denationalization': in spite of 45 years in exile, the
author has kept such a command of his native tongue
which is superior to that of many émigrés native
speakers of Russian.
    Consequently, what did changed since the
author left Kirghizia is Soviet Kirghiz itself.
This text, therefore, as text XIV and, to a certain
extent, text XV, bears a precious testimony to what
the living, 'autochtonous norm' (C-195) was, as it
developed (Texts XI) during the 1920-40 period and
most certainly continues to be used in such fields
where the double process of russification/russiani-
zation (cf. Texts XII and VIII) has been less inten-
sive. Most of the 'surprising' features noted here
are those which constitute as well the 'oddness' of
texts XVI (from Xinjiang, cf. below).
    The Soviet Kirghiz speakers' reaction allows
us to measure the exact impact, on the language itself and on its peakers (C-176), of an official
policy which, linguistically speaking, was pointless:
Kirghiz had at its disposal during the early 1940s
all the linguistic internal means necessary for any
kind of communication in a modern world.

For parsing, cf.

        1.5: K-1216, 2170   1. 5-9: K-1277,1602
        1.14: K-2015   1.64: K-1209
                    1. 71: K-1886

TEXT XIV-A

KALPÖTÖŠ

1- Bir Kalpötöš degen bar eken. 2- Köp kalpötöš degen teŋtep adam eken. 3- Bir kün: "atamnın arwayıga baxšıš kılıp ataymın" dep "xay-
rat kılamın" dep "uy soyup eldi kıčıramin"
dep eldi kıčırat. 4- El kelgiče kazanga uydun
göšün salıp koyup: "el keč kaldı" dep özü
döŋö čıgıp ketet. 5- Katını: "bul tentek uydun
göšünü elge beretigen boldu" dep "kanday kıl-
sam eke" dep göštün barını aškanasıga alıp
kirip bekitip koyot šorpo-morposu menen.
6- Kalpötöš döŋö čıksa bir moldo bar eken
moldo kele jatıptır. 7- Ogočo moldo kirip kelet Kalpötöš döŋdö. 8- Moldo kirip kelip katı-
nıga aytat: "bu Kalpötöš keče: 'men atamnın
arwayıga baxšıš kılıp uy soyomum erte bargıla'
degen ede. 9- Soygon uyu kana baxšıš kılgan
xayratı kana" deyt. 10- Dese katın aytat: "bir
katta zor taštı soku taštı maylap otko kaktap
koygon eken". 11- Aytat: "men uy soygonunu bil-
bedim moldo kelse kuyruguga šu taštı matıramın" dep oturat ede" deyt. 12- Moldo bečara
korkkonunan kačat. 13- Ogočo Kalpötöš kirip
kelet: "o katın moldo kana". 14- "Moldo kana
degende, katın aytat. "Kazandagı göštü šorpo-
morposu menen kötürüp alıp moldo alıp ketti.
15- Men ne bilemin sen ayttıŋ bi" deyt. 16- degende aytat: "ırıskı ede": 'bir parčanan ber-
gin šorpogo matırıp menin oozumga salayın'"
deyt. 17- Bir maalda bir parča nandı katın Kal-
pötöškö beret. 18- Kalpötöš nandı alıp: "toxto
moldo matıramın" dep kuuyt. 19- Har kanča kuusa
moldo: "kuyruguma taštı matırat eken" dep kačıp
beret. 20- Göštü katın aškanıya alıp kančaga
jep šorpo-morposu menen oŋop kalıptır.

KALPÖTÖSH

1   Once upon a time, there was a (man)
called Kalpötösh. He was a (very cleaver)
man who was every bit as good as many of
his fellow creatures. One day, saying: "I
intend to make a sacrifice to the spirits
of my ancestors, to give alms, to slay a
cow and invite people", he invited people.
While waiting for people to come, he put
the cow's meat (to cook) in a cauldron;
(then), saying to himself "People are
late", he climbed up a hill (to watch them

5   coming). His wife said to herself: "This
featherbrain now must give the cow's meat
to others; what can I do? and she took all
the meat and the whole broth with it,
hiding it behind the ashkana. While
Kalpötösh was climbing the hill - there was
a mollah - the mollah came. At this moment,
the mollah entered (their house). Kalpötösh
was on the hill. The mollah came in and
said to the wife: "Yesterday Kalpötösh told
me 'Come tomorrow, I'll slay a cow and make
a sacrifice to my ancestors' spirits'.
Where is the cow to be slain, where are
the alms to be distributed?" he said. With
these

10   words, the wife answered: "He greased a
big stone, the mortar stone and put it to
the fire to heat up", she said: "He simply
said 'I don't know how to slay a cow; when
the mollah comes, I'll drive this stone
into his rump". The poor mollah fled away
in fear. Then, Kalpötösh came back home:
"Wife! where's the mollah?" Upon hearing
these words, the wife said: "He took the
meat which was in the cauldron, the whole
broth with it, that mollah and went away.

15   What do I know? did you tell (me)
anything?" she said. She added: "There
(still) was (some) food: 'Give me a piece
of bread to dip in the broth and put it

into my mouth', he said". Then the wife
gave Kalpötösh a piece of bread. Kalpötösh
took the bread and shouted: "Stop, mollah,
I'll drive...". However hard he pursued
him, the mollah saying "He'll drive the
stone into my rump" fled

20   even quicker. The wife took the meat from
behind the ashkana, stuffed herself with
the meat, the broth and the rest and thus
had the last word.

TEXT XIV-B

T O Y

1   Owal jūču warat. Üč dört adam kızga jūču wa-
    rat. O kız atası kīzını beret. Ol üčöwgö pata
    kılıp bir eki koydu soyot. O kızdın üstünö
    toy wolot. Bir eki čapan bir jawat: üč adam
    bolso üč čapan; tört adam bolso tört čapan.
    Onon kaytıp kelet. Onon toygo warat. Kızdın
5   üstügö warıp toy kılat. Owal pata toyu wolot.
    Ogo pata toydun göšünü kapka salıw özunu tü-
    yöt. Ogo bir eki jüzdük özuga tiget. Onu ka-
    tındar čogulup barı sögöt. Onu sögalwasa ja-
    zık tartat. Onon "Bizi talaš!" deyt. Un čačat.
    "Pata toy kele jatat!" deyt... kızdın üstündö.
    "Ha" dep biri birige un cacat, "Bizi talas!"
10 deyt. Kız jaktan tartıwalsa ūl jaktı jazıktar
    kılat; ūl jaktan tartıwalsa kızdı jazıktar
    kılat. Ek(i) üč kün toy wolot. Onon küyöwgö
    jeŋerleri üč nazdım tört nazdım tawag aparat;
    toguz tawag aparat ogo: baškısı koydun göšü...
    šondoy jaxšı jaxšı tawaktard(ı) aparat. Onon
    küyöwdü ırdatıp kelet. Bir üygö kirgizet; egin
15 kiygizet. Küyöwdü taze jaxšı ırdatıp kelet.
    Eki jaginan eki küyö joldoš ırdayt. Kol jōluk
    karmatat... jeŋeleri. On(u) alıp bir üygö kiy-
    gizet. Onon kız küyöwdü taŋat... jeŋeleri.
    Kečinde bir koy soyuw otko kirgizet. Beš altı
    koydu soyot. Ulak čawat... kızdın üstündö.
    Katındar bir üydö oturat; erekteler bir üydö
20 oturat. Kızga köšögö tartat. Onon nika kıygan
    mālda barat. Barı čogu oturat. Mollolor nika
    kıyat. Kız wakilini bir adama kaytarat; ūl wa-
    kilini bir adama kaytarat. Onon kız gıŋšılatat.
    Onon bir adam "Ha" dew 'Ölöŋ' aytat. Bay bolso
    pul čačat; kambagal bolso jemiš nan čačat.
    Tügögüčö Ölöŋ aytat. "Čač sılar" deyt; čačını
25 sılayt. Jüzdük baylayt. Onon bir eki mollo ke-
    lip nika kıyat:
        - Kızdı kabul tuttup bu? deyt.
        - Kabul tuttum, deyt.
        - Ūldu kabul tuttuŋ bu ? deyt.
        - Kabul tuttum, deyt.
30   - Adama wakilini kaytardıŋ bı ? deyt.
        - Kaytardım, deyt.

THE WEDDING

1   First comes the match-maker. Three or four people go to the girl's (house as) match-makers. The girl's father gives her away. Having said (some words of) blessing for these three, he skins two or three sheep. The wedding will take place at the girl's place. He spreads out some coats: three coats if there are three people, four if there are four. Then they go back (home).

5   Then they come to the wedding. They come to the girl's place, and prepare the wedding. First, the benediction (engagement) ceremony takes place. For that, having put the meat of the engagement banquet into a bag, they tie it up. They sew some rings to it. The women, having assembled, grab it. The one which doesn't grab it, pays a forfeit. Then they tell her: "Vie with us!". People throw flour. People say: "The engagement is coming!"... at the girl's place. Shouting 'Ha!', people throw flour at each other, saying: "Vie

10   with us!" If the girl's side wins, the boy's side pays a forfeit; if the boy's side wins, the girl's side pays a forfeit. The wedding lasts two or three days. Then, the matrons bring three times, four times a dish to the groom: they bring him nine dishes: first of all, mutton... very very good dishes they bring (him) like this. Then, they have the groom sing. They usher him into a yurt. They

15   dress him. They have him sing nice songs. On each side (of him) two groomsmen of his friends sing. Matrons... have them take the scarf. Having taken her (the bride) to a yurt, they dress her. Then they... the matrons tie the bride to the groom. At night, having skinned a sheep, they roast

it. Five or six sheep are skinned. A
'buzkachi' is organized... at the girl's
place. Women sit in one house, men in
another. The curtain is drawn on the

20   girl. Then comes the time to celebrate the
nika (religious wedding). Everyone sits
down. The mullahs celebrate the nika. The
girl entrusts a man to be her witness; the
boy entrusts a man to be his witness. Then
the girl wails. Than a man shouts 'Ha!'
(and) sings Ölön. If he is rich, he throws
money, if he is poor, he throws food,
bread. He sings Ölön until he finishes. He
says : "They'll stroke her hair" - people
stroke her hair. They slip a ring (on

25   the bride's finger). Then come some
mollahs and celebrate the nika. They say:
"Do you accept the girl?" - "I accept her",
he says. "Do you accept the boy?" - "I
accept him". "Did you entrust

30   somebody to be a witness?" - "I did". the
mollah celebrates the nika. Allah is the
greatest. It's finished.

COMMENTS

These two texts have been recorded in Afghanistan by Rémy Dor, the first one in June 1973 in the Great Pamir from a local chieftain called Osman Aji, the second one one July 5, 1972 in Tergen Gorum (Small Pamir) from Orun Bibi, first wife of the khan's elder son.

The second text, because it is even more spontaneous than the first one, gives a good idea of the local spoken language and of its pronunciation. Both have been included into R. Dor's Doctoral Thesis (Orature Kirghize) which he presented in 1980 at the Sorbonne. He kindly allowed us to publish the transcription of his tapes together with his own comments.

About those 3 to 4,000 Kirghiz-speakers (most of them previous refugees from neighboring countries) who up to 1978 lived in the Wakhan Corridor, one can read R. Dor's "Brève information sur les réfugiés kirghiz", Central Asian Survey, vol. 1, n° 2-3, Oct. 82-Jun. 83, pp. 85-89. and D. Denker: "The Last Migration of the Kirghiz of Afghanistan?" Central Asian Survey vol. 2, n° 3, Nov. 83, pp. 89-98.

About their dialect (which is part of the "Southern Variant") cf. K, vol 2: R. Dor: "Le Dialecte kirghiz Pamirien".

The Latin alphabet used here is practically the same as in text XII.

TEXT XIV-A

1. 1: Kal + pötöš = kal: a person suffering from ringworm: a popular shrewd character in Turkic legends. Pötösh (Small Pamir: bötösh): an element to be compared with lit. kirg. 'arampöösh': little rascal. Cf. Turkish: kel: scab.
1. 2: teŋtep: lit. kirg. tengde-
1. 3: arway: lit. kirg.: arbak ~ arbay
baxšiš: lit. kirg.: bakchi: shaman
wayrat: lit. kirg.: kayrat: strength, glorious deed
kičir: lit. kirg.: chakir-: to invite, Y-500

304

l. 4: göš: meat, lit. kirg.: et
l. 5: eke: a shortened form of eken
      aškana: a kind of folding screen separating
      the yurt into two parts. Behind it, kitchen
      ustensils are kept. In lit. kirg.: kitchen,
      canteen
      šorpo-morpo: K-1042
l. 11: matıramın: retrogressive assimilation for
      batıramın
      kuyruk: in lit. kirg.: tail
l. 16: ırıskı: in lit. kirg.: daily bread (bibl.)

                    TEXT XIV-B

The sound noted with a 'w' represents the last
stage of spirantization of /b/=[β]→[w]. Note also
the imperfect Vowel Harmony.

l. 1:   owal: lit. kirg.: obolu
        o: lit. kirg.: al
        jū: in lit. kirg.: to come nearer
l. 2:   üčöw: lit. kirg.: üchöö:a group of three
        pata: lit. kirg.: bata: benediction (K-527)
l. 6:   salıw ōzunu: a sandhi phenomenon: salıp:
                      /p/= [φ]→ [w]
        jüzdük: lit. kirg.: shakek: a ring
l. 11: küyöw: lit. kirg.: küyöö: fiancé, groom
l. 12: nazdım: lit. kirg.: mertebe, jolu
        tawag: lit. kirg.: tabak: a dish
        aparat: lit. kirg.: alıp barat
l. 14: egin: Y-943,II: clothes
l. 15: taze: extremely
l. 18: ulak čawat: lit. kirg.: ulak tartat: the
        famous buzkachi game, also called kök
        börü (grey wolf), a kind of rough polo which
      is played with a sheep carcass as the ball
l. 19: erekte: lit. kirg.: erkek
l. 20: mollo: lit. kirg.: moldo
l. 21: wakili: ar. a representative
l. 22: gınšılatat: lit. kirg.: kıngshıla-: to wail
        Ölöŋ: a popular melody
l. 23: kambagal: lit. kirg.: kedey
        tügö-: to finish, lit. kirg.: ayakta-. A
        verb typical for Southern and Xinjiang kir-
        ghiz

The Quranic formula, the use of 'wakili' and also
of 'xalas' (ar. finished) testify to a Muslim

influence among Afghan Kirghiz - at least among
those of the speaker's milieu - apparently much
stronger than in other parts of Kirghizistan.

Y-669 gives another, more romantic nika formula:
'süydümgö chakırt-': to summon the bride in order
to know whether she accepts the groom. If she does,
she answers: süydüm: I fell in love.

ИОАННДАН
ЫЙЫК ИНЖИЛ

К Ы Р Г Ы З   Т И Л И Н Д Е

2—БӨЛҮМ

1. Ыйсанын биринчи ажайыбы: сууну мусалдаска айлан-дыруу. 13. Соодагерлерди ийбадатканадан кууп чыгаруу. 19. Өзүнүн өлүүсү жана тирилүүсүн Ыйса алдын ала айтып берет. 23. Анын ажайыптар урматына көп киши Ага ишенип калат.

1. ҮЧҮНЧҮ күнү Галилеялык Канада үйлөнүү той болчу, жана Ыйсанын энеси да ошо жерде болгон.

2. Ыйса да жана Анын шакирттери да үйлөнүү тоюна чакырылган болчу.

3. Жана мусалдас жетпегендиктен, Ыйсанын энеси Ага айтат: аларда мусалдас жок.

4. Ыйса Ага айтат: Менин жана Сенин ишибиз эмне, аял? Менин убагым келелек.

5. Анын энеси кызматчыларга айтты: Ал силерге эмне десе, ошону кылгыла.

6. Ошол жерде Иудейлердин тазалоо адаты боюнча коюлган, эки же үч чен *(80—120 литр)* бата турган, таштан жасалган алты суу сактагыч бар болуп турган.

7. Ыйса аларга айтат: идиштерди суу менен толтургула. Жана аларды эрдөөсүнө чейин толтурушту.

8. Жана аларга айтат: эми сузуп алгыла жана той башкаруучуга алып баргыла. Жана алып барышты.

9. Той башкаруучу мусалдас болуп калган суунун даамын көрүп,- *бул мусалдас* кайдан алынганын билбеди, аны жалаң гана сууну сузуп алган кызматчылар билди,- ошондо той башкаруучу күйөөнү чакырат

10. жана ага айтат: ар адам эң мурда жакшы мусалдасты алып берет, анан мас болгондо, андан жаманыраагын; сен болсоң жакшы мусалдасты ошого чейин сактадың.

11. Ошентип, Галилеялык Канада Ыйса ажайыптардын башталышынын негизин салды жана Өзүнүн атагын көрсөттү; жана Анын шакирттери Ага ишеништи.

12. Мындан кийин Өзү жана Анын энеси, Анын бир туугандары жана Анын шакирттери Капернаумга келди, жана ошо жерде бир аз күн болушту.

13. Иудейлердин Пасхасы *(диний майрам)* жакындаган, жана Ыйса Иерусалимге келди.   5. Мус. 16,1.

14. Жана ийбадаткананын ичинде өгүздөрдү, койлорду жана көгүчкөн саткандарды жана акча майдалоочулардын олтурганын тапты.

Матф. 21,12. Марк. 11,15.Лук. 19,45.

15. Жана аркандан камчы жасап алып, ийбадаткананын ичинен баарын кууп чыгарды, ошондой эле койлорду жана өгүздөрдү, жана майдалоочулардын акчасын төгүп салды, үстөлдөрүн болсо ала салдырды;

16. жана көгүчкөн сатуучуларга айтты: муну бу жерден алып кеткиле жана Менин Атамдын үйүн соода үйүнө айландырбагыла.

17. Ошондо Анын шакирттеринин эсине: «Сенин үйүң жөнүндө күнүлөөчүлүк Мени жутат» деп жазылганы түштү.   Забур 68,10.

18. Ошо жөнүндө Иудейлер Ага жооп берип айтышты: ошондой кылуу үчүн бийлик бар болгонун Сен бизге кайсы нышаан менен далил көрсөтөсүң?

19. Ыйса аларга жооп айтты: бул ийбадаткананы кыйраткыла, жана Мен үч күндө аны тургузамын.

Матф. 26,61; 27,40. Марк. 14,58; 15,29.

308

TEXT XIV-C

20. Ошо жөнүндө Иудейлер айтышты: бул ийбадаткана кырк алты жылда курулду, жана Сен аны үч күндө тургузасыңбы?

21. Ал болсо ийбадаткана деп, Өз Денеси жөнүндө айткан болчу.

22. Ал өлгөндөрдөн тирилгенден кийин, Анын шакирттеринин эсине Анын айткандары түштү, жана Жазууга жана Ыйса айткан сөздөрүнө ишеништи.
Забур 15,8. Исаия 55,3. Матф. 17,23. Ап. ишт. 2,25; 13,34.

23. Жана Ал Иерусалимде Пасха майрамыңда болгондо, ошондо көп адам Ал көрсөткөн ажайыптарды көрдү жана Анын атына ишеништи.

24. Бирок Ыйса өзү Өзүн аларга ишенип тапшырган жок, анткени алардын баарын билген, Матф. 9,4. Марк. 2,8.

25. жана адам жөнүндө бирөөнүн күбө болуусунун кереги жок болчу; анткени адамдын ичиндеги болгонун Өзү билген. Забур 7,10. Иер. 11,20. Иоан. 6,64.

CHAPTER 2

AND the third day there was a marriage in Cana of Galilee; and the mother of Jesus was there:

2 And both Jesus was called, and his disciples, to the marriage.

3 And when they wanted wine, the mother of Jesus saith unto him, They have no wine.

4 Jesus saith unto her, Woman, what have I to do with thee? mine hour is not yet come.

5 His mother saith unto the servants, Whatsoever he saith unto you, do it.

6 And there were set there six waterpots of stone, after the manner of the purifying of the Jews, containing two or three firkins apiece.

7 Jesus saith unto them, Fill the waterpots with water. And they filled them up to the brim.

8 And he saith unto them, Draw out now, and bear unto the governor of the feast. And they bare it.

9 When the ruler of the feast had tasted the water that was made wine, and knew not whence it was: (but the servants which drew the water knew;) the governor of the feast called the bridegroom,

10 And saith unto him, Every man at the beginning doth set forth good wine; and when men have well drunk, then that which is worse: but thou hast kept the good wine until now.

11 This beginning of miracles did Jesus in Cana of Galilee, and manifested forth his glory; and his disciples believed on him.

12 After this he went down to Caper'-na-um, he, and his mother, and his brethren, and his disciples: and they continued there not many days.

13 And the Jews' passover was at hand, and Jesus went up to Jerusalem,

14 And found in the temple those that sold oxen and sheep and doves, and the changers of money sitting:

15 And when he had made a scourge of small cords, he drove them all out of the temple, and the sheep, and the oxen; and poured out the changers' money, and overthrew the tables;

16 And said unto them that sold doves, Take these things hence; make not my Father's house an house of merchandise.

17 And his disciples remembered that it was written, The zeal of thine house hath eaten me up.

ЕВАНГЕЛІЕ ОТЪ ІОАННА.

2. ¹ На третій день былъ бракъ въ Канѣ Галилейской, и Матерь Іисуса была тамъ. ² Былъ также званъ Іисусъ и ученики Его на бракъ. ³ И какъ недоставало вина, то Матерь Іисуса говоритъ Ему: вина нѣтъ у нихъ. ⁴ Іисусъ говоритъ Ей: что Мнѣ и Тебѣ, Жёно? еще не пришелъ часъ Мой. ⁵ Матерь Его сказала служителямъ: что скажетъ Онъ вамъ, то сдѣлайте. ⁶ Было же тутъ шесть каменныхъ водоносовъ, стоявшихъ по *обычаю* очищенія Іудейскаго, вмѣщавшихъ по двѣ или по три мѣры. ⁷ Іисусъ говоритъ имъ: наполните сосуды *водою*. И наполнили ихъ до верха. ⁸ И говоритъ имъ: теперь почерпните и несите къ распорядителю пира. И понесли. ⁹ Когда же распорядитель отвѣдалъ воды, сдѣлавшейся виномъ,— а онъ не зналъ, откуда *это вино*, знали только служители, почерпавшіе воду,— тогда распорядитель зоветъ жениха

¹⁰ И говоритъ ему: всякій человѣкъ подаетъ сперва хорошее вино, а когда напьются, тогда худшее; *а* ты хорошее вино сберегъ доселѣ. ¹¹ Такъ положилъ Іисусъ начало чудесамъ въ Канѣ Галилейской и явилъ славу Свою; и увѣровали въ Него ученики Его. ¹² Послѣ сего пришелъ Онъ въ Капернаумъ, Самъ и Матерь Его, и братья Его и ученики Его; и тамъ пробыли немного дней. ¹³ Приближалась Пасха Іудейская, и Іисусъ пришелъ въ Іерусалимъ ¹⁴ И нашелъ, что въ храмѣ продавали воловъ, овецъ и голубей, и сидѣли мѣновщики денегъ. ¹⁵ И сдѣлавъ бичъ изъ веревокъ, выгналъ изъ храма всѣхъ, *также* и овецъ и воловъ, и деньги у мѣновщиковъ разсыпалъ, а столы ихъ опрокинулъ; ¹⁶ И сказалъ продающимъ голубей: возьмите это отсюда, и дома Отца Моего не дѣлайте домомъ торговли. ¹⁷ При семъ ученики Его вспомнили, что написано: «ревность по домѣ Твоемъ снѣдаетъ Меня» (Псал. 68,

18 Then answered the Jews and said unto him, What sign shewest thou unto us, seeing that thou doest these things?

19 Jesus answered and said unto them, Destroy this temple, and in three days I will raise it up.

20 Then said the Jews, Forty and six years was this temple in building, and wilt thou rear it up in three days?

21 But he spake of the temple of his body.

22 When therefore he was risen from the dead, his disciples remembered that he had said this unto them; and they believed the scripture, and the word which Jesus had said.

23 Now when he was in Jerusalem at the passover, in the feast *day*, many believed in his name, when they saw the miracles which he did.

24 But Jesus did not commit himself unto them, because he knew all *men*,

25 And needed not that any should testify of man: for he knew what was in man.

10). 18 На это Iудеи сказали Ему въ отвѣтъ: какимъ знаменіемъ докажешь Ты намъ, что *имѣешь власть* такъ поступать? 19 Iисусъ сказалъ имъ въ отвѣтъ: разрушьте храмъ сей, и Я въ три дня воздвигну его. 20 На это сказали Iудеи: сей храмъ строился сорокъ шесть лѣтъ, и Ты въ три дня воздвигнешь его? 21 А Онъ говорилъ о храмѣ Тѣла Своего. 22 Когда же воскресъ Онъ изъ мертвыхъ, то ученики Его вспомнили, что Онъ говорилъ это, и повѣрили Писанію и слову, которое сказалъ Iисусъ. 23 И когда Онъ былъ въ Iерусалимѣ на праздникѣ Пасхи, то многіе, видя чудеса, которыя Онъ творилъ, увѣровали во имя Его. 24 Но Самъ Iисусъ не ввѣрялъ Себя имъ, потому что зналъ всѣхъ, 25 И не имѣлъ нужды, чтобы кто засвидѣтельствовалъ о человѣкѣ; ибо Самъ зналъ, что въ человѣкѣ.

TEXT XIV-C

COMMENTS

Bible translators have been busy for a long time with virtually all known languages, but began translating into Kirghiz excerpts from the New Testament only recently. Although different forms of Christianity (essentially, Nestorianism) have been known in Kirghizstan for centuries, either directly or indirectly (through Islam - hence the form Iysa for Jesus, Turkish Isa, Arabic 'Isa), Christian teaching remained for long a mere and very secondary component, among many others, in the complex philosophical (mainly 'shamanistic') reference system of the Kirghiz.

The Russian Church, contrary to its policy in Tatarstan, made few attempts to propagandize Orthodoxy. As for the first, Russian-trained, post colonization generation of Kirghiz intellectuals who might have overcome the post-1863 reaction of intensified zeal for Islam (as self-defense), it was too deeply involved in various modern secular issues to be tempted by far off Western Christianity.

Paradoxically but logically enough, it took almost half a century of official intense atheistic propaganda (and parallel, nationally induced rediscovery of some sort of 'idealism') to make Christian teaching a cultural and social problem fully included into the stock of knowledge deemed necessary for modern, well-read, broad-minded intellectuals (cf. Chingis Aytmatov's latest controversial novel: Plakha/Batalga, in Novyi Mir, 1986, n° 6,8,9). No doubt that Baptists (ex-Volga Germans), exiled to Kirghizia after 1941, played a certain role in this process.

The translation given here has been done in England in collaboration with Kirghiz native speakers. This may explain the Russian form of some proper nouns such as Ioann (Saint John), Galileia, paskha, etc. The choice of 'Ierusalim' or 'iudei' (Russian biblical/historical forms for 'Jews' - Turkish: yahudi) may have been dictated by extralinguistic reasons.

The number of rare/unknown lexical items has

been kept to a low minimum while, in the best Bible
translation tradition, words with broad enough,
similar connotations have been skilfully integrated
as 'technical' terms (shakirt: disciple, now considered obsolete by Y-897 refers as well to any
'follower' or to an 'apprentice').

Musaldas ~ musalda ~ musalla: wine made out
of grapes, different from arak, sharap, etc.

Chen is a measure unit (in lit. kirg.: a cup).

Ajayıp is given in Kh. Karasaev, J. Shukurov,
K. Yudakhin: Russko-kirgizskii slovar', OGIP, Moscow
1944 as rus. chudo: miracle, but in Y-24 as rus.
charodeistvo: witchcraft, sorcery.

Injil: Gospel, not in Y.

Iybadat + kana: temple (Y-296: rus. molel'nia:
meeting house, chapel.

On verse 18 nısaan seems to be a misprint for
jısaan ~jısana: a sign.

Çijnavcï: S. BET—ALMAN

MANAS

(„Manas" dastanïnïn ulandïsï „Semetej" den bir bölüm)

Cïçaruvcï ve başredaktor:
VELİ KAJUM•CHAN

Millij Türkistan Komitetinin janïndaçï ədebij-ilimij .
bölümünin tarapïnan cïçarïlqan
2. kitap.

MANAS

1

(Manas dastanının — Semetejden bir bölümi)

Qasïrqï, biznin aldïmïzda turqan bir maqsat, oquuçularïbïzdï eski qalq murazdarï turasïndaqï çazïlqan eski aqïndarïbïzdeʼi çana çazuuçularïbïzdïn cïqarmalarï menen taanïştïrïp, quraldandïruudur. Nundan bir
5
nece çïldar murun ötkön murazdïq-tarïjxïj cïqarmalardï bilüv keleçektegi aqvaldarqa çanïnlïşsïz tüşünüşke çardam beredi.

Qandaj qana cïqarmalardï alïp qarasanïzda, al cïqarmalar öz dooründaqï bolup turqan çana bolup ötkön vaqïjalardï köz aldïna elestetip, oşol çaşap turqan qoom quruluşun çana oşol qoomqo tijişti ajrïm köz qaraş-
10
tardï toluqu menen süretdep bere aladï.

Qajsï bir cïqarmalardïn özgöçö bir qasïjetï, oşol çaşap turqan doordoqu qoom quruluşun çaqtap-maqtap ajtuvïnda qana bolboj, aqa sïn köz menen qarap, qalqqa zïjanduu çerlerin tüzetüvge çardam etip keleçegïn körgösüp çazïşïndadïr.

15
Mïna oşonduqtanda, eski qalq cïqarmalarïnïn esteligin çanï vaqïjalar menen, çanï cïqarmalar menen salïştïrïp birdej pajdalanïş mümkünçülügü, bizdin oquuçularïbïz çana çanï çazuuçularïbïz üçün ötö zarïl nersedir. Adabïj cïqarmalarqa nïndaj köz qaraş, eski adabïj bulaqtarïnïn keremet-
20
tüülügün açuqa çana oşol cïqarmalardaqï madanïj çazuuçuluq sözdörünün zor rolunu iş çüzündö ajqïn körgösüp, keleçekte pajdalana bilişke belgili çol açadï.

Bizdin Türkestanïbïzda belgilüü bir uaaqtarqa cejin, ajrïm, ülkenülken fontazïjalï epozdor-dastandar, angemeler, çomoqtor kilep bolup
25
cïqarïlbastan, oozdo1-oozqo köçüp ajtïlïnïp kelindi. Braq, qalq körüngen nerselerdi qana alïa berbesten, orcundu, oruundu özülerinin kündelikti turmuşuna sajkes kele turqan zor maanige ee boluuçu dastandardï basïp çolbostoп, köcetip ajtuularïna qaraqanda, oşol ajtïlqan dastandardïn içindegi „Qaarma..dar" qasïr bolsoçu degendej tilek tilegendikteri belgili bolup cïqadï.
30
Mïna uşundaj qïzïçtuu qalq eposunun, qalq dastanïnïn biri „Manas" eposu bolup atala li. Coqoruda ajtïlqandaj, Manas eposuda, oozdon-oozqo köçüp ajtïlïp çürgendikten, Manastï kim çazqandïqï uşul ubaqqa cejin

belgisiz. Tek qana qïrqïzdïn Tïnïbek[1]) çana Qaramoldo[2]) sïJaqtï el çomoqcularïnïn aJtqandarïnan alïnïp kiJinki kezderde çazïlqan.

35 Bu keremettüü qalq eposu Manas, özünün realdïq fontazïJaqa baJlïqï çaqïnan, ademiligi, qïzïqtuuluqu çaqïnan rustardïn „Bïlïnasï", çana KarelïJanïn „Kalevalasï" mïndaJ tursun, eski Alman qalqïnïn „Nibelung"sï, Fransuzdun „Şanson de Roland"sï, Farsïnïn „Şaxnama"sï, Grextin „Jllijas-odisseJi" sïJaqtï qalq epos cïqarmalarïnan artïp tüşpese kem cïqpaJdï.

40 Manas tuuralu Coxan VəlijXan uulu özünün cïqarmasïnda[3]): —„Noqoj doorundaqï[4]) eski qïrqïz uruvunun eŋ birinci eposu Manas. Manas, Qïrqïzdardïn artqa qaltïrïp oturuucu barïïq keremettüü çomoqtorun, bir ubaqta, bir mezgilde, bir kişinin — baatïr Manastïn çanïna toptoşturuloqan

45 entsiklopedialïq çïJnaqïdïr. Bul, dala Jllijasï sïJaqtï — qïrqïzdardïn, turmuşu, adatï, süJüşpenciligi çana çaqrafiJalïq, dinimiJ-meditsinslïq çönündögü tüşünügüdür. Oşonu menen birge türlü el aralïq qatnaştarda uşul zor epos icinde belgili orun aladï.

Manas toluq nersedeJ bolup körüngön, bir nece epizotdordon-bölümcelerden turadï. Manastïn ulandïsï bolqan başqa bir epos SemeteJdi alsaq

50 ta, Manastïn çolun çoldoJdï. Qïrqïzdardïn aJtuularïna qaraqanda, Manastï eşitiş ücün üc künü uudasï menen aJtsada tügenbeJdi, çana qalq eşiliştçn çalïqpaJdï deşedi. Al, SemeteJdi aJtïş ücünda bir nece kün kerek bolso kerek. (71-72-bet. Ruscadan qotorqon — Bet-Alman.)

55 Birinci poemanïn baatïrï Manas, CüJden[3]) Talasqa, Talastan AnçïJanqa[4]) ceJinki NoqoJloroqo üstömdük etip turqan Çaqïp degendïn balasï bolso kerek. Manas ata tegi çaqïnan aq sööktörgö çatpasada, qandardan barqï kem bolboqon. Manastïn atasï Çaqïp: „Men çaş Manastïn atasï çaqïmduu CüJden Talasqa cejin eelejmin, men qan emesmin, braq qandan kem emes, qan Çaqïp menmin." dep aJtqan eken. (72-bet).

60 Birinci poemada Manastï mïndaJ dep münezdeJdi: — "Al, (Manas) Ançïlandïn cala bïşqan nanïn çep, kök almasïn kemirip-semirip, Ançïlanda özüp conoJqon adam. 12 çaşïnda çaa ata bilip, 13 çaşïnda özünön ülken

baldardï aldan oodara tartïp duşmandarqa soqqu bere bilgen, AJïldardaqï suluu qïzdardï ala qacïp, qarşïlïq qïlqan er çürök baatïrlardï çelkeden

65 alïp: — „Etïn oorusa qoquJ, qoquJ dep qïcqïrqïn" dep maçburlaqan. 14 çaşïnda qapcïqaJlardaqJ çaşaqan bötön aJïldardï köcürüp-bölüp, bijik toolordoqu özgö duşman çïlqïlarïqa tijip, quup, 15 çaşïnda sansïz qalqtardïn başçïsï bolo bilgen. Manas uzun boJluu, uzun qaştï, suuq çüzdü, qara qandï, braq aq etti, qursaqtuu, arqasï kök boloqon deJdi. Çürektüü Manas kimge uqşaJdï? — „Ol kök çalduu kekcil qarïşqïrqa uqşaJ edi" — deJdi. Manas

70 acuulanqanda ötö qorqunuctuu bolup körünüp, murutu tik tuup, közünön ucqundar cïqïp, oozunan icke qaJïnqa oqsoqon izqaarlar cïqïp, tanalarï alacïqtaJ kööp ketüücü eken. (Alacïq — Qïrqïzdardïn kijizden çazaqan kicinekeJ boz üJü.) (72-73-bet. qotorqon. Bet-Alman.[1]

75 Birinci poema çaş Manastïn, öz atasïn — beti aq qardaJ, betinin ortosundaqï qïzïlï, qardïn betine tamqan qandaJ, caci soqoncoquna çetip, qara qunduzdaJ, çïtï çïpardaJ, tişi kürüctöJ 15 çaştaqï — „Qara qan degendïn qïzï, Qanïkejge quda tüş" dep çibergeninen baştaladï. Manastïn atasï Çaqïp, balasïna qoluqtu tabïş ücün, atï Irqaidaj [1] bolup arïqtaqanca, köp

80 çerlerdi qïdïrïp, Qara qandïn aJïlïn tabat. Braq, qandan on çoop ala albaJ, — „Menin qïzïm qan uuluna ilaJïq, senin uuluna bijdin erke qïzï ilaJïq" degen çoop aladï.

Munu uqq.ından kijin, Manas Qara qanqa soquş çarijalap, çenip zorluq menen alat. Al kijinki epizotdorunda, özünün elin-çerin talamciliqqa
85 uçı·ratpaj, saqtap turuş ücün, qalmaqtarqa qarşı soquşqandiqin köröbüz.
Oşol kezdegi Manqol qanl Çolojdun qarşiliq qiziminin natijçasinda qasir-
qi Isiq-köl tarabindaqi qirqizdar Qara-ertişke batiş Altajqa qaraj siqil-
lişip bara çatqandiqtan, Manastin başciliqi menen barliq başqa muzulman
qalqi qarap turuşpastan Manqoldor menen soquşup turuşqan.
90 Manas Çoloj qandi öltürgön. Al qana emes Qitajqa qarsi çoruqtar qi-
linip, Qitaj baatiri Qonurbajda öltürülgön. Mina uşundaj soquştardin natijçasinda, Manas Manqol qanl Naz-qorurun qolunan ölgön. Manas ölgön-
dön kijin, Manastin çolun çoldop, qunun quup balasi Semetej ciqadi" —
dep çazilqan. (73-74-bet. Qotorqon. Bet-Alman.)
95 Coxan Valijxan uulu ajtqandaj, Manas dastaninin başqa qalq dastan-
darinan artiqciliqi çana özgöcölügü, vaqijanin başi Manastan baştalsa-
da, aqirinda Manastin çolur ,oldoqon, Semetej, Almanbet, Külcoro, Qau-
coro sijaqtl çüzdegen çetkincekteri ciqip, Manastin atin tarixtan ücürbej-
di. Mina oşondluqtanda, keremettüü Manas eposu ajniqsa dala Türkestani-
100 bizdin ichde, uşul bügünkü künge cejin unutulbastan ajtilmaqta.

(. . .)

Qizilqan ubaqtarda, Türkistan qalqina, Manas sijaqti baatirlar ülken
bel bolup köründü. Maselen: — Manas dastaninin ulandisi. Semetejdin
bir bölümündö, Çediger¹) degen eldin, Cinqoço, Toltoj degen baatirlari
Semetej baatirdin bolocoq qoluqtusu Aj—cürektin atasi, Aqun qendi—, Qi-
105 zindi ber" — dep qamap çatqanda, Aqun qan Cinqoço çana Toltojjorqo
elci çiberdi. Elcige barqan adam, duşmandin könülün majtarip, esin ciqa-
rip, Semetejdin danqin kötörüü ücün: —

— „Cinqoço, Toltoj elinen,	Qatinin alsan ölörsün.
Er öltürüp salbasam,	Qajtip ketkin üjünö,
110 Eski dooqo qalbasam,	Minerine at berem,
Kündöj bolqon balanidi, 125	On-eki qapqa şaarimdan,
Küjgüzüp qarmap bergendej —	Tandasan suluu qiz berem.
Künöö 'qilip albasam.	Alistan qabar kep uqar,
Menin canam kelbese,	Er Semetej baatirin,
115 Bul er Semetej baatirdin,	Aj—cürek aldi — dep uqar.
Ala turqan qajni eken. 130	Attanip ciqar çol çürüüp,
Asili işin çön bolbojt,	Altimiş türkün qol alip,
Aj—cürek alsan on bolobojt,	Qizip salar elindi.
Uruşsan ujat bolosun,	Ketirip salar belindi.
120 Qarmaşsan qorduq körösün,	Sojup salar atindi.
Er Semetej baatirdin, 135	Çojup salar qalqindi" —

— dep ajtadi. Buda bolso Semetejdej erdi betke uştap, duşmandi qajta qaj-
tarip çiberiş taktikasi edi.

Bul, keremettüü Manas dastaninda, bul sijaqti vaqijalar mindep kezi-
gişe beredi. Manas çe bolboso Semetejler çaşap turqan doorlordo asmanqa
140 ucuu tuurasinda, ec qacan başqa kelbej turqan axval boisoda, bul Manas
dastaninin icinde, bul sijaqtuu realdiq fontazijalar köp kezigişedi. Maselen:
Aj—cürektin asmanda ucup çürüşü çönündö:

TEXT XV

145
— „Aqundun qïzï Aj—cürek, 150 Ančijan menen Külöjdü,
Aq quu kebin kijdi emi, Almatï menen Ceiekti,
Qanatïn küngö qaqqïlap, Ošondon bəri qïdïrïp,
Qujruqun suuqa capqïlap. Keŋ Talas öndüü çer tappaj,
Kün batïş közdöj uctu emi. Semetej öŋdüü er tappaj,
Aq quuraj başïn qïdïrïp, 155 Altï tünü, çeti kün —
Asmandap ucup cïqtï emi. On-üc künü uctu emi.“

— dejdi. Munu öz dooruna salïştïrïp qaraqanda, bul ajtïlqan sözdör bolo-
coqtu bolçop kerenıet ajtïlqan sözdür.

160
Manas dastanïnïn daqï bir qasilettüü çeri, oşol dooruloqu öz elinin
qoom quruluşun, kulturasïn, ürp — adetterin ajta kele: özüntün çoruq qïlïp
kelgen duşman ölkölörünündä qoom quruluştarïn çana aqa bolqou türlüü
köz qaraştardï köz aldïŋa elestetip sïpattap beredi.

(. . .)

165
Azïrïnca, bizdin qolubuzda Manas dastanï tuurasïnda çetkiliktüü ma-
terijaldar çoq bolqonduqtan, oquucularïbïzdïn köŋülün tïndïrïp, til suutu
qïluu ücün, Manas dastanïnïn ulandïsï, Semetej baatïrdan bir bölümün
berip oturabïz. Bul cïqarına başïnan ajaqïna ceiin 7—8 muundu ir - ölön
menen çazïlqan.

Bul bölümündö:

170
Semetej baatïrdïn çaş kezinde quda bolqan qajnï Aqun qan, Aqun
qandïn qïzï Aj—cürek Semetejdin qoluqtusu bolqon. Çediger degen elden,
Cïnqoço, Toltoj degen baatïrlarï, Aj—cürektï tartïp alabïz dep, qol çïjïp
barïp, Aqun qandïn şaarïn qamap çatqanda, Aj—cürek Semetejge barïp,
Aq—şunqar degen quşun ala qacïp kelgen. Semetej aq—şunqardï artïnan
175
izdep barïp üstünön cïqïp, Cïnqoço, Toltojdu çenïp, Aj—cürektï alïp qajt-
qan. Biraq, munun baarïsï tügöl emes, Cïnqoço, Toltoj, Aqun qanqa —
„Qïzïndï ber“ — dep qaniap çatqanïnan baştalatda, Semetej baatïr Aq—
şunqardï izdep barïp Aqun qandïn şaarïna çanïdan çetkenine toqtolodu.
Bul cïqarmanïn sözü belgilüü Qïrqïz çomoqçusu Tïnïbektikï, çïjnaqan
Arabaj uulu.

180
Türkistan Millij Qomitasïnïn
Ilimij bölümünün tapşïrïqï bojunca,
İştep çïqqan:

Ş. BET ALMAN.
185
Berlin. 1943-çïl.

M A N A S

1   (An excerpt from Semetey - part of the
Manas Epic)

Now, one aim set before us is to brace
ourselves by acquainting our readers with
the works of our past writers and poets
about our ancient popular heritage. To know
the historical-

5   hereditary works of past years helps
understand without error the situations of
the future.

No matter what works you examine, they
make the events of the past and the things
that happened in their time appear before
your eyes, they can portray the social
structures developed by that time and the
particular viewpoints corresponding to that

10   society.

This is a peculiarity of every piece of
these works: they do not only support and
praise the social structure developed by
that time, they examine it with a critical
eye, they are written to show the future
and to help correct the aspects that are
harmful to the people.

15   This is why it is extremely
important for our readers and new
writers to compare new works and new
events with the literary popular
monuments of the past and to be able
to use them in the same way.
Examining thus the literary works
opens a well-defined road toward the
knowledge of how to use them in the
future, showing clearly and actually
the important cultural role of the

20   authors' message in these works - and
      toward the discovery of the magic of
      the ancient literary sources.

      In our Turkestan, during a well-known
      period of time, in particular because
      tales, legends, very big epics-dastans of
      romance fiction were not published as
      books, they came down to us through
      recitation, passing from mouth to mouth.
      However, the

25   people have not only sung what they saw,
      have not only published epics enhancing
      the great value constantly given to the
      numerous peculiarities of their everyday
      life by comparing this to what was
      glorified, they expressed in a certain way
      the people's innermost wishes as if saying
      "If only we could have now heroes like
      those sung in these epics!".

30   Among such interesting popular epics and
      popular dastans, one is called the Manas
      Epic. As stated above, in the Manas epic,
      since it came down to us by word of mouth,
      nobody knows up to now who wrote it.
      Simply, it has been written down lately in
      conformity with what Kirghiz popular story-
      tellers like Tınıbek and Karamoldo sang.

35   Such a fictional epic as Manas, because
      of its realistic, myth-related richness,
      its high attractive value, its enthralling
      character, is to be put side by side with
      the Russian 'Byliny', the Carelian
      'Kalevala' and doesn't stand out less if
      one puts it higher than such popular epics
      as the 'Nibelungen' of the ancient Germans,
      the French 'Chanson de Roland', the Persian
      'Shahname' and the Greek 'Iliad and
      Odyssey'.

40   Chokan Valikhan-uulu writes in his own
      works about Manas: "Manas is the very first
      epic of the old Kirghiz tribe in the Nogoy
      age. Manas is an encyclopaedic collection
      concentrating in one man - Manas the Hero -

at a given time and moment, all the
mythical tales of these Kirghiz who
remained behind (that is, did not migrate).
This, exactly as the Iliad, is an
explanation of

45   the life, customs, passions, geography,
beliefs and medical knowledge of the
Kirghiz. At the same time, various inter-
ethnic relations play a certain role in
this large epic.

Manas is to be considered as a complete
whole, made out of different episodes and
subparts. If we take another epic -

50   Semetey - it is the sequel of Manas and
follows the same path as Manas. According
to what Kirghiz say, in order to hear
Manas, if one recites for three days at a
stretch, one doesn't finish and they say
that people won't be bored to hear it. In
the same way, in order to recite Semetey,
it would probably take a few days" (pp 71-
72. Translated from Russian.B.A)

The hero of the first poem, Manas,
probably is the son

55   of Jakıp who wields authority on the
Noogay from the river Chü to Talas and
from Talas to Andijan. Although Manas'
father pertained in no way to the 'white
bones', his importance was no less than
the khans'. Jakip, Manas' father, is said
to have declared: "As young Manas' father I
am happily in power from the Chü to Talas;
I am not a khan, but no less than a khan: I
am Jakip-khan" (p 72).

60   In the first poem, Manas is
characterized thus: "He (Manas), having
eaten the barely baked bread of Andijan,
having gnawed, fattening on them, green
apples, grew and reached manhood in
Andijan. At 12 he could wield a bow, at 13
he could unhorse stout fellows, deliver a
blow to the enemies, kidnap beautiful girls

in encampments, catch by the nape of the
neck the daring

65   heroes who opposed him, saying while
      compelling them: 'When your flesh will hurt
      you, shout: help, help!'. At 14 he could
      drive out and scatter alien settlements
      pitched in gorges and chase and capture
      other enemy horses in the high mountains;
      at 15 he hold sway over innumerable
      peoples. Manas was said to be tall in
      stature, heavy-browed, with severe
      features; his blood was black but his skin
      was white, his belly full, his back grey.
      To whom did

70   brave Manas bear a resemblance ? it is
      said: "He was like a grey-maned, resentful
      wolf". When Manas was angry, he looked
      extremely dreadful, his moustache bristled
      up, sparks would fly out from his eyes, out
      of his mouth icy streams similar to thin
      birch trees would spurt and his chest would
      swell to the size of a small yurt"
      (alachik: a small yurt made out of felt. pp
      72-73, translated by B.A).

75   The first poem begins with young Manas
      sending his own father to say: "Seek
      Kanigey in marriage for me, the daughter of
      Kara Khan" - a 15-year old beauty with
      teeth like (grains of) rice, an aromatic
      smell, whose hair as black as an otter
      hangs down her back, with a snow-white
      face with rosy spots on it similar to
      (droplets of) blood dotting the snow.
      Manas' father, Jakıp, in order to find a
      fiancée for his son, with his horse as raw-
      boned as a June-berry bush, travels up and
      down through many
      countries

80   and finds Kara Khan's encampment. But
      unable to get the right answer from the
      Khan, he is told: "My daughter is worthy of
      a khan's son, our erke's daughter is worthy
      of your son".

After hearing this, Manas declares war
on Kara Khan and having won, takes the girl
by force. After these episodes, so as not
to let his own people be plundered and to
protect them, we

85   see him fighting the Kalmyks. As a result
of the hostile onslaught of Joloy, the
Mongol khan of that time, those Kirghiz who
dwell now around (lake) Issık köl, after
having flocked toward the Black Irtysh in
Western Altay with Manas at their head,
without waiting for all the other Muslim
peoples, went on to wage war on the
Mongols.

90   Manas killed Joloy khan. He did not only
march against the Khıtay, he also killed
Konurbay, the Khıtay khan. As result of
similar battles, Manas died at the hand of
Naz-Koru, the Mongol Khan. After Manas'
death, following Manas' path, his son
Semetey is reported to have come out and
washed his blood". (pp 73-74. Translated
by B.A.).

95   As Chokan Valikhan-uulu says, the
specificity - and superiority - of the
Manas tale over other popular epics (lies
in the fact that) if the starting point of
the events begins with Manas, at the end
appear, following Manas' path, heirs by the
hundred, similar to Semetey, Almambet,
Külchoro and Kanchoro, who do not wipe
Manas' name out of history. Because of this
and more

100   particularly in our Turkistan, the magic
Manas epic continues to be sung for not
having been forgotten until nowadays.

    (....)

In tense (incancescent) times, for the
people of Turkistan, heroes such as Manas
are considered an enormous strength. For
example: in one part of Semetey - the
sequel of the Manas tale - when the hero

Chingocho and Toltoy of the Jediger people
besiege Akun khan, the father of Aychürek
(the future fiancée of the hero Semetey)
telling him: "Give me your daughter!", this

105   Akun khan sends an emissary to Chingocho
and Toltoy. The man who goes as an
emissary, in order to take the enemy down a
peg or two, make him remember and enhance
Semetey's reputation, says:

"I won't take the field to kill the hero
from Chingocho and

110   Toltoy's tribe, I will not become
responsible for an old squabble (= take
revenge). I cannot commit a crime such as
giving my child similar to the sun, having
caught and saddened her. I cannot doo

115   that. Because this Semetey the Hero has
taken her (since long) as an in-law, your
plan is bound to fail. If you take
Aychürek, it won't be right. If you fight,
you'll disgrace yourself. If you

120   constrain her, you'll be humiliated, If you
take Semetey the Hero's wife, you'll die.
Hurry back home, I'll give you a horse to
ride and I'll give you any beauty you want,
chosen from the twelve-

125   grated city. The news would heard from afar
and Semetey the Hero would hear it:
'Someone kidnapped Aychürek'. Taking the
field on
130   horseback, levying all sorts of
troops, he'll rush up to punish your
tribe and break your spine, to
slaughter your horses and

135   annihilate your people" says the emissary.
Thus, having proved a hero similar to
Semetey, he suggests the tactic to send
back the enemy.

In this epic tale Manas, such episodes
can be found by the thousand. At the time
when Manas or Semetey lived, even as

140   for flying up to the heavens, never is
there any impossible situation and in this
epic such realistic fantasies often follow
one another. For example - about Aychürek
flying up in the sky

    "Akun's daughter, Aychürek
Wore now the garments of a
   white swan,

145   Flapping her wings toward the sun,
Flapping her tail toward the river,
She ascends toward the West,
Looking for the heads of thistles.
She is now flying in the sky.

150   After Andijan and Külöy
Alma Ata and Cheyek,
From there she wanders hither
But doesn't find the wide Talas a
   suitable place,
But doesn't find Semetey a suitable hero

155   Six nights, seven days,
She flew thirteen days".

    In comparison with that time, these
words are magic words which forestall the
future. Yet another superiority of the
Manas

160   tale is to describe at large the social
structure, the culture, the habits and
customs of its own people at that time and
to show vividly the viewpoints which were
typical for it and the social structure
they noticed in the countries of their own
enemies.
    (....)

    As for the present, because we do not
have enough material concerning the Manas
tale, in order to satisfy our readers'
hearts

165   in order to wet their tongue, we offer them
          one part of 'Semetey the Hero', a sequel of
          the Manas tale. This work, from the
          beginning to the end, is made of 7-8
          syllable songs and stanzas.

          In this excerpt (it is said): Semetey
          the hero in his

170   young age became a relative of Akun khan
          and Aychürek - Akun khan's daughter became
          his wife. The heroes Chingocho and Toltoy
          from the Jediger tribe, having decided to
          kidnap Aychürek, rally an army and march,
          besiege Akun khan's city; Aychürek goes to
          Semetey and runs back with his gerfalcon
          Aksungar. Semetey, following in her steps
          in search of Aksungar, runs into Chingocho
          and Toltoy, vanquishes

175   them and brings back Aychürek. But
          this is only part of it. It begins
          when Chingocho and Toltoy besiege
          (the city), telling Akun khan: 'Give
          us your daughter!' and ends when
          Semetey the Hero in his quest for
          Aksungar reaches again Akun khan's
          city. The text of this work is that
          of Tinibek, a famous Kirghiz story-
          teller, as collected by Arabay-uulu.

180   Elaborated in conformity with the
          instructions of the Scientific
          Section of the Turkestan National
          Committee by S. Bet

185   Alman.
                    Berlin, 1943

COMMENTS

The origin and the date of this document
speak for themselves. For an overall view of the
problems linked to the 'Eastern Legion', cf. A.R.
Alexeiev: "Soviet Nationalities Under Attack", in
Soviet Nationalities in Strategic Perspective, ed.
by S.E.Wimbush, Croom Helm, London 1985, pp. 61-
74.
        From a sociolinguistic viewpoint, the main
interest of this text lies in the fact that it testifies to the continuation, well into the 1940s,
of a tradition for which we have no written proof
since the end of the 1920s. As indicated below, the
kind of 'Kirghiz' used here sharply differs from
today's literary norm in that it includes a great
many forms which, today, would rather be characterized as 'Kazakh'.
        However, as already stressed about texts 1-E
and 1-G, the author does not use here some cheap
macaronic jargon, nor displays an excessive taste
for 'dialectisms'. For extralinguistic reasons, he
remains faithful to the pre-1923 comprehensive
meaning of the 'Kirghiz' ethnonym which covered then
Kazakh and Kirghiz. He thus tends to continue the
elaboration of an 'ortok til'.
        Such a widening of its scope so as to present
it as 'Türkestaner': Turki - a pan-tribal, pan-
regional language in the making - tends to integrate
many linguistic features typical for 'Kirghiz'
stricto sensu, but remains centered, as all local
newspapers, reviews, etc. since 1905, on a rather
'Kazakh' norm.
        Without oversimplifying too much an unstable,
not standardized (because not acknowledged as official) reality, this oral variety of intelligentsia
Kirghiz can be described as morphologically Kazakh,
but phonetically and lexically Kirghiz.
        As a comprehensive form of language, it is
more open to traditional 'Chagataisms' than to the
modern literary norm and its loose, imperfectly
rational syntax is very similar to that of earlier
texts (1-G for example).
        Nevertheless, the author, who, obviously, has

a good command of Russian, is not at all impervious
to Soviet ideological influence (l. 1-10) and,
consequently, to Russian lexical loanwords and
idiomatic calques. These are particularly numerous
- more numerous even than in the sociolinguistically
similar text n° XIII - without however ever putting
the 'kirghizity' of the language in jeopardy. For
example:
1.2: bizniŋ aldïmïzda tuɼɔan bir maqsat: the aim
which stands in front of us = rus. цель, которая
стоит перед нами
1.3: eski qalq murazdarï: the old popular monuments = rus. старые народные памятники
1.4: quraldandïr: to arm = rus. вооружать
1.18: adabij bulaqtarï: literary sources = rus.
литературные источники
1.23: fontazijalï epoz: fabulous epics = rus.
фантастический эпос
1.36: ədemilik (lit. kirg.: körkömdük): high
artistic value = rus. художественность
qïzïqtuuluq: diverting character = rus.
занимательность
belgilüü: well-known = rus. известный
etc., etc.

The variety of Latin script used here corresponds
to the one used in Soviet Kirghizia during the 1930s
with only minor, typographical changes: ö instead
of ө and ï instead of ь. Except for ɔʲ , it corresponds also to the system used in Text XIII.
From a more purely linguistic viewpoint, the only
truly 'dialectal' features to be noted are the inter-
changeability, in comparison with the modern literary norm (K-43,47), of 'z' and 's' forms:
qasïrgï   lit. kirg.: azïrkï
muraz ösüp   muras ösüp
müzülman   musulman
and a tendency to mix up the distributional differences between /š/ and /s/, /č/ and /š/ which exist
between literary Kirghiz and literary Kazakh:
1. 45: süjüspencilik   kaz.: süjispenshilik
One should not analyze either as morphological
features what maybe are mere orthographical problems:
the 'da' particle is not written here separately
as in lit. kirg. (cf. also 1.50)
braq is in fact a phonetical rendering of lit.
kirg. birok
such renderings as aqval (ar. ahwal) for lit.

kirg.: abal: situation, or vaqija for lit. kirg.:
okuya: event may conceal very similar pronuncia-
tions. Y-41 does have an 'aqıbal' form and Latin
'v', just as cyrillic 'в' stand both for [β] :
K-95. The initial 'o' in 'okuya' transcribes a
sound very similar to the one rendered by 'u' in
'ubakt(ı)': time (often spelled vakıt), both graphemes standing in fact for [w~ ʌ] (cf. uqşaş =
lit. kirg.: okshosh). Same remark for mundan =
mından.

A problem, similar to this one (that is
implying the spirantization of an occlusive: K-498),
occurs in an intervocalic position where this more
or less complete spirantization may give birth to
a long vowel or to a diphtong:

$$V + Occl. + V \longrightarrow V + Spir. + V = \begin{smallmatrix} \rightarrow \\ \rightarrow \end{smallmatrix} \begin{smallmatrix} \bar{V} \\ \underset{V}{\overset{v}{}} w \end{smallmatrix}$$

Considering the general instability of certain
long vowels in Kirghiz (K-185) as well as that of
some diphtongs in Kazakh, it is not sure whether
the orthographical choice made by linguists (working
separately) do reflect or not an actually very different phonetical reality.

The spelling 'uruvu(nun)' on l. 41 for example,
suggests therefore a pronunciation very close to
- and not different from - that of the official,
lit. kirg. spelling: uruusu(nun) (cf. text 1-G for
other variants in the spelling of the same word).

The same problem arises with such apparently
strange forms as 'Kazakh' bilüv, ajtuvĭnda, tüzetüv=
lit. kirg. bilüü, aytuusunda, tüzötüü (l. 27),
that is about the adequacy or non-adequacy of the
spelling of the /Ū~Ō/ suffix (K-389, 1261) (Cf.
J.R.Krueger: Introduction to Kazakh, Teaching Aids
for the Study of Inner Asia, Indiana University
Research Institute in Asian Studies, Bloomington
1980, pp. 13-17). In any case, the oral, phonetic
reality concealed behind those forms poses - whatever it is - no difficulty to any native speaker.

An inadequate orthographical choice may also
be responsible for what would amount (if confirmed)
to serious discrepancies in the rules of Vowel
Harmony. Forms such as bölümi, tüzetüvge, tüşpese,
özülerinin, bölümcelerden, özen, etc. instead of
lit. kirg.: bölümü, tüzötüügö, tüshpösö, özülörünün, bölümchölördön, özön would signal - if actually pronounced as written - that Bet Alman's

idiolect knows no <u>labial</u> Harmony (and therefore
is not Kirghiz).

In fact, we do find irregular traces of such
Labial Harmony in this text: özgö, doᴄᴐᴐɑ, etc.

Ultimately, we are maybe dealing here simply
with a 'Kazakh' orthographical aberration: labial
<u>graphemes</u> are not written in suffixes and are
replaced by the corresponding non-labial graphemes
even if actually <u>pronounced</u> as labials:

Cf. Kruger's <u>Introduction to Kazakh</u>, p. 14:
ölen is therefore pronounced ölön
tütin   "   "   "   tütün
öte   "   "   "   ötö, etc.

The same lack of phonological principles is
probably also responsible for an alleged violation
of the rules of Consonantal Harmony in

1. 10: süretdep   (K-408) lit.kirg.:süröttöp
1.63: atdan   "   "   attan
(a problem distinct from 1. 50: alsaqta, lit. kirg.:
alsak da: sandhi phenomenon)

The remaining, really linguistic discrepancies
with the literary norm are few and concern minor
points:

- Genitive:
1. 2: bizniŋ lit. kirg.: bizdin. Cf. texts
1-E,G and Krueger's <u>Introduction</u>... p. 23.
but: 1. 38: Fransuzdun, etc.

- Present:
1. 6, etc.: beredi lit. kirg.: beret; aladï =
alat; turadï = turat, etc. This is a truly Kazakh
form: cf. Krueger, p. 49.

- Determiner suffix:
1. 47: belgili lit. kirg.: belgilüü: K-1098,
1102 and Krueger, p. 44.
but 1. 22: fontazijalï lit. kirg.: fantaziyalık:
K-1054 and Krueger, p. 46.
orcundu lit. kirg.: orchunduu
but 1. 30: qïzïqluu. Id.: sïjaqtï = sıyaktuu;
cüzdü = jüzdüü; etti = ettüü.

TEXT XV

PARSING

cíjnavcí, cíojaruvcí: lit. kirg.:jıynoochu,
chıgaruuchu

1. 3: tuurasïndaojí: lit. kirg.: jönündögü
1. 6: çaŋïŋlïşsíz: probably a misprint for
jangılıshsız
1. 11: qasijet: obsolete, lit. kirg.: özgöchülük
1. 14: körgösüp: lit. kirg.: körgöz- or körgönsü-
cf. Y-428
1. 19: acuoja: lit. kirg.: achuuga
1. 20: rolunu (cf. 1. 35: realdíq, 1. 36: Rustar)
K-217, lit. kirg. Orustar. Most probably
pronounced with an initial ultrashort vowel
when not in intervocalic position as here:
...zor (r)olunu...
1. 26: sajkes: ? say (Y-621,II-2?)+kez? or kech?
1. 28: bolsocu = bolso+cu: lit. kirg.: chı, particle Y-880, K-375
1. 31: atala lí: lit. kirg.: atalat ele
Manas eposuda: lit. kirg.: eposusıda
1. 33: Tïnïbek, Qaramoldo: famous bards
1. 36 ǝdemilik cf. Y-22: ademi: beautiful
1. 40: Noojoj dooru: the XII century
1. 44: dala: lit. kirg.: dal
dinimij: lit. kirg.: diniy
1. 46: qatnaş: lit. kirg.: katıshuu
1. 51: eşitiş: lit. kirg.: uguu
uuda: Kaz.: udayı, lit. kirg.: üzülböy,
dayıma
1. 52: çaliq-pajdi: lit. kirg.: zerik-peyt
1. 54: Ançïjan: an Uzbek form, lit. kirg.: Andıjan
1. 56: aq sööktör: the 'white bones': the blue-
blooded ones, the hereditary aristocracy
1. 65: maçburlaojan: lit. kirg.: zorduk kılgan
1. 66: bötön: lit. kirg.: bashka
1. 68: bolo bilgen: bil- as an auxiliary verb;
lit. kirg.: kir al- (cf. Text XIII,1. 20)
1. 70: edi: lit. kirg.: ele
1. 72: tana: ? most probably ir.: tan: body, chest
here maybe lungs; plural of majesty.
1. 73: alacïq: Y-46
kööp: from köp- (Gerund; Labial harmony)

1. 79: Irɔaj: Mespilus Amelanchier Med. (Rosaceae)
1. 81: erke: Y-961: organizer of festivities? or
biy: judge? In any case, a 'junior officer',
an inferior
1. 84: zorluq: lit. kirg.: zorduk, K-429
1. 90: Qȋtaj, or Qaraqitai ~ Qitan. Cf. Luc Kwanten:
Imperial Nomads, University of Pennsylvania
Press 1979, p. 66.
çoruq: lit. kirg.: araket, jürgüzüsh
1.103 :Çediger: a Khitay tribe
1.110: dooqo qal-: lit. kirg.: öch al-: Y-603
1.117: Y-77
1.131: altȋmȋş türkün: lit. kirg.: türküm türdüü,
ar türdüü
qol: an army
1.136: betke uştap: to show
1.144: kep kij: Y-375, lit. kirg.: kiyim
1.147: aq quuraj: Y-455, Salsola ruthenica (Cheno-
podiaceae)? A variety of thistle used for
obtaining soda ash.
1.180: millij: lit. kirg.: uluttuk
qomita: Republican Turkish.

F - THE KIRGHIZ LANGUAGE IN CHINA

XINJIANG   KIRGHIZ   XVI

a)- Before the 'Cultural Revolution':

- Süyüktüü ata-meken   Text XVI-A
  (Shınjang el basması, Ürümqü 1956)

- Junggo kırgız tilinin orfogra-
  fiyası   Text XVI-B
  (Qızıl Suu Gazeta basması, Artısh 1957)

- Algı söz   Text XVI-C
  (Algı Irlar, Shınjang el basması, Ürümqü 1957)

- Jumakun Mambet: "Jarıq tang"   Text XVI-D
  (id., p. 24-25)

- Amantur Bayzakov: "Beyjing'   Text XVI-E
  (Kerme Too, Shınjang el basması, Ürümqü 1962)

b)- After the 'Cultural Revolution':

- Qızıl Suu Adabiyatı, 1980, 1-2   Text XVI-F(a)
  (Alphabetical chart)

- Alippe   Text XVI-F(b)
  (Shınjang el basması, Ürümqü 1981, p. 85.)

- Amantur Bayzak: "Quttuqtoo"   Text XVI-G
  (Shınjang Qırgız Adabiyatı, 1981, 1, p. 3-4.)

- Two articles from "Qızıl Suu Geziti",
  (November 20, 1982):
     . Partiyanın küjürmöndülügü idiya jana sayası
  jaqtagı jogoru birdeyliginde   Text XVI-H(a)
     . Aptonom rayonduq uluttar ıntımaqtıgı
  boyuncha   Text XVI-H(b)

Süyüktüü ata-meken The Beloved Fatherland
Shınjang el basması 1956 The people's typography
in Xinjiang

اتا ملكه نبزدمن تووللورو مدندن دأريالاری

تارىم ويدۇكۇ

ماملكه تىك چه ارا ‎——‎
اجىراتلباعان حدلارا ‎- - -‎

Ata-mekenibizdin tooloru menen daryaları
    _____ : Mamlekettik chek-ara
    - - - : Ayıratabagan chek-ara

Mountains and rivers of our Fatherland
State border
Unsettled border

TEXT XVI-A*

1 ۰۰6 · بۇربۇرۇبۇز بەيجىن ـ اتا مەكە
نەيزدىن جۇرۇ گۇ

بەيجىن شااری ۇلۇو اتامەكەنەيزدىن بۇربۇر شاارى.
ۋۇۇۇۇۇۇۇ 500- جىلدىن الننەا بەيجىزشاارى پادشالاردىن بۇيـ
5 رۇۇۇ تۇنزرۇ تۇرغان ۇرنۇسۇ مەلە؛ تاك 1949 ـ جىلىچۇگە
خزا ا مەل ر.سپۇ بلىكاسى نۇزۇ لگۇن كۇندۇن باشتاپ بۇل با
يرقى شاار مەلدىن ۇز بۇربۇرۇنا ايلاندى.

بەيجىن مىل جۇ مارك جانا مارك قۇرۇۇ شاار. دۇينودۇ مندايـ
ساتاناتۇۇ، مندايـ قۇرۇۇ بايرقى شاار از ۇجۇرايت.
10 بۇربۇرۇبۇزدا مندان 4 ـ 5 جۇز جال مۇردا سالىـ
ان سپاىمر بار بەيجىندە بجكى جانا تەشقى دەپ مەكى
شاار بار. بجكى شاارنەن بچندە مۇرداىى حان سارانى بار،
حان سارانىن بچندە پادشاىنۇن ۇردۇسۇ ۇردۇسۇ بار. بۇل سپاىدەر
بنرى مەدىن بنرى نۇتاشپ 30 كىلومىتر ۇزۇندۇقتۇ مەلۇت.

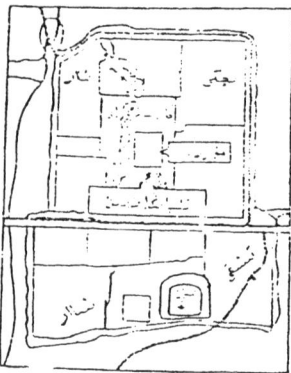

15 بەيجىن شاارنەن تۇبۇسۇنۇن فاراساكنز كوپ ـ كوك
جاشلدىقتىن ارىمسان جارقراعان التىن نۇردۇ كۇرۇسۇز.
ال التىن نۇر دەگىنەز، كۇنگۇ جامەلىشپ جارقراپ تۇرـ
عان مۇردامى پادىشا ۇردۇسۇنۇن مۇنارى. بۇل حاندىن
ۇردۇسۇ ازبر مۇزۇ ۋەگۇ ايلاندىرىلدى. كوك جاشىل كۇرۇنگۇن

ممنـد دەسەگىن، بايجمادە ولتۇرعان أربـدر ژې ـ ژاۇ سوال
دوردۇن بـالرىنا ارنۇردۇز بـای ئىككەن. وشوندۇئتان جا ـ
شىل بولزب كورۇنوت.

حان ساراینىن تۇشنۇك دارىبازاسىندا دائقتزۇ تىيانكان
مەن بار. ماۇجۇشى ار جاى بۇرنجى مايدا جانا بۇرنجى
وكتابردە تىيانكانىن ترنۇناسنا جمعپ قالق بارادىن كور- 25
دون كىچمەت. تىيانكانىن ايانتمان 60 ادام. بىر ساپ بو-
لزب ونۇژگو بولوت. ازس سجس ادام مۇردا بۇل جردن
شىـەرتندلر دوبوـۇ بوأىوندۇئۇن دسمندا كەلتىرە الببت.

شىرتندىلار دوبوـۇز دەشبىز مەنەن مە قالق بوش 30
تونۇئتان مۇرداعى بەيجمندى مسنـد كەلتىرەت. ال ۇباقىتـا
شاردەن بچمندە 60 مىڭ تونا شىـەرتندىلار جاتتى. انىـەن
نىن وچ كەمدىن جاتاعـردا بولمون مەس. ارباقتارى تنمپ قال
عان. كۇن جاسا كوچونۇ كورزنۇوس قاسپ سۇۇ قابتاپ
كەتجۇ، بوشتونۇئتان كيـن بيجـن بويۇن كوتوردۇ، باش ـ 35
تانى قەيىب ەلە جالجى سارى سۇۇلار جاناتۇرعان لـۇكـۇ
شۇيگو تەندۇرماپ، 5000 مەتردن اشق ۇستـ جاباغـان
ارى نۇرۇلدۇ. حان ساراینىن بچندەگى 3 جولۇ كولدۇن
(بېيجاي، جۇڭكاي، نانجاي) كولدۇن باردمى جۇنقۇر قا ـ
زلدى. مۇردا مڭ پلاس بولعون شجاجاي كولۇ. (مل مڭ 40
مۇردا شجاجاي كولزن «شىرندى كول» دەپ، اتاشجۇ)ازر
تازا كواكگو ايلاندى. ال جردە ابرم ادام تـۇژشوتۇرعمان
كولادور جانا دەم الزۇ باركتارى ۇرۇلدۇ. بىيجمندن مەلى
جايدەن كـۇنندۇرۇ ۇشـۇل كولگو بارپ سۇۇعا تـۇژشۇب
ۇاۇشوت.

حان ساراینىن تۇشنۇك باتىش تارابىندا جۇڭنانجاي كولۇ 45
بار. بىزربوردۇق مل وكموتۇتۇن ۇئۇ وشول جردە. انى

TEXT XVI-A***

مەنىڭ دەمكەچلەردىن بىيغاي پاركتن بئرەله كوبوروو ابردب
تۇرات. سىز بىيغاىا بارىپ تۆشتوك تارايتى تاراپ نوىوسۆزداء
تەپتىڭى،ماۇجۇ شى شتەپ جانتان جاردەپ ۋىلوپسۇ زىجىكگىزدەن
بئزدىن كەلبىەكتدگبىز قانداي بولىوق؟ ال كىزدە بەپ   50
جىندىن جىعش جانا تۆشتوك تارابى ونور جاي رابونبو-
لاز. كوبنوگون رازودودور وشزل جرگە نرىتوشوت. زا-
زودوردىن جانىا كوبنوگون باقچالار. بالدار ياسلى سپرت
ماىدانى جانا تۆزدوو جرەالجلق شتەدن باشقاراتورعان
جانا سالامانتق ساقتوو ورونداري قۇرۇلات. اۇ بئر رابون-   55
دورو جلمۆشجۇلاروزجۇن قنزمات نلا نورعان بوربوردوق
ورۇن بار بولوت.انىن بجندە سپورت اياتتارى، نەانر-
لار، مادانيات ساراپلارى جانا دوحورقانالارى بار بولوت.
جلمۆشجولاردن جاناق قاناسى زازوو رابونونون جانتدا بو-
لوپ، مونون باردعى جاعى قۇرۇلات.   60

كوردنىزنۇ قوۇز بايجەندىن تۆشتوك باتش تارابى

مادانى اغاتۇو رابونو بولوت. انن كولبو ازر-
قى بايجەنن نىچ بولۇگۇنۇزدا جولاڭ بۇنكۇل ماملكەتتن
جوعورۇو نلم تۇزلدوو ورگانى - جوككو پلمىلەر اكادە-
مياسى جانا 30 - 40 جا اتاقتۇو ونىۋەرستاتتر تحنىگر-   65
مدوو وشول جەرلەرگە قۇرۇلات. وشۇنن مەنن بۇل جەرلەر
كەلاجكتە بۇنزون ماملكەتتىن ملك ماانلىزۇو مادانى اعارتۇو
بوربوروو بولۇپ قالات.

مادانى اعارتۇو رابونونون باتشىندا شپبان وروۇ-   70
نۇ بار. بۇل ملک كوۇركوۇ رابون.

شبباندى ەل وكۇوتۇ كەلاجكتە بايجەندىن قادىمكى
داۇكا زالىوز مىراستارى بار ورۇندارمەدىن داربا جانا كوۇ-
لوكواۇز جولدور ارتلۇوو نۇتاشتەرىپ جاسوونو بلاندەپ جا-
تات. مۇزۇو مەنن بايجەندىن اۇ بئر جۇرى باقچانن اربئر   75
بولۇككۇرۇزنو ايلانات.

ۋالۇز بوربوردۇبۇز بايجىن قالقىىزدن قۇلازدا كەلە-
جەكتە سالتانانتلۇو جانا قوۇز بولۇپ بەرەت.

1   6)- Borborubuz Beyjin ata mekenibizdin jürö-
       gü.
       Beyjin shaarı uluu ata mekenibizdin borbor
       shaarı. 800 jıldın aldında Beyjin shaarı padı-
5   shalardın buyruq tüshürö turğan ordosu ele;
       teng 1949-jılı Junghua el respublikasi tüzül-
       gön kündön bashtap bul bayirqı shaar eldin
       öz borboruna aylandı.
       Beyjin eng chong jana eng qooz shaar. Düynödö
       minday saltanattuu, mınday qooz bayirqı shaar
10   az uchurayt. Borborubuzda mından 4-5 jüz jil
       murda salınğan sepilder bar. Beyjinde ichki
       jana tıshqı dep eki shaar bar. Ichki shaardın
       ichinde murdaqi han sarayı bar, han sarayının
       ichinde padishanın ordosu bar. Bul sepilder
       biri menen biri tutaship 30 kilometr uzunduq-
       tu eeleyt.
15   Beyjin shaarının töbösünön qarasangız köp kok
       jashıldıqtın arasınan jarqırağan altın nurdu
       körösüz. Al altın nur degenibiz, küngö chagıl-
       lïsïp jarqırap turğan murdaği padısha ordo-
       sunun munarası. Bul handın ordosu azır müzöy-
       gö aylandırıldı. Kök jashıl körüngön emne
20   desengiz, Beyjinde olturğan ar bir üy-bülö
       joldordun baarina ar türdüü baq tikken. Oshon-
       duqtan jashıl bolup körünöt.
       Han sarayın tüshtük darbasında dangqtuu
       Tıyannganmın bar. Maujushıy ar jılı birinchi
       mayda jana birinchi oktabrde Tiyannganmin
25   tribunasina chıgip qalq paradin közdön kechi-
       ret. Tıyannganmın ayantınan 60 adam bir sap
       bolup ötüügö bolot. Azir ech bir adam murda
       bul jerdin sïpırındılar döbösü bolğondugun
       ishine da keltire albayt. Sıpırındılar döbö-
       sü deshibiz menen ele qalq boshtonduqtan mur-
30   dagi Peyjindi eshine keltiret. Al ubaqıtta
       shaardın ichinde 60 ming tonna sıpırındılar
       jattı, anı menen ech kimdin jalağıda bolğon
       emes. Arıktarı tınıp qalğan. Kün jaasa ko-
       chönü körüngüs qalıp suu qaptap ketichü,
       boshtonduqtan kiyin Beyjin boyun kötördü,
35   bashqani qoyup ele chalchıp sarı suular jata
       turğan Lungshuygo tındırılıp, 8000 metrdin

ashıq üstü jabîlǧan arıq quruldu. Han sarayı-
nın ichindegi 3 chong köldün (Beyhay, Jung-
hay, Nanhay) köldün bardıǧı chungqur qazıldı.
Murda eng iplas bolǧon Sichahay kölü. (El eng
40   muŋda Sıchahay kölün"sıpırındı köl" dep atash-
chu) azır taza kölgö aylandı. Al jerde ayrım
adam tüshö turǧan köldör jana dem aluu park-
tarı quruldu. Beyjindin eli jaydın kündörü
ushul kölgö barıp suuǧa tüshüp oynoshot.
45   Han sarayın tüshtük batısh tarabında Hung-
nanhay kölü bar. Borborduq el ökmötünön üyü
oshol jerde. Anı menen emgekchilerdin Beyhay
parkın bir ele köpüröö ayırıp turat. Siz Bey-
hayga barıp tüshtük taraptı qarap qoyosuzda
teetigi, Maujushıy ishtep jatqan jer dep oy-
50   loysuz ichingisden 'Bizdin kelechektegibiz
qanday bolmoq?' Al kezde Beyjindin chıǧıshı
jana tüshtük tarabı önör jay rayonu bolup.
Köptögön zavoddor oshul jerge toptoshot. Za-
voddordun janina köptögön baqchalar, baldar
yaslıy sport-maydanı jana türdüü jırgalchı-
lıq ishterin bashqara turǧan jana salamattıq
55   saqtoo orundarı qurulat. Ar bir rayondordo
jumushchular üchün qızmat qıla turǧan borborduq orun bar bolot. Anın ichinde sport
ayanttarı, teatrlar, madaniyat sarayları jana dohtorqanaları bar bolot. Jumushchulardın
jataqqanası zavod rayonunun janında bolup,
60   munun bardıǧı jangı qurulat.
Körünüshü qooz Beyjindin tüshtük* batısh
tarabı madanı aǧartuu rayonu bolot. Anı kö-
lömü azırqı Beyjindin 1/3 bölügünöz da chong,
bütkül mamlekettik joǧorqu ilim izildöö or-
ganı - Junggo ilimder akademiyasî jana 30-
65   40cha ataqtuu universitetter, tehnigomdor
oshol jerlerge qurulat. Oshonu menen bul
jerler kelechekte bütün malmekettin eng maa-
nilüü madani aǧartuu borboru bolup qalat.
Madani aǧartuu rayonunun batıshında Shıysan
70   öröönü bar. Bul eng körköm rayon.
Shiysandı el ökmötü kelechekte Beyjindin qa-
dımkı dangazaluu mırstarı bar orundar menen
darya jana kölökölüü joldor arqıluu tutash-
tırıp jasoonu plandap jatat. Munu menen Beyjindin ar bir jeri baqchanın ar bir bölük
75   türünö ayalanat. Uluu borborubuz Beyjin qal-
qıbızdın qolunda kelechekte saltanattuu jana
qooz bolo beret.

TEXT XVI - A

1   Our capital city, Beijing, is the heart
of our fatherland.

The town of Beijing is the capital city
of our great fatherland. 800 years ago,
Beijing was the seat of the Emperor's

5   court from where orders came; in 1949,
beginning with the formation of the Chinese
People's Republic, this ancient city became
the capital of the people.

Beijing is a very big and very pretty
town. One can find few towns so pretty and
imposing in the world. In our capital,
there are remparts built 400 or 500 years
ago. There are two

10   towns in Beijing, called the Inner and
Outer city. In the Inner City is the former
Emperor's palace and inside this imperial
palace, the Emperor's suites. The remparts,
in one long stretch,

15   are 30 kms long. If you look on Beijing
from above, you can see, amid a
greensward, a gleaming golden light. The
light we are speaking about is that of the
towers of the old imperial suites which
shine, reflecting the sun. These imperial
suites have now been transformed into a
museum. As for the greenery we said one

20   could see, it is the many gardens planted
by each family on all the streets of
Beijing. This is why (the city) looks
green. At the Southern Gate of the
Imperial Palace is the well-known Tian An
Men (square). Each year Mao Zhuxi
(President Mao) on May 1st

25   and October 1st appears on the tribune and
hails the people as they march past. On
Tian An Men 60 people can march abreast.
Nobody remembers now the hill of refuse

which rose in this place. Through the tale of the Refuse Hill, the people recall the former

30   pre-Liberation Beijing. At that time, there were 60,000 tons of refuse in the town and besides there was no garbage dump. Canals were full. Rain made streets invisible, flooding them suddenly. After the Liberation, Beijing was emancipated. Among other things,

35   after letting the muddy, yellowish water of the Longxugou ditch settle, more than 8,000 meters of covered canals were built. Three big, deep lakes were dug inside the palace: Beihai, Zhonghai and Nanhai. The Sheshahai lake, formerly very dirty (people before

40   called Shesha lake the 'Refuse Lake') was transformed into a clean lake. Swimming pools and Rest Parks were built there. On summer days, the Pekinese come to the lake to play and bathe. On the

45   South-Western side of the Palace is lake Kongnanhai. There is the seat of the Central People's Government. A simple bridge separates it from the Beihai Workers' Park. When you go to Beihai, facing South, you'll be thinking deep down inside: "Over there is the

50   place where Mao is working. What will our future be like?"

      Earlier, the East and South districts of Beijing were industrial districts. Most factories were concentrated there. Around these factories numerous kindergartens, nurseries, sport grounds and various facilities designed to enhance welfare and

55   promote health are being built. In each district there is a catering center for worker. There one can find sports grounds, theaters, cultural and medical centers.

60 Workers' housing estates are near the
factories and have been newly built.

To the West of a picturesquely
landscaped Beijing lies the cultural-
educational district. Its surface
represents 1/3 of present day Beijing.
There the pan-national higher scientific
research center, the Chinese Academy of
Sciences and 30 or 40

65 famous universities and technical
institutes are being built. In this way,
the district will become in the future the
most important center for cultural
development in the whole country. West of
the cultural and educational district is
the Xisan valley. It

70 is a very picturesque place. In the
future, the government has planned to link
Xisan to the famous spots of Beijing rich
in ancient monuments through a river and a
tree-lined road. Thus,

75 each district in Beijing will look like
part of a garden. Our great capital city in
the hands of our Pekinese will continue to
be wonderful and pretty.

TEXT XVI - A

PARSING

1 1 20, etc.: Beijing is rendered as beyjin, or peyjin. Other, less known place names are given in more stable phonetical transcription;

1 42: beyjindin eli: calque for ch. Beijing ren: Pekinese

1 60: körünüsü qooz beyjindin tüshtük batys... an obvious error, read tündük.

Note the typical mixture of Russian (lexical idiomatic) and Chinese influences.

ЖУҢГО КЫРГЫЗ ТИЛИННИН

ОРФОГРАФИЯСЫ

(Башталгыч проекти)

« Кызыл- Суу Газета Басмасы

Артыш   1957

1- АЛФАВИТ

1- КЫРГЫЗДЫН ЖАҢЫ АЛФАВИТИ.

Кыргыздын алфавити, славян алфавитиндеги 31 тамга 2 белгисин толук алуунун сыртында, аган кыргыз тилинин эрекчелигине карап «Ө, У, Ң,» тамгалары кошулат, тамганын жалпы саны 36.

АЛФАВИТ

арапча	басма	жазма	окулушу	арапча	басма	жазма	окулушу
١	А	а	а	س	С	с	эс
ب	Б	б	бэ	ت	Т	т	тэ
و	В	в	вэ	ۇ	У	у	у
گ	Г	г	гэ	و	V	у	у
د	Д	д	дэ	ف	Ф	ф	эф
ه	Е	е	е	ح	Х	х	ха
يو	Ё	ё	ё (йо)	تس	Ц	ц	ца
ج	Ж	ж	жэ	چ	Ч	ч	ча
ز	З	з	зэ	ش	Ш	ш	ша
ى	И	и	и	ش	Щ	щ	ша
ى	Й	й	ый	ر			ичкертуу белги
ك	К	к	ка		Ь	ь	
ل	Л	л	эл	ى	Ы	ы	ы
م	М	м	эм				ажыратуу белги
ن	Н	н	эн		Ъ	ъ	
ڭ	Ң	ң	ың		Э	э	э
و	О	о	о	ٶ	Ю	ю	ю (йу)
ٶ	Ө	ө	ө	يا	Я	я	я (йа)
پ	П	п	пэ				
ر	Р	р	эр				

TRANSLATION   TEXT XVI-B

        - The Orthography of the Kirghiz Langua-
ge of China (Initial Draft)
        Printing House of the Qızıl Suu Geziti,
Artısh 1957.

        - Alphabet
        The New Kirghiz Alphabet
        The Kirghiz alphabet adopts in its
entirety the 31 letters and 2 signs of the Slavic
alphabet, adding to it the letters Ө, Y, Ң in view
of the peculiarities of the Kirghiz language; all
in all, it has 36 letters.

in Arabic / Printed form / Handwriting / How it reads

الـــعى سرلار

معـنجالةءل باسـباــس
1957 - جل ؤرؤمچَى

An excerpt from 'Algı Irlar' (First Songs),
Shınjang el basması, Ürümqü 1957 - the first
Kirghiz language anthology to be published after
1949.

الغى سۇز

جوڭگو كوممۇنىستىك پارتئياسى جەتەكچىلىك قىلغان
قاتى رەۋولۇتسئياسىنىڭ جەڭگىسى بىز وڭمۇۋ ئلم ـ مادانـ
مئانتىا ارتا قالغان از ۋاۇتاردى دا قاراڭغىلقى دۇيۋىشۇنوڭ
ازات ەتىپ، قالقىمىزدى ەكونومكائق جاعنداقى مرلۇۇ
جوۇكون ئلم جانا مادائىيات جاعنداقى زوشاۇۇجۇاۇقتان
ەكىزنىن قۇتناردى. قالقىسىردن نجنە بىرەك بىرلىك ورـ
نوب جرعالئۇۇ بئن زامان باشتالدى ۋەئمۇشتوكئ قاۇق
تۇرۇشۇندا بولغون ۋىرە ئىشى ۋۇن كوردۇ ەشن كورگون
بىزدەن اتالرىمىز ەشى ەشلرىمىز، اعلارىمىز ەشن جەگـ
لرىمىز جانا قۇرۇ ـ قۇردائىتارىمىز ۇشۇ كۇنگو ۋر زامانـ
ىمىزدەن جنئى باقئىتاۇۇ ەكئنئە كوز جۇگۇرنۇ كەلىپ،
قاۇ حانئر ۇۇتۇنا. جوڭگو كوممۇنىستىك پارتئياسىنا
كوسوۇبۇر مائزدىۇگا جس جزروكتون قىمش ايتات.

مئنا ۇشۇل جاعدايدى ۋرئن جاشتا كاگىن بولمۇ
مامات اقساقال جزروكتۇ تۇتۇندائىزۇجۇ سوزدۇر مئنن
نوما قوشوت:

گومسنداك زالىم بارىندا،
قايمدان جزروك جەر بولعون.
جوڭگودوڭ مومۇن ادامى.
جامقورلورعو جەم بولعون.

1   ALGI   SÖZ

      Junggo kommunisttik partiyası jetekchilik
      qilğan qalq revolutsiasının jengishi biz
      öngdüü ilim-madaniyatta artta qalğan az
      uluttardı da qaranggılıq düynösünön azat
5   etip, qalqibızdı ekonomikaliq jağındağı
      ezilüüchülüktön, ilim jana madaniyat jağın-
      dağı tushaluuchuluqtan negizinen qutqardı.
      Qalqıbizdın ichine bereke, birlik ornop jır-
      ğalduu bir zaman bashtadı. Ötmüshtögü qalq
      turmushunda bolğon oor azapti öz közü menen
10   körgön bizdin atalarıbiz menen eneleribiz,
      ağalarıbiz menen jengeleribiz jana qurbu-
      qurdashtarıbız ushu küngö öz zamanıbızdin
      chınği baqtiluu ekenine köz jügürtö kelip,
      ulu hansu ulutuna, Junggo kommunisttik par-
      tiyasına kösömübüz Maozıdongga chin jürök-
      tön alqish aytat.
15   Mına ushul jağdaydın özün 62 jashga kelgen
      moldomaymat aqsaqal jüröktö tolğondatuuchu
      sözdör menen ırğa qoshot.
                    Gomindang zalım barında
                    Qayğığan jürök cher bolğon
20   Junggonun momun adamı
                    Jemqorlorgo jem bolğon.

1   FOREWORD

The victory of the people's Revolution
under the direction of the Chinese
Communist Party, through the liberation
from the obsurantism of backward (as far as
scientific and cultural fields are
concerned) minorities similar to us
basically freed our

5   people from oppression in the economic
field and from its shackles in the
scientific and cultural fields. The
Revolution strengthened the unity and
happiness of our people, so that a period
of bliss began.

Our contemporaries, our brothers and
sisters, our fathers

10   and mothers who have witnessed with their
own eyes the harsh agonies in the life of
the people of yore, upon discovering that
their own present day epoch is actually
happy, from the bottom of their heart say
'thank you' to our leader Mao Ze Dong, to
the Chinese Communist Party and to the
great Han people. It is precisely

15   this contribution which Moldo Mambet
aksakal, having reached the age of 62, adds
to his poem in heartfelt words:

At the time of the Guomindan oppression,
My heart was harsh with sadness;
The wise man of China
Was cattle fodder.

TEXT XVI-C

PARSING

l. 2:   in Junggo, the -go element (ch. guð ▨) is
        pronounced [gc] and not [ɤc].
        jetekchilik kılgan: ... at the head of. In
        lit. kirg.: jetekchiligi astında.

l. 8:   ötmüshtögü: former. Not in Y; from öt-(Y-
        601) +/mIš/+/DAGI/: K-1096. In lit. kirg.:
        ilgerki.

l. 15: jagday: (Y-210) circumstance, factor.

l. 21: jemkor: cattle and monster, ogre, cannibal.
        In lit. kirg.: a gluttonous person.

2 — جاريق تاڭ

1   جعمش جافقان جارقمراپ،
جاجنى نۇرۇن جاريق تاڭ.
ازاتتىقتا جەتىشىنك.
ارىپ احقان باردىق جان.
5   قالقىم ۆجۆن العا دەپ،
قاىناب جەنتى جارىق زك.
مىكتىن قىزىلى باىراعىن،
قارماپ جەنتى جاريق تاڭ.
بىلاپ جاتقان ۋلەردى،
10   كۆلدۆردۆڭ سىن جاريق تاڭ.
ۆجكۇن ۋرمۇن ـ تۇقۇيدۇ.
ۋندۆردۆڭ سىن جاريق تاڭ.

ايتىپ، ايتىپ تۇگۇنگۆس،
ازىق بەردىك جاريق تاڭ.
15   باردىق دلگە تدىنەگىز،
باقىت بەردىك جاريق تاڭ.
مىـ ايال، قارى ـ جاش دەپمى،
ھەرجىمىز سەنى ارتىكداى.
تۇبولوك باقىت كەلتىرەدىك.
20   تۇگۇندۇ ارمان قالغىكداى.

TRANSLITERATION   TEXT XVI-D

Jumakub MAMBET   :   JARIQ TANG

1   Chiġish jaqtan jarqirap,
     Chachtı nurun jarıq tang.
     Azattıqqa jetishtik
     Arıp achqan bardıq jan.
5   Qalqim üchün alġa dep,
     Qaynap chıqtı jarıq tang
     Eriktin qızıl bayraġın,
     Qarmap chıqtı, jarıq tang.
     Iylap jatqan elderdi,
10   Küldurdüng sen, jarıq tang.
     Öchkön ormon-toqoydu
     Öndürdüng sen, jarıq tang.
     Aytıp, aytıp tügöngüs
     Azıq berding, jarıq tang.
15   Bardıq elge teptegiz,
     Baqıt berding, jarıq tang.
     Er-ayal, qarı-jash debey,
     Eerchiybiz senin artıngdan.
     Tübölük baqıt keltirding
20   Tügöndü arman qalqıngdan.

THE RADIANT DAWN

1   Glittering from the East
     The radiant dawn radiates its light.
     We have conquered freedom:
     Each soul discovers this marvel.

5   Hurrying onward my nation,
     The radiant dawn rises up quivering;
     The red flag of freedom
     The radiant dawn has brandished.
     To the groaning peoples

10   You brought joy, radiant dawn;
     The devastated forest
     You made grow, radiant dawn;
     With your songs, endlessly,
     You nurture us, radiant dawn;

15   To each nation, quite equally,
     You give happiness, radiant dawn,
     Men and women, young and old,
     We followed your steps.
     You instituted the final bliss,

20   You fulfilled the people's cherished dream.

TEXT XVI - D

PARSING

1 1: Chıgısh yaqtan: an allusion to the
       political motto: 'The East wind
       prevails over the West wind'.

1 13: tügön-güs : K-1186

1 15: teptegiz : K-1110

1 20: arman: J-69

كەرمە توو

(برلاز جيناغى)

جوڭگو جازغۇچىلار قوومۇنىڭ شىنجاڭ ۋ‍ ‍ـ
ەۇر اۇتونوم رايونلۇق بۆلۈمچىسى جىعىن
باسماعا دايارلايدى.

شىنجاڭ ەل باسمانسى
1962 — ۈرۈمچى

KERME TOO * (A Collection of Verses)
Prepared for printing by the Xinjiang-Uyghur
Autonomous District section of the Writers' Union
of China. The Xinjiang People's Printing House,
Urumqi 1962.
*: A mountain ridge in the Qızıl Suu Qırgız
District. It links the Tien Shan range to the
Pamirs.

ا. بايزاكوڭ

بەيجىن

١
بور بور ۇمىزۇلڭ ديسق ۇلۇۇ چولڭ بەيجىن،
جۇرەكمىزۇلڭ قان جۇكۇرتكۇن دەنەمدىن.
جاڭى جۇككو، جاڭى زامان قۇرۇۇدا،
پەرۇلەتاردىن تىكىلىف قىزىل جەلەككىن.

٥
باشتاعان سەن ەلىمىزدى جاڭشىككا،
چولڭ بۇرۇلۇش زالۇار بيمىك جاڭشىتە.
تۇزوق كىزندىن كىزىگۇن ورتۇن وچۇرۇپ،
جەتكزكەن سەن ەمگەكچىنى تەئدىككە.

قۇرۇزاما نسيك جاڭى بەيجىن باعىما،
١٠
سىيىمىقتانام قۇت تۇنەوزنو تالا ا.
وندۇرۇشتۇن ۇركۇندۇگۇن تەمىنە،
ەسكى تارىح باشىن ىيدى جاڭما.

بەيجڭىم سەن باقىت تالايدىن كىزۇزۇلڭ،   بەيپىلدىككتىن تەرەكسىك بەيجىككىم،
كۇيل باقمادىن باتراايتۇرمان كۇنۇزۇلڭ.   كەنەن ئجتىك مول بايلىقتىن ئيشكىن،
مەكەنىمدە باردىم ۇلۇت ئلدەمرىن،   ەل ارالىق ئدەبەردى دىتورۇپ،
قولدون الى كبزۇز اجقان ۇزۇۇقمزن.   ٢٠ تالا قالىمردىلڭ بۇتكۇل دۇينو ئلدەمرىن.

                                         سىنتماقبىز ۇيۇلتاشتاي بەرككەن،
                                         جاراتابىز باقىتمىزدى مەگەكتەن.
                                         باتىش ئلدەن بات جاتىندا ۇزۇبۇز،
                                         دوس قۇبانىپ، جات ورتۇنۇۇن جاڭشىتەن.

                                         ٢٥ سەنوت ساناپ ۇنۇكۇزۇدو مەكەنىم،
                                         كۇلدۇ جايناپ قالا مەنەن قىرلارىم،
                                         بەيجىن سەبكەن قىزىل ۇرۇق چەچەكتەپ،
                                         كۇلۇپ بەرسەن تروودان بيمىك تالابىم.

TRANSLITERATION   TEXT XVI-E

Amantur BAYSAK   :   BEYJING

1   Borborumsung, jiq uluu chong Beyjing
     Jürögösüng qan jügürtkön denemdin
     Jangı Junggo, jangı zaman quruuga,
     Proletardın tikting qızıl jelegin.

5   Bashtaqan sen elibizdi jenqishke,
     Chong burulush zalqar biyik jengiste.
     Tozok kündün küygön örtün öchürüp,
     Jetkizgen sen emgekchini tengdikke.

     Qurulgansıng jangı Beyjin bagıma.
10   Sıyıqtanam qut qongongo tagıma,
     Öndürüshtün örköndögön tempine,
     Qarı tarıh bashın iydi jangga.

     Beyjinggim sen baq tallaydın könüsüng.
     Gül baqchamdın batpay turgan künüsüng.
15   Az sandagan tuugan ulut elderin
     Qoldon alıp közün achqan özüngsüng.

     Beypildiktin tiregising Beyjinggim.
     Kenen achtıng mol baylıqtın eshigin
     El aralıq engsebizdi kötörüp,
20   Tang qaltırding bütkül düynö jer jüzün.

     Intımaqıbız uyul tashtay birikken
     Jaratıbız baqtıbızdı emgekten.
     Batısh elden bat jaqında ozobuz,
     Dos qubanıp, jat örttönsün jengishten.

25   Minüt sanap önügüshtö zamanım.
     Güldü jaynap qala menen qirlarım.
     Beyjing sepken qızıl uruq chechetep,
     Güldey bersin toodan biyik talabım.

                    1959 jıl, 10 ay.

BEIJING

1   You are my capital, grand sacred Beijing,
     The heart which makes blood flow in my
           body.
     In order to build a new China, a new epoch
     You hoisted the proletarians' red flag.

5   You led our people toward victory,
     The Great Bend is in this tremendous,
           sublime victory.
     Putting out the burning blaze of hellish
           days,
     You led workers to equality;

     You're being built, new Beijing, for my
           happiness,

10   I identify myself with whom brings luck to
           my shoulder.
     To the increasing rhythm of production,
     Old History bends its head on its breast.

     My Beijing, you are the heart of happiness
           imparted to me,
     The sun which never sets on my flower
           garden,

15   The one which opens the eyes, takes by the
           hand
     The blood-related minority peoples.

     You are the rempart of prosperity, my
           Beijing,
     You opened wide the door of opulence,
     You enhanced our international prestige,

20   You astonished the whole world.

     Our symbiosis is (like) that of embedded
           stones,
     We'll built our happiness through our work.
     In a near future, we'll overtake the
           Western countries,

Delighting thus our friends, let's
frustrate the enemy through our
victory.

25   My epoch develops minute by minute.
My hills and towns come into bloom,
The red seeds sown by Beijing (already)
    bloom,
May my noble yearning blossom higher than
    the mountains!

October 10, 1959

PARSING

1 21: ujul tashtay: not in Y; hewn building
stone. Y-814 gives another meaning
(quite close in this context): an
excrescence on the trunk of a tree.

1 27: Chechekte - not in Y. to blossom

فنلسۇۇ ادابياتى

2-1

1980

قـىرغىزچا تامغالاردـىن جـازىلىشـى جانا وقۇلۇشۇ

	تاءمغا				№		تاءمالار				№	
	اتاسى	چىك كاتى	اخىرتى كاتى	ورتوو كاتى	باتقا كاتى		اتاسى	چىك كاتى	اخىرتى كاتى	ورتوو كاتى	باتقا كاتى		
ö	,	,	,	,	,	16	!	١	١	ﺍ	١	1	a
p	ﻢ	ﻤ	ﭗ	ﻭ	٤	17	ﻢ.	ﺏ	ﺑ	ﻪ	ﺑ	2	b
r	ﺮ.	ﺮ	ﺮ	ﺮ	ﺮ	18	ﭫ	ﺏ	ﺐ	ﺑ	ﺑ	3	v
s	ﺲ	ﺲ	ﺲ	—	—	19	ﮒ	ﮎ	ﮒ	ﮎ	ﮒ	4	g
t	ﺕ	ﺕ	ﺖ	ﺗ	ﺗ	20	ﺩ	ﺩ	ﺪ	ﺩ	ﺩ	5	d
u	ﺞ	ﺞ	ﺠ	ﺟ	ﺟ	21	ﺝ	ﺝ	ﺠ	ﺟ	6	J
ü	ﺰ	ﺰ	ﺰ	ﺰ	ﺰ	22	ﺯ	ﺯ	ﺰ	ﺯ	ﺯ	7	z
f	ﻒ	ﻒ	ﻔ	ﻓ	ﻓ	23	ﯼ	ﯼ	ﯾ	ﺋ	ﺋ	8	i
h	ﮫ	ﺡ	ﺡ	ﻫ	ﻫ	24	ﯼ	ﯽ	ﻯ	ﯾ	ﯾ	9	y
ch	ﺞ	ﺝ	ﺡ	ﭽ	ﭽ	25	ﻚ	ﻚ	ﻜ	ﮎ	ﮎ	10	k
sh	ﻨﺎ	ﺶ	ﺷ	ﺶ	ﺶ	26	ﻞ	ﻝ	ﻼ	ﻟ	ﻟ	11	l
ı	ﯽ	ﯼ	ﻯ	ﻩ	,	27	ﻢ	ﻢ	ﻣ	—	ﻣ	12	m
e	.	.	ﻪ	ﻪ	.	28	ﻦ	ﻥ	ﻧ	ﺗ	ﺗ	13	n
ġ	ﻟ	ﺥ	ﺥ	ﻪ	ﻪ	29	ﺞ	ﺝ	ﺥ	ﮒ	ﮒ	14	ng
q	ﻦ	ﻕ	ﻗ	ﺰ	ﺰ	30	,	;	ﻭ	ﻭ	;	15	o

Transliteration/Translation
          Qırgızcha tamgalardın jazılıshı jana oqulushu
          The way of writing and reading letters in
                    Kirghiz
            Letters   Letters
Name. Isolated form. Final form. Middle f. Initial f.

NB! The alphabetical order is half Arabic and half
                    Russian

ۋن جەلدىققا ئارنالغان بۇتۇن كۈندۈۋ باشتالغمچ
مەكتەپ وقۇۋ كتەبى

(۱ - جەلدىقتىن العاچقى جارىم جەلددەس ۈچۈن)

الىپپە

شىنجاڭ ئاعارتۇۇ باسماسى

TRANSLITERATION/TRANSLATION

An excerpt from 'Alippe' (p. 85)

On jildıqqa arnalgan bütün kündüü bashtal-
gich mektep oquu kitebi (1 jildiqtın algach-
qi jarım jıldigı üchün)

Shinjang agartuu basmasi 1981

A daily primer for 10-year primary schools
(for the 1st semester on the 1st year)

Xinjiang Pedagogical Printing House, 1981.

الپىپەنى وقؤپ بۇتۇردۇم ‏ 1

كەچمىنەكەي ەاتاي ەەكتەپتەن كەلسە، اتاسى
ۇيدو جوق ەكەن. ال اتاسىنىن كەلىشىن اشمەشتىق
مەنەن كۆتتۇ. ال اتاسى ەشىكتەن كىرەبەردى مە-
نەن ەلە وتو قۇبانىچدا: ‏ 5

– اتا! مەن بۇگۆن «الپىپە»نى وقؤپ بۇتۇر-
دۇم. ەمى «الپىپە»نى قىمىنالباي شمەدىروقؤي الامىن.
«الپىپە»نىن باردىق ارىپتەردىن بىلىپ الدىم، – دەپ
قولۇندىاعى الپىپەسىن كۆرسۆتتۇ.

اتاسى، بالاسىنىن الپىپەنى وقؤپ بۇتۇرگۆن- ‏ 10
دۇگۆنو ايابای قاتتۇ قۇباندى.

– ەمى، ساعا مەن «تىل – ادابئيات» وقؤۇ
قۇرالىن الىپ بەرەمىن بالام، – دەپ ۇۇلۇنۇن ماڭ
دايىنان ۆپتۇ.

85

1   ALIPPENI OQUP BÜTÜRDÜM

Kichinekey Eltay mektepten kelse, atası
üydö joq eken. Al atasının kelishin ashıgıshtıq
menen küttü. Al atası eshikten kire berishi-
5   nen ele ötö qubanıchda:
Ata! men bügün 'Alippe'ni oqup bütürdüm. Emi 'Alippe'ni qıynalbay sıdır oquy alamın.
'Alippe'nin bardıq arıpterın bilim aldım - dep
qolundagı alippesin körsöttü.
10   Atası, balasının alippeni oqup bütürgöndügünö ayabay qatuu qubandı.
Emi saga men 'Til-Adabiyat' oquu
quralın alıp berermin, balam, - dep uulunun mang-
dayınan öptü.

1   I FINISHED READING THE PRIMER

         When little Eltay came back from school,
his father was not home. He waited
impatiently for his father to come back.
As

5   soon as his father crossed the threshold,
he greatly rejoiced: "Daddy! Today I
finished reading the primer. Now I can
read without difficulty and without
faltering; I managed to overcome all the
witchcraft of the primer" said Eltay,
showing the primer he was holding in his
hand.

10   His father was extremely delighted about
his son having finished reading the
primer. "Now I can buy the text-book
called 'Language and Literature', my son",
said he and kissed his son on the
forehead.

372

TEXT XVI - F(b)

PARSING

1 5: qubanıchda: a nominal predicate in /DA/
cf. text XIII 1 5

1 10: bütürgöndügünö... qubandı = bütür-
/GAn/+/LIk/+/(s)I/+ Dative case. K-1168, 1331,
1345

1 12-13: oquu quralı: cf. text I-G II-1

شىنجاڭ
قەرەز ئادەبىياتى

1

1981

TEXT XVI-G

قۇتتۇقتۇو

امانتۇر بايزاق

حاڅى مۇڭكۇ قۇرۇلغاندان كىن بارتىبازردىن ماركىسزىم . ئەنيبنزردەدك ۇلۇتتۇق سايباسان
شن حارغىرلغان نۇرىندا مامھكەمبىزردەكى باشقا ازىاندو ۇلۇتتار قاتاربندا قىرغىز ۇلۇتۇد
ۇزۇقتان بەرى زاربما كۇزكۇن ماقباتبنا جنتكەن مله. ٥٥٥٥ . جلى قىرغىزۇز قىرغىز ۇبلاستى قۇرۇ-
لۇب، ۇز تىل حابرۇ-زۇن حوامو قوبۇب تولۇتتۇز ورتوو جەيىن قىرغىز باللدارى ۇزۇنىتلنىشدە
وقۇزۇ قىرغىز ورتو مەكتەي دا قۇرۇلغان مله.

5

تىباننشان، باشبر متەتكندەكى كەرمەتوو اراسدامى تارقاق جاللايتەان
قىرغىز حارساحسلارى مانامكەت قابارىن، دۇنۇيو قابارىن، جمىرلك قابار-
لارى بر كۇزۇۇردۇ. ۇزتلادەوزگەرزدن قزرلىزۇگەرزدن ۇزتلىشە وقۇب سايسى دەتسىاتى. مادبى
امارتۇ حاتتان كۇزۇدوزشكو قاراب دەت العان مله. ٥٥٥٥ . جلى باشتالغان مله مله سول-
جۇلدۇزقتۇن كەبەبندەن بارتىبازردن ۇلۇتتۇق سايباسى بوزمۇنجىۇلۇقتا ۇچۇرادى، بۇزا
ۇلاشىپ كەلكەن لىن سىباز حانا «توزت كەشلدك» توبۇتۇن ١٥ جل حزركزۇزكىن قلمىشبارى

10

ايتىپ تۇگكۇكۇزۇ باقتت-زردنئارنا الىپ كەلدى. مادازىبات كۇقتورۇشۇز. دەب اتالغان وكۇ-
مونتۇزەزۇله شىلدك حۇركۇزۇۇب بارتىبازدن ۇلۇتتۇق سايباستى بۇزۇزانشتتەلكەن ادال .مكەله
تەرزبزدى بارس حومۇ حمارردى. «ۇلۇتتۇق مرەكجەلدك». «ۇلۇتتۇق بولكۇجۇۇلك». «مسكنى تىر-
لدىرۇۇ» «زاراملدىن.» «بارتنبازلىن قارىس جتساحلار نۇزۇۇ. «مشۇحدلقجۇربجلار.» مدت ماكىه

15

ماللاعازدارەم. «قاملمان مى» حانا باشقالار دەب قارا جابتادى. ايمم حەراهردە ۇلۇت قابار-
ندا حارا-ا» حوزۇزادى. بۇنۇ قابارىدا حاتتبىنا قابان . ئوبۇزۇ جمسارىب كەلانقبان حاش
حارۇز مۇزلارسرىا حانتامرداني حوق حالالاردى تاقدى. قابباى كىگكىرردى. اجنارلق كۇرۇشكو قارت
نى حاباب بوبۇز ادامگىرحلدك اسروۇى . زرماتىن. ووزرداريىىادا ابى استى قلدى بۇحۇزۇق
نۇرۇب حاشتادى. حابزۇ كرست. وئۇزۇلۇتتان. توبۇو ۇدۇز. قىرغى زاۇزۇ حوبۇز وئنۇرعان اكمجىلدك

20

ئاسومۇز بوۇب ماشتادى. قامازدىم بىر نۇرجۇزا جاللاۇبۇب حالان سباباى سوۇب قزرلىزۇز

3

دەگىن ،كى سوز، ئاتاىدان باشقا مىتەمە قالغانى جوق.

فرەز جارباۇلارنىن نورمۇسىدا وقتوبوعون داراجادا تومۇندووي باشتادى.

"جورت كشلك نوپ" نۇن ئالياى ئاشقا جادا ئەندان كىن عانا مليزدەكى بوورردوش ۇلۇت 25
ئاىرا كەلتۇرىبادى. جانا كەلتىرلمەكتە. بىل ۇجۇن قرعەز ملى. جۇككو كومىنتەر بارتىياسىنا
ئابىبوم رابونبۇق مل وكومونۇنو. جانا ئابونوم رابسونۇبوززداقى بووردوش ۇلۇت ملنە چىن
ۇرروبتون ئاتابز. بۇككۇن باقتلۇۇتاۇدا "قرعەز ادابياتى" مل مەنەن جۇزكورۇۇشۇپ 30
وباربابى قرعز ملى تارىجەندا مەمگەبىسز زور قوبانىش! بىز بۇ زور قۇبانىشتى قۇزتۇۇتاعان
كەربزدى باشقا ساۇلارعا، وقتوبوش مله كوركوم ونوروجەمارماجەلمىستادادا بەجال قالعانبزدى مىكە الىپ
قالام قابراتكەرلەرى جولدوبىتور كۇندۇ۔ نۇنكو ۇلاب قايراتقا قايرات قوشۇپ، "تورۇتتۇ" زامات
دابروۇز بۇزۇزىمامىستىن تالابسا لايتى، "قرعەز ادابياتى" جورنالنىن سابا۔بن جوەورۇكوتورۇپ،
نۇرمۇستون نۇبۇى كۇزكۇ۔نسوايلاندىرشمىز كەرەك۔ قرعز ملنن نورمۇشو "قرعەز ادابياتى"
جورنالىنى ازمتبى قانار بولامى. وشونداۇتان تۇزمۇشتۇ نەرلك ۇبرونۇۇۇز، ملىزدەكى بو۔ 35
وردوش زاۇلتارلدان ۇبرونۇۇۇز، مۇزۇزنۇ جانا ازىرقى زامان مل ارالىق ادابيات چەمارماجا۔
لەخان ۇبرونۇۇۇز كەرەك. وشونداۇى مله ئىدىبالىق ئانانبەردى مادانيات ئىلم ۔ ونور بىلە۔
بزدى قۇزز ونور جەۇمارماجە۔لاس جاقتان قابلياتى، جەبەردەكبىزدى
تەرەپ و۔نۇزۇپ ،ئنبردس ،ساى باقتىۇۇ ئايت نوبۇرامندا "قرعەز ادابياتى" ىن كۇجۇۇزۇون
دۇئا مەگكە مەمن نەرلك جبادبز تارتقازۇ ۇجۇن ئاعا باسىپ، ملىزدەن ،مكمەق مادانيەتتن 40
دائدا دەككمكى، كوجورۇس، ۇجۇن جان ئايامباى مىە قوشوباز!

TRANSLITERATION

Amantur BAYSAK

QUTTUQTOO

1   Jangı Junggo qurulgandan kiyin partiyabızdın
marksizm-leninizmdik uluttuq sayasatı-/
nın jarqıragan murunda mamleketibizdeki bashqa az sanduu uluttar qatarında Qırgız ulutu
da/ uzaqtan beri zarıga kürkön maqsatına jet-
ken ele. 1954-jılı Qızıl Suu Qırgız Oblastı
quru-/lup, öz til jazuusun jolgo qoyup, to-
luqsuz ortogo cheyin Qırgız baldarı öz ene
5   tilinde / oqudu. Qırgız orto mektebi da qurulgan ele.
Tianshan, Pamir etegindeki Kerme Too arasın-
da tarqaq jaylashqan/ Qırgız charbachıları,
malmeket qabarın, dünöyö qabarın, jerlik
qabar-/ lardı, ır, küülördü, öz tilinde ugup,
"Qızıl Suu Geziti" öz tilinde oqup, sayası
ıqtısatı, madani / agartuu jaqtan güldönüsh-
kö qarap bet algan ele. 1957-jılı bashtalgan
10   eng ele "sol"chulduqtun kesepetinen partiyabızdın uluttuq sayasatı buzgunchuluqqa uchuradı. Buga / ulashıp kelgen Lin Biyav jana
"tört kishilik" toptun 10 jıl jürgüzgön qıl-
mıshtarı / aytıp tügötküsüz baqıtsızdıqtardı
alıp keldi. "Madaniyat köngtörüshü" dep atal-
gan ökü-/mötsüzdük biylik jürgüzülüp, partiyabızdın uluttuq sayasatı boyuncha ishtelgen
adal emgek-/terbizdi barın joqqo chıgardı.
"Uluttuq erekchelik", "uluttuq bölgünchü-
15   lüq", "eskini tir-/ildirü", "ubarachılıq",
"partiya qarshı chıqınchılar tubu", "syu-
jıngjuychılar", "chet elge / baylagandar",
"qagılgan mıq" jana bashqalar dep qara chap-
tadı. Arım jerlerde ulut qatar-/ında jazaa-
ga uchuradı. Ushu qatarda jangı gana qanat-
quyruq chıgarıp kele jatqan jash / jazuu-
chularıbızga qapqaydaqı joq jalaalardı tang-
dı. Qalpaq kigizdi. Achınarlıq küröshkö
tart-/tı. Qamaq quydu. Adamgerchilik abiroy-
urmatın, oor darajada ayaq astı qılıp,
20   tumchuq/turup tashtadı. Jazuu geziti, oquu-
luqtar toqtotuldu. Qırgız ulutu choguu ol-
turgan ak(i)mchilik / rayondu bölüp tashtadı, qagazdın bir burchuna chala jugup qalgan

síaday bolup Qızїl Suu / degen eki söz, tam-
gadan bashqa eshteme qalganı joq.
Qırgız charbachılarının turmushu da oqshobo-
gon darajada tömöndöy bashtadi. "Tört kishilik top"tun talpagı tashqa jayılgandan kiyin
25 gana elibizdegi boordosh ulut-/targa oqshosh
Qırgız elinin tangı atıp jangı doorgo qaray
qadam qoydu. Murunqu jogotulgandardın barı /
qalıbına keltirildi jana keltirilmekte. Bul
üchün Qırgız eli, Junggo kommunister partiya-
sına / aptonom rayonduq el ökümötünö jana
aptonom rayonubuzdaqı boordosh ulut eline
chın / jüröktön alqish aytabız. Bügün baqt(ı)-
luu tangda "Qırgız Adabiyatı" el menen jüz
köröshüp / oturganı, Qırgız eli tarıhında
ebegeysiz zor qubanısh! Biz bu zor qubanısh-
30 tı quttuqtagan / kezibizde, bashqa salalarga
oqshosh ele körköm önör chıgarmachılıgında
da, bechel qalgan(ı)bızdı eske alıp / qalam
qayratkerleri joldoshtor kündü-tüngö ulap,
qayratqa qayrat qoshup, "Törttü **zaman-/dan-**
dıruu"uluu mildetinin talabına layıq, "Qırgız Adabiyatı" jurnalın(ı)n sapasın jogoru
kötürüp, / turmushtun tunuq küzküsünö aylan-
dır(ı)shıbız kerek. Qırgız elinin turmushu
"Qırgız Adabiyatı" / jurnalının azıqtıq qay-
nar bulagı. Oshonduqtan turmushtu tereng
35 üyrönüshübüz, elibizdegi bo-/ordosh uluttar-
dan üyrönüshübüz, murunqu janaazırqı zaman
el aralıq adabiyat chıgarmachı-/lıgınan
üyrönüshübüz kerek. Oshondoy ele idiyalıq
taanımıbızdı, madaniyat ilim-önör bilim-/
bizdi qooz önör chıgarmachılıq jaqtan qa-
bılıyat, cheberdigibizdi / tır(ı)shıp ös-
türüp, elibizdin bay baqt(ı)luu ayant-topu-
rag(ı)nda "Qırgız Adabiyatı"n güjürmön-/dük
emgek menen tereng jıldız tartqızuu üchün
alga basıp, elibizdin engselü madaniyatın-/
40 dagı da denggelge kötörüsh üchün jana ayabay esc qosholu!

       Quttuqtap aytam ırımdı,
       Qubanchım boygo tıgıldı.
       Jurnaldın atın uqqanda,
       Monchoq jash közdön ırgıdı.

45   Jurnaldın chıgar qabarı,
Chaqmaqtay elge taradı.
Changqaqtı qımız bashqanday,
Qırgızdın qandı qumarı.

50   Jonghua elim bay terek,
Güldönüp shagı tengselet.
Bir shagı anın Qırgız el,
Baq nuru turat sebelep.

55   Ay jarıp turmush ongoldu,
Aq bulut oqshoyt qoy tobu.
Qomuzgu zoosun jangırtıp,
Qordolgon küchtüü bozosu.

60   Jol achıldı saparga,
Jurt ilimge attana.
Önör-ilim bolboso,
El tuzun q(ı)yın aqtarga.

THANKS-OFFERING

1   After the building up of the New China,
in the blinding light of our Party's
marxist-leninist national policy, together
with other minority peoples of our State,
the Kirghiz people too had reached the goal
it had aspired to since long. After the
foundation in 1954 of the Kızıl-Suu Kirghiz
children began to study in their

5   own language up to the incomplete
secondary school. A Kirghiz secondary
school had been founded too.

The Kirghiz cattle-breeders who practise
transhumance in small groups in the Kerme
Too on the slopes of Tian Shan and Pamir,
when hearing news of the State, of the
world, of their own land, poems and songs
in their language, when reading in their
own language the newspaper "Kızıl Suu", had
taken over the control of their
pedagogical, cultural, economic and
political development. As soon as 1957,
because of the abjectness of ultra-leftism,
the national

10   policy of our Party suffered from
deviationism. For ten years, the crimes of
Lin Biao and of the Gang of Four who
followed this line brought about
innumerable calamities. The so-called
'Cultural Revolution' ushered in the rule
of anarchy and all the exhausting, honnest
work carried out according to the national
policy of our Party was annihilated.
'National particularism', 'ethnic
separatism', 'resurrection of the past',
the 'unrest', 'the groups of anti-Party

15   saboteurs', the 'revisionnists', 'the
foreign henchmen', 'the hidden dissidents',
etc. obscured everything. In some places,
whole ethnic groups were submitted as such
to repression. In such a danger, our young

writers who were just beginning to dawn
were slandered in the most impossible way.
A bonnet was put on their heads. This
offense led to a struggle. They were
jailed. Putting everything topsy-turvy in
a heavy manner, this almost crushed
humanish, decency

20   and honor. The written press and education
were suspended. The self-governing
district where the Kirghiz people is
concentrated was on the verge of being
divided. Those two words, black as ink,
"Kızıl Suu", vaguely placed side by side on
a piece of paper, were supposed to be
nothing more than letters. The Kirghiz
cattle breeders' life deteriorated to an
unbelievable degree.
    As soon as the hide of the Gang of Four
was spread on the ground, a new dawn broke
for the Kirghiz people as well as for the

25   sister nationalities of our people which
marched toward a new era. Everything which
had been previouly destroyed was and is
being restored. For this, the Kirghiz
people wholeheartedly thanks the Communist
Party of China, the local people's
government and the ethnic brother
population of our autonomous district. In
the light of today's happy new dawn, the
fact that "Kirghiz Literature" recovered
its people is, in the history of the
Kirghiz people, a tremendous happiness.
Upon celebrating this extremely great
happiness and remembering how clumsy we
still are in the field of artistic

30   production - as in other sectors - we,
comrades, enthusiasts of the pen, laboring
day and night, adding energy to energy, in
comformity with the urge of the great duty
of the Four Modernization, increasing even
higher the quality of the review 'Kirghiz
Literature', must transform ourselves into
a faithful mirror of life. The Kirghiz
people's life is the frothing, nourishing

spring of the review 'Kirghiz Literature'.
This is why we must study life

35   in depth, draw our inspiration from the
model of brotherly peoples of our nation,
of the works of contemporary and ancient
international literature. In the same way,
assiduously developing our skill, the
aesthetic acceptability of our works, our
technical and artistic cultural
proficiency, our ideological knowledge, let
us make our contribution, without sparing
our souls, to rise ever higher the level of
culture toward which our people strive,
striding forward so that 'Kirghiz
Literature" may deserve, thanks

40   to a most heroic labor, to take root
deeply in the rich and happy territory of
our people.

    Upon offering my congratulations, I sing
        my song;
    Joy pierces my breast.
    Upon hearing the name of the review
    A pearl came bursting to my eyes.

45   The new about its publication
    Spread like a spark among our people;
    Just as kumys quenches thirst,
    It quenched the Kirghiz' passion.

    My people in China is an aspen

50   Its branches sway and blossom;
    One of them is the Kirghiz people,
    A ray of joy bathes it.

    The moon is shining, life returned to
        normal,
    The white cloud is a little flock of
        sheep,

55   Restoring to health the komuz
    The strong bozo became rejuvenated.

    The way is open for travelling,
    My people, on horseback toward Science!

It is a hard task for whom has no
knowledge

60   To pay one's debt toward the people.

TEXT XVI-G

PARSING

1. 4: toluksuz orto: incomplete secondary school
(8 instead of 10 years) cf. rus.: неполная
средняя (школа)

1.15: shyujıngjuyı+chı+lar: note the Kirghiz suffix /čI/ = -ist added to a han word: xiu-
zhengzhuyi

1.17: qanat-quyruq: young, inexperienced writers
are compared to fledgelings

1.38: ayant: not used in the oral language

1.56: kordolgon...bozo: an alkoholic sweet and
sharp beverage made with grain (with or
without hops), similar to the Slavic 'bra-
ga', to which sugar or honey has been added
(chaptalization) to make it stronger

1.58: attana = attan (Y-80) + a!

1.60: el tuzun...aqta: Y-39: to thank for one's
salt, i.e. to pay one's debt to...

✥ ✥

«ﻞ ﮔﯦﺰﯨﺘﻰ» ﺑﺎﺵ ﻣﺎﻗﺎﻻ ﺟﺎﺭﯨﻴﺎﻟﯩﺪﻯ: 1

ﭘﺎﺭﺗﯩﻴﺎﻧﯩﯔ ﻛﯚﭼﯚﺭﻣﻮﻧﺪﯛﻟﯚﻛﯚ ﺋﯩﺪﯨﻴﺎ ﺟﺎﻧﺎ ﺳﺎﻳﺎﺳﻰ

ﺟﺎﻗﺘﺎﻋﻰ ﺟﻮﺋﻮﺭﯛ ﺑﯩﺮﺩﻩﻳﻠﯩﻜﯩﻨﺪﻩ

ﺷﯩﻨﺰﺍﯕﻪ، ﺑﻪﻳﺠﯩﯖ، 10-ﻧﻮﻳﺎﺑﯩﺮ ﻗﺎﺑﺎﺭﻯ. « ﻞ

5   ﮔﯦﺰﯨﺘﻰ» ﺑﯜﮔﯜﻥ ﭘﺎﺭﺗﯩﻴﺎﻧﯩﯔ ﻛﯚﭼﯚﺭﻣﻮﻧﺪﯛﻟﯚﻛﯚ ﺋﯩﺪ-

ﻳﺎ ﺟﺎﻧﺎ ﺳﺎﻳﺎﺳﻰ ﺟﺎﻗﺘﺎﻋﻰ ﺟﻮﺋﻮﺭﯛ ﺑﯩﺮﺩﻩﻳﻠﯩﻜﻜﻪ

ﺩﯦﮕﻪﻥ ﺗﻪﻣﺎﺩﺍ ﺑﺎﺵ ﻣﺎﻗﺎﻻ ﺟﺎﺭﯨﻴﺎﻟﯩﺪﻯ.

ﺑﺎﺵ ﻣﺎﻗﺎﻻﺩﺍ ﻣﯘﻧﺪﺍﻱ ﺩﻩﻟﻪﺕ: 12-ﺗﯚﺭﺯﯛﻟﺘﺎﻱ

ﻗﺎﺑﯩﻠﺪﺍﻏﺎﻥ ﭘﺎﺭﺗﯩﺎ ﺋﻪﺭﺟﻪﺳﻰ ﺋﯩﺪﯨﻴﺎ ﺟﺎﻧﺎ ﺳﺎﻳﺎﺳ-

10   ﺟﺎﻗﺘﺎ ﺟﻮﺋﻮﺭﯛ ﺑﯩﺮﺩﻩﻳﻠﯩﻚ ﺑﻮﻟﯚﻧﯩﯔ ﭘﺎﺭﺗﯩﺎ ﻗﯘﺭﯗﻟﯚﺷﯩﻨ-

ﺩﺍﻏﻰ 3 ﺗﯚﺭﺩﯛﯕ ﻧﻪﮔﯩﺰﻛﻰ ﺗﺎﻻﻳﯩﺘﯩﻦ ﺑﯩﺮﯨﻨﭽﻰ ﺑﺎﻻﺑﻰ

ﻏﻪﻟﺪﻯ. ﺑﯩﺰﻝ—ﭘﺎﺭﺗﯩﺎ ﺑﯩﺰﺩﯨﻦ 60 ﺟﯩﻠﺪﺍﻥ ﻛﯚﭘﯜﺭﯛﻭﻙ

ﺯﺑﺎﻏﺘﺎﻥ ﺑﻪﺭﻛﻰ ﺑﺎﺋﺘﯩﺮﺩﯨﻖ ﻣﻪﻧﻪﻥ ﻛﯚﺭﯗﺵ ﻗﯩﻠﻐﺎﻥ

ﺋﺎﺟﺮﯨﺒﺎ-ﺳﺎﺑﺎﻗﺘﺎﺭﯨﻨﯩﻦ ﺗﻪﺭﯦﻞ ﻗﻮﺭﯗﺗﯚﻧﺪﯛﺭﯛ، ﺷﯘﻥ

15   ﺩﻭﻱ ﻣﻪﻟﻪ ﺟﺎﻏﻰ ﺗﺎﺭﺟﯩﺨﻰ ﺩﻭﺋﻮﺭﺩﯛﻥ ﺋﺎﺭ ﺑﯩﺮ ﭘﺎﺭﺗﯩﺎ

ﺋﺎﻥ -ﺋﺎﺑﺎﺗﺎﻧﯩﺌﯚﯕﯚ ﺟﺎﻗﺘﯩﺮﻩﺳﻰ.

ﺑﺎﺵ ﻣﺎﻗﺎﻻﺩﺍ ﻣﯘﻧﺎ ﺑﯚﻻﺭ ﻛﯚﺭ-ﺳﯚﺗﯚﻟﯚﺕ: ﺋﺰ—ﺭ.

12-ﺗﯚﺭﺯﯛﻟﺘﺎﻱ ﻭﺟﻮﺗﻮﺭﯛﻥ ﺯﯨﺒﺮﯗﻧﯚﯕ ﺋﺎﺭﻗﻪﻟﯩﯚ، ﺑﯚﺗﻜﯚﻝ

ﭘﺎﺭﺗﯩﺎﻧﯩﻦ ﺗﺎﻧﯩﻤﻪﻥ 12-ﺗﯚﺭﺯﯛﻟﺘﺎﻱ ﻗﺎﺑﯩﻠﺪﺍﻏﺎﻥ ﺑﻪﺭﻭ-20

ﮔﯩﺮﺍﻣﺎ ﻧﻪﮔﯩﺰﯨﻨﺪﻩ ﺑﯩﺮﺩﯨﻜﻜﻪ ﻛﻪﻟﺘﯩﺮﻭﭖ، ﭘﺎﺭﺗﯩﻴﺎﻧﯩﻦ

ﺋﺎﺭ ﺩﺍﺭﺍﺟﯩﻠﯚﯘ ﺯﯨﺒﯚﻣﺪﺍﺭﻯ ﺟﺎﻧﺎ ﺑﺎﺭﺩﯨﻖ ﻛﯚﻣﭙﺎﺭﺗﯩﺎ

ﺋﯚﭼﯚﻟﻮﺭﯗﯓ ﺋﯩﺪﯨﻴﺎ ﺳﺎﻳﺎﺳﻰ ﺟﺎﻗﺘﺎ ﭘﺎﺭﺗﯩﺎ ﺑﻮﺭ-

ﺑﯚﺭﺩﯛﯕ ﻛﯚﻣﻪﺗﻪﺗﻰ ﻣﻪﻧﻪﻥ ﺟﻮﺋﻮﺭﯛ ﺩﺍﺭﺍﺟﺎﺩﺍ ﺑﯩﺮ-

ﺩﻩﻱ ﺑﻮﻟﻮﺗﯚﺭﻣﺎﻥ ﻗﻪﻟﯚﯘ-ﻛﻪﺯﻩﻛﺘﻪ، ﺑﯚﺗﻜﯚﻝ ﭘﺎﺭﺗﯩﺎ-25

ﻧﯩﻦ ﺋﯩﺪﯨﻴﺎ ﻗﯚﺑﯜﻟﻐﺎﻥ ﻣﺎﺋﻠﯚﯘ ﻣﻪﻟﺪﻩﺗﺘﻪﻧﻪﻣﻪ. ﺑﯩﻞ—

ﭘﺎﺭﺗﯩﺎ ﺑﯩﺰﺩﯨﻦ ﺗﺎﺭﯨﺞ ﺗﺎﻳﺸﯩﺮﻏﺎﻥ ﺯﻭﺭ ﻣﻪﻟﺪﻩﺗﺘﻪﻧﻪﻣﻰ

ﺋﯚﺯ ﺋﯚﺗﯚﻧﯚ ﺋﻟﯚﯘ ﺟﻪ ﺋﺎﻻﻻﺑﺎ-ﺳﺘﻤﻨﺪﺍ، ﺑﯚﺗﻜﯚﻝ ﻣﺎﻣﻠﻪ-

ﻛﻪﺗﺘﻪﮔﻰ ﺋﺎﺭ ﺯﯚﻟﯚﺕ ﻣﻠﻨﻨﯩﻦ -ﺳﯚﺗﺴﯩﺎﻟﯩﺴﺘﯩﻚ ﺯﺍﻣﺎﻥ

ﺩﺍﺷﺘﺮﯗﺯ ﻗﯚﺭﯗﻟﯚﺷﯩﻨﺪﺍ ﺟﺎﻟﺒﻰ ﺑﻪﺗﻜﯚﻯ ﺟﺎﻏﻰ ﻗﺮ-30

ﺩﺍﺍﻟﺪﻯ ﺑﺎﺭﺩﯨﻘﻘﺎ ﻛﻪﻟﺘﯩﺮﯦﺸﻨﻪ ﺟﻪﺗﻪﻛﭽﯩﻠﻤﻚ ﻗﻪﻟﯚﯘ

ﺟﻪ ﺋﺎﻻﻻﺑﺎ-ﺳﺘﻤﻨﺪﺍ ﺑﺎﻳﻼﻧﯩﺸﯩﻨﯚﯘ ﺯﻭﺭ ﺋﯩﺶ.

ﺑﺎﺵ ﻣﺎﻗﺎﻻﺩﺍ ﻣﯘﻧﺎ ﺑﯚﻻﺭ ﻛﯚﺭ-ﺳﯚﺗﯚﻟﯚﺕ: 11-ﺗﯚﻭﺕ-

نىك بوربوردۇق كومتەت 3 حالىى حىنالىــىنان
بەرى، بارنىۋا بوربوردۇق كومتەتى جەندەتتى، ئاڭك
يانتان ئزدووو ۋشوندوى ەلە ئالتىاتتى نەگـــز
قىلىۇۇا بەكەم تزرۇپ، جوءورتۇ جەتەكجەلەك نت
مەردەكى مەنەن جەچكن ئدنس ئولدوئۇپ، باش-
الامانجەلمەتى، ۋگشوپ، مارگسمزمەدنك لۇشىمەندىجان-
نا ئۇردۇۇ ەمزماتتارئا جەتەكجەلەك قىلاتزرەان بىر
ئاتار فاگجەن، سايا-اتتاردى بەلگماەپ جانا نزجە-
دەشتىرۇپ اتقارۇپ، مامەلەكەتمبزدن ارقايسى جاق
تارىندا وتو زور قۇبانارلۇۇ وزگەرۇشتوردۇ بارەتە-
ئا كەلتەردى. ئاماتىات بۇتكۇل بارتىياداءى جول-
دوشتوردۇ تاربىيالادى، ئبرەجا ح بارتىيابزدن-
مامەلەكەتبمز ئوزۇۇاماندان بەرتى ئارىجاتتەمىەتشەلۇۇ
بىر قاتنجا ەا-ەلە جونۇ ندوگۇ جەجمەسىنە بولەونزىۇ-
رونۇشتۇ كەگرى قۇلاج جابدىروۇ ارەملۇۇ، بۇتكۇل
بارتىيانن ئدىدا جانا سياسى جاقاىئاءىبەردەدەكگن
زور داراجادا ئلكەرەلەتتى.

35

40

45

50

(ژلاندەسى 3 ۇ بەتتە)

TRANSLITERATION

1   "El Geziti" bash makala jarıyaladı:
     PARTIYANIN KÜJÜRMÖNDÜÜLÜGÜ IDIYA JANA SAYASI
            JAQTAGI JOGORU BIRDEYLIGINDE
5   Shinhuashe, Beyjin, 10-noyabır qabarı. "El
     Geziti" bügün Partiyanın küjürmöndüülügü idi-
     ja jana sayası jaqtagı jogoru birdeyliginde
     degen temada bash makala jarıyaladı.
     Bash makalada mınday delet: 12 qurultay
     qabıldagan partiya erejesi idiya jana sayası
10   jaqta jogoru birdeylik boluunu partiya qurulu-
     shundagı 3 türdüü negizgi talaptın birinchi
     talabı qıldı. Bul - partiyabızdın 60 jıldan
     köbüröök ubaqıttan berki baatırdıq menen kürösh
     qılgan tajrıba - sabaqtarının tereng qorutun-
15   dusu, oshondoy ele jangı tarihıy doordun ar
     bir partiya uyumu jana ar bir partiya müchö-
     sünö qarata chıgargan saltanattuu chaqırıgı.

     Bash makalada mına bular körsötülöt: azır
     12-qurultay öjöttörün üyrönüü arqıluu, bütkül
20   partiyanın taanımın 12-qurultay qabıldagan
     pirogiramma negizinde birdikke keltirip, par-
     tiyanın ar darajaluu uyumdarı jana bardıq
     kompartiya müchölörün idiya jana sayası jaq-
     ta partiya borborduq komiteti menen jogoru
25   darajada birdey bolo turgan qıluu kezekte,
     bütkül partiyanın aldına qoyulgan maanilüü
     mildettenme. Bul --
     partiyabızdın tarıh tapshırgan zor mildet-
     tenmeni öz üstünö aluu je ala albastıgına,
     bütkül mamlekettegi ar ulut elinin sotsia-
30   yalistik zamandashtıruu qurulushuna jalpı
     betkey jangı qırdaaldı bardıqqa keltirishine
     jetekchilik qıluu je qıla albastıgına bayla-
     nıshtuu zor ish.

     Bash makalada mına bular körsötülöt: 11-iret-
     tik borborduq komitet 3-jalpı jıynalıshınan
35   beri, partiya borborduq komiteti chındıqtı
     amalıyattan izdöödö, oshondoy ele amalıyattı
     negiz qıluuda bekem turup, jogorqu jetekchi-
     lik ishmerdigi menen chechekin adıs qoldonup,

TEXT XVI-H(a)

bash alamanchılıqtı ongshop, marksizmdik
40 lushyendi jana türdüü qızmattarga jetekchilik
qıla turgan bir qatar fangyın,sayasattardı
belgilep jana izchildeshtirip atqarıp, mamle-
ketibizdin ar qayshı jaqtarında ötö zor qu-
banarluu özgörüshtördü bardıqqa keltirdi.
45 Amalıyat bütkül partiyadagı joldoshtoru tar-
biyalardı, ayrıqcha "partiyabızdın mamleketi-
bizdi qurulgandan berki tarıhına tiyeshelüü
bir qancha masele jönündögü chechimi"ni bolgon üyrönüshtü kengiri qulach jaydıruu arqıluu, bütkül partiyanın idiya jana sayası jaq-
50 tıgı birdeyligin zor darajada ilgeriletti.

(Ulandısı 3-bette)

TEXT XVI - H(a)

1   The 'People's Daily's (Ren Min Ri Bao)
    leading article reports:

    The Party's dynamism lies in its high
    degree of Unity (Like-mindedness) in the
    ideological and political fields.

5   A dispatch from the New Agency
    Xinhuashe, November 10, Peking:

    The leading article of today's 'People's
    Daily' turns on the theme: "The Party's
    dynamism lies in its high degree of unity
    in the ideological and political fields".
    In the leading article it is said: the
    Party statutes adopted at the 12th Congress
    consider

10 a high degree of unanimity in the
    ideological and political fields to be the
    first among the three basic demands in the
    building of the Party. This is the profound
    conclusion drawn from the lessons and the
    long experience gained by our Party through
    more than 60

15 years of heroical struggle: similarly it is
    a solemn challenge for a new historical era
    to each cell and each member of the Party.

    The leading article points out: Now,
    through the study of the documents of the
    12th Congress, having brought down to
    unity the whole Party's knowledge on the
    basis of the program adopted by the 12th
    Congress, each Party cell at all levels and
    each member

20 must remain united to the highest degree
    with the Party's Central Committee in the
    ideological and political fields - such is
    at

25 this moment the crucial task set before
    the whole Party. This hard test is linked
    to the possibility or impossibility for

our Party to bring down to a coordinated
whole the new situation during the

30 development of the socialist modernization
of each nationality in the entire state, to
the capacity or incapacity for our Party to
take charge of the difficult tasks demanded
of it by History.

The leading article points out that:
since the 3rd general meeting of the 11th
Central Committee, the Party Central
Committee

35 has carried through to a successful
conclusion all the very heartening changes
which took place in various fields in our
state, carrying out, after fixing and
exploring them, its policies and a series
of political campaigns enhancing various
services and the Marxist line, putting an
end to anarchy, using decisive methods

40 with the skill of a high leadership,
looking for the truth on the basis of the
activities (=facts) and, for this very
reason, remaining steadfast in the
fulfilling of its task. Action has

45 educated all the comrades of the Party
and, in particular, has improved to a high
degree the whole Party's ideological and
political unanimity thanks to a wide
expansion of the study of the "Decisions
about a series of problems concerning the
history of

50 the Party since the foundation of our
state".
(to be continued on p 3)

PARSING

Compare the political jargon of this text with that of text XII. Note the strinking mixture of Russian and Han political terms and catchphrases.
The former are less visible, as idiomatic calques, but are often underlying:

birdikke keltir-: to reduce to unity = rus.: свести к единству
jogoru darajada: to the highest degree = rus.: в высшей степени
...tarıh tapshirgan zor mildettenme: the difficult problem placed upon the Party by History = rus.: трудная задача, возложенная на Партию историей
mildettenmi öz üstünö al-: to take upon oneself the burden = rus.: взять на себя задачу

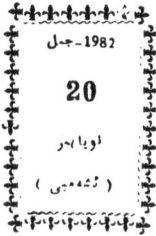

قىزىلسۇۋگە زىنتى

1982-جىل

20

(ئشمەسى)   اويا بار

克改勒苏报   (ح. ح)

419 - نال – نال

اپتونوم رايوندۇق ۇلۇتتار ىنتىماقتەمى بويۇنچا   1
ماقتاپ-سىلىۋو جىنالىشى جەگىشتۇۋ ئاقتادى

جىنالىشى اپتونوم رايوندۇعۇ ارۇلۇت ئەاى، دەلك جەر ۋزدۇشتۇ-
رۇۋ جوركەرلەرى جانا مل ازاتتىق ارمىياسمنىن كۇماندىر-
جوركەرلەرىندە چەمارىدلغان ۇندىرونۇ قابىلدادى   5

شەنجاش، بەيجىن، 16-نويابىر قا-
بارى، بىز ارۇلۇت ئەاى تەمىز ىنتەن
ماقتاشىپ، ۋرتوق كۇرۇش قىلماق ئلە-
12-قۇرۇلتاي ۋرتوۋەو قوبەون كۇجۇر-   10
مىن باعەتى ئشكە اشىر الاابىز. بىزل،
15-نويابىر نۇشتون كەيىن ۇرۇ-جۇ-ۇدۇر
اياتقاان شەنجالك زىبەۇر ايتونۇم را-
يوندۇق ۇلۇتتۇز ىنتىماقتق بويۇنچا
اىدنتق كولاكتىمىپ جانا ۇلگگولۇ-رۇ   15
جەكەلەرى ماقتاپ-سىلىۋو جىنالمىشنا
قاتىشقان 500دون كوبۇرووك ئل زلۇت
وكۇلدۇرۇزۇنۇن ۋرتوق جۇرۇك -وزۇ-
شەنجالك زىبەۇر ايتونۇم را-ون
ۇلۇتتۇز ىنتىماقتق بويۇنچا چاقىرعان   20
بۇل نرەتكى-جولك جىنالىمىش—شەنجالك
ازات بولمون 33جلدان بەركى العاچى
جىنالمىش،6. كۇن ۇلانتمالعان بۇل نرەت-
كى سالىت نازتىۇز جىنالمىسشنا ار
زلۇت- وكولدۇور تولۇپ-تاشقان قد-   25
زۇزۇلۇق مەنەنبارتىياسنن ۇلۇتتۇز سا-
ياساتىدن ۇزجەملادىشتىروۇ، ۇلۇتتار دنتە-

ئاقتمەن كۇچۇپتۇۇزۇن ۋتو ماگىزدۇزلۇ-
ۇۇن بايانداشتى، شەنجالك زىبەۇر ايتو-   30
نوم رايوندۇق پارتكومدۇن بىرىنشى
سەكرەتارى ۋالئ ئنماۇ شەنجاگدىنزلۇت-
تار ىنتىماقتەمى جاقتاعى چولك جاقشى
قەمداالدى 7 جاقتان سۇلى—دۇ. ال
مىنداي دەدى: ازىرقى دوور—شەنجاگ-   35
دا زلۇتتار دنتەمى ئلە جاقشى بول-
مون تارىخەى دوورلۇردۇن ئشرى،
ۋەوندۇى ئلە شەنجاگدىن سايا-سى،
رقتىسادى ئلە جاقشى بولمون تارىخەى
دوورلۇردۇن ئشرى.   40

جىنالمىش اياقتاانندا، جىگگوكوۇ-
ۇۇز-تەمك پارتىياسى بۇربۇردۇق كوم-
تەت سەكرەتارىياتنن كازندرماك سەك-
رەتارى جاباۇشى جەتەكچى جولدۇشتۇر ۇلۇتتۇق   45
ىنتىماقتەمتا سالىم قۇشقون 500 دون
كوبۇرووك ارۇلۇت وكۇلدۇرۇنۇ ماقتۇۇ
تۇزۇ-زۇ سىداق قاعازى جانا سىملىق،
بۇيۇمدارى تارقاتتى.

(ۇلاندىرسى 3- بەتتە)

(ۇلاندىرسى 3- بەتتە)

QIZIL   SUU   GEZITI
1982 jıl   20 noyabr   ishembi

1   APTONOM ROYONDUQ ULUTTAR INTIMAQTIGI BOYUNCHA
    MAQTAP SIYLOO JIYNALISHI JENGISHTÜÜ AYAQTADI.

Jıynalısh aptonom rayondogu ar ulut eli,deng jer
özdöshtürüü jookerleri jana el azattıq armiyasının
komandır-jookerlerine chıgarılgan ündöönü qabıldadı.

         Shinhuashe, Beyjin 16-noyabr qa-
         barı. Biz ar ulut eli tıgız intı-
         maqtashıp, ortoq kürösh qılsaq ele,
         12-qurultay ortogo qoygon küjür-
10   mön bagıttı ishke ashır aalabız. Bul-
         15-noyabr tüshtön kiyin Ürümchüdö
         ayaqtagan Sınjang-Uygur aptonom ra-
         yonduq uluttuq ıntımaqtıq boyuncha
         aldıngı kollektiv jana ülgülüü
15   jekelerdi maqtap_sıyloo jıynalıshına
         qatıshgan 500-dön köbüröök ar ulut
         öküldörünün ortoq jürök sözü.
         Shınjang-Uygur aptonom rayon
         uluttuq ıntımaqtıq boyuncha chaqırgan
20   bul iretki chong jıynalısh - Shınjang
         azat bolgon 33-jıldan berki algachqı
         jıynalısh. 6-kün ulantılgan but iret-
         ki saltanattuu jıynalıshına ar
         ulut öküldörü tolup-tashqan qı-
25   zuuluq menen partiyanın uluttuq sa-
         yasatıq izchildeshtirüü, uluttar ıntı-
         maqtıgın küchöytüünün ötö mangızduulu-
         gun bayandashtı, Shınjang-Uygur apto-
         nom rayonduq partkomduq birinchi
30   sekretarı Wang In Maw Shınjangdıq ulut-
         tar ıntımaqtıgı jaqtagı chong jaqshı
         qırdaaldı 7 jaqtan süylödü. Al
         mınday dedi: Azırqı door - Shınjang
         da uluttar ıntımagı eng jaqshı bol-
35   gon tarıhıy doorlordun biri,
         oshondoy ele Shınjangdin sayası,
         ıqtisadı eng jaqshı bolgon tarıhıy
         doorlorun biri.

TEXT XVI-H(b)

Jıynalısh ayaqtaganda, Junggo kom-
40 munistik partiyası borborduq komiteti sekretariyatında kandidat sekretarı Chyaw Shı jana Wang In Maw sı-
jaŋtuu jetekchi joldoshtor uluttuq
ıntımaqtıgın salım qoshqon 500-dön
45 köbüröök ar ulut öküldörünö maqtoo
tuusu, sıylıq qagazı jana sıylıq
buyumdarı tarqattı.

(ulandısı 3-bette)

TEXT XVI - H(b)

QIZIL SUU GEZITI
Saturday, November 20, 1982

THE SOLEMN MEETING DEDICATED TO UNITY
AMONG THE NATIONS OF THE AUTONOMOUS
DISTRICT ENDED IN A SUCCESS.

1   The meeting approved the call issued to
        the soldiers and officers of the
        Liberation Army, to the soldiers bringing
        new lands under the plough and to each
        nation of the autonomous district

5   Xinhuashe, November 16, a dispatch from
        Peking:

        "If we, multinational people, tightly
        close ranks and wage a common struggle,
        we'll be able to put into practice the
        glorious

10   drive made common by the 12th Congress".
        Such is the whole-hearted statement (made
        by) more than 500 multinational delegates
        participating in the meeting honoring
        exemplary individuals and

15   front-rank associations (and) dedicated to
        inter-ethnic unity in the Xinjiang-Uyghur
        autonomous district as it ended in Urumqi
        in the afternoon of November the 15th. This
        great and regular meeting called on behalf
        of inter-ethnic unity in the Xinjiang-
        Uyghur

20   district is the first one since the
        liberation of Xinjiang, 33 years ago.

        The multinational delegates to this
        regular solemn meeting which lasted six
        days, expressed with unbounded warmth the
        exceptional(ly important) meaning of the
        strengthening of inter-ethnic

25   unity (and of) the implementation of the
        national policy of the Party and the First

Secretary of the Party Committee of the
Xinjiang-Uyhgur Autonomous District Wang En
Mao described, from

30   seven viewpoints, the excellent state of
unity among the nations of Xinjiang. He
said thus: "This period is one of the
epochs in History when inter-ethnic
relations are very good in Xinjiang

35   and the same (holds true) for economy and
politics".

At the end of the meeting, Qiao Shi,
candidate to the

40   Secretariate of the Central Committee of
the Chinese Communist Party, Wang En Mao
and other comrades-leaders handed rewards,
honorary diplomas and honorary pennants to
more than 500 multi-ethnic

45   delegates who made their contribution to
(inter) ethnic unity.
(to be followed on p 3)

COMMENTS

Even quicker than in the 1920s in the USSR, a
similar 'policy of development of the minority languages' was implemented for the Turkic-speaking
peoples of Chinese Xinjiang as soon as 1952.
Specialists were formed, often under the gui-
dance of Soviet linguists on long-term secondment
mission who, after surveying in a first phase the
sociolinguistic situation on the spot, took the
most direct part in the second phase: the development of an alphabetical/orthographical system, the
delimitation of a morpho-phonological norm and, in
general, all the technical problems linked with
the new functions and written uses of the ethnic
languages.

A)- The script
As in Soviet Central Asia, the touchiest problem for the 90,000 Kirghiz living along the Sino-
Soviet border (whose territory had just been transformed into different autonomous 'zhou's) was that
of the script.
A choice had to be made among three possible
solutions.
- Latinization: It had been unofficially and
intermittently experienced during the 1930s as long
as the local government in Xinjiang had been colla-
borating with the USSR. The system then in use was
the same as in Soviet Central Asia (cf. texts XI),
this choice being however much more theoretical
than practical.
When, after 1949 and in spite of this touchy
precedent, this solution was envisaged, it was, in
a dramatic contrast with 1926 Soviet Kirghizia, not
by the native intelligentsia (cf. below), but by
the Chinese central government, in the wake of the
Han-centered movement of 'Romanization/Latinization'
(cf. Ma Xueliang: "The Relationship between the
Plan for Phonetic Spelling of Chinese and National
Minority Written Languages", Language Reform in
China, P.J.Seybolt and G. Kuei-ke Chiang Ed., Sharpe
Inc., New York 1978 and J. De Francis: Nationalism
and Language Reform in China, Octagon Books, New
York 1972).

A variant of the 'pin yin' system (itself
different from the one illustrated by texts XI) was
designed (cf. G. Jarring: "The New Romanized Alphabet for Uighur and Kazakh and some Observations on
the Uighur Dialect of Kashgar", Central Asiatic
Journal, 1981, 25, pp. 230-245) which tended to
make a compromise between the Han pinyin and the
Soviet, pre-1941 script:
ə = ö; ü; e = ı; ê = e; ng; y; x = sh; q = ch;
ķ = q; k; ơ =g; g; j.
Cf. for example, the same sentence as in text XI-B:
    1922 jele, azerbayjanen jange alipêgê ətüp
    jatķanen uķķanda, joldox Lênin "bul kün qeơexta
    əzgerüx" dêp joop ķaytarơan.
This system was viewed as an important asset
for modernity, but was not officialized. It was
used only intermittently and mainly for scientific
publications. Its ultimate failure seems to be linked
less to the official change of attitude toward the
Arabic script and Islam (this aspect was far less
delicate among Kirghiz than among Uyghurs) than to
a whole set of political, extralinguistic problems
which arose between Moscow and Peking (cf. Hans
Bräker: "Nationality Dynamics in Sino-Soviet Relations", Soviet Nationalities in Strategic Perspective, S.E.Wimbush Ed., Croom Helm, London 1985).

- Cyrillic was considered for a while a possible
solution. Hence a research program (Kırgız tilinin
dialektardın teksherüü programması, Pekin 1956, in
cyrillic script) and the draft proposed in 1957
(cf. Text XVI-B), later completed by Jangı jazuunu
üyrönüü materiaları, Kızıl Suu 1957.
Its main advantage was to allow a linguistic
and cultural reunification of Kirghizstan which
would have made possible the use, on Chinese territory, of all publications printed in Soviet Kirghizia. It would have satisfied most Soviet experts
working in China and officialized a deep Soviet
influence already implemented in this part of Xinjiang well before 1949.
Of course, such a solution was acceptable only
as long as relations between Peking and Moscow were
to remain exceptionally good. Together with serious
changes in this field, difficulties began to arise
after the 'One Hundred Flowers' movement which were
ultimately to lead to the excesses of the 'Cultural
Revolution'.

- The preservation of the Arabic script appeared
thus as a convenient, neutral solution. It had been
used long before 1949 and printing houses existed
in Urumqi, mainly however for Uyghur.
   The system then adopted (cf. Text XVI-A,C,D,E)
was that of the 'Reformed Alphabet' (cf. Text 1-G)
completed by new diacritic marks which allowed a
clear distinction between front and back labials:
ﯗ = ü   ﯗ = ö
y = ﮚ is distinct from i and ı, but the ﺀ diacritic
mark used to distinguish i from ı is irregularly
used.
   This system in any case provides Kirghiz with
a clear and simple orthography. It has remained unchanged ever since.
   Although the·publication of the Qızıl Suu
Gazetası had already been stopped, a few texts in
Kirghiz continued to be printed in 1962 (Text XVI-E).
   After a decade spent in the wilderness of the
'Cultural Revolution', publishing in Kirghiz was
restored in 1980 with the same alphabet (Texts XVI-
F,G,H and 1-A(a)).

   B) The Language itself
   After 1949, the Kirghiz language spoken in Xinjiang was submitted to contradictory, although complementary influences which, as much as a long iso-
lation from Soviet Kirghiz, are responsible for
some of the discrepancies which can be perceived
between these two local variants of the same tongue.
   Morphological differences are practically non-
existent. Nevertheless, shifting from Soviet to Xinjiang Kirghiz triggers a feeling of strangeness,
especially in intellectual/journalistic texts. Yet,
one must be aware of the fact that text XVI-G, for
example,(Quttuqtoo) is as much normative in Xinjiang
as text V or VIII are in Soviet Kirghizia, the former being however much less 'sinicized' than the
latter are 'russified'.
   Discrepancies between the two norms are, super-
ficially, of syntactical origin (Xinjiang Kirghiz
having remained nearer to the oral tongue, i.e.
laxer in this respect), but, basically, lexical.
   One can note:
- a temporary tendency, before the 'Cultural
Revolution', to introduce phonologically adapted
Russian loanwords which, outside intellectual circles, were not understood. Such is the case of

revolyutsia, ekonomika, etc.: as a general rule
they did not succeed in replacing equivalent terms
of Arab (ınqılab, ıktısad) or Turkic origin (köngtörüsh) which were - and remain - of current use.
    This restriction of Russian influence remains
the main source of misunderstanding between Chinese and Soviet Kirghiz. But nothing in Xinjiang
ever resembled the anti-purist witch-hunt of the
1930s: simply, the 'loan level' remained in Xinjiang
where it was in Soviet Kirghizia before World War
II, i.e. limited in number, in form and in scope.
Cf. for example: respublika, dohtor, zavod, rayon,
yaslıy (nursery), teatr, organ, akademiya, park,
parad, müzöy, oktabr, pirograma, noyabır, proletar,
etc. In the same way, the semantical and idiomatic
calques common to both Kirghiz norms are those
which developed during the 1920-30s: borbor: capital city; köngtörüsh: reform; tieshelüü: concerning. This allows us to quantify the process of
russification/russianization as it developed in
Soviet Kirghizia during the 1940-50s.
    - a more stable tendency toward differenciation
through the use of
    . lexemes now considered 'obsolete' in Kir-
ghizia but currently used in Xinjiang:
algı söz: preface, instead of bashı/kirish söz
kurultay: conference, instead of s"ezd
ıqt(ı)sad: economy, instead of charbachılık
sap: rank; öyöt: document; kösöm: leading billy-
goat → leader.
    . lexemes typical for Xinjiang Kirghiz but
considered 'dialectal' in the USSR or having a special, local meaning. These are numerous enough to
call for the elaboration of a small Xinjiang Kirghiz Dictionary:
tügö-: to finish >uyghur: tügä- and Y-776, instead
of ayakta-
alkısh: thanks (lit. kirg.: hlessings)
boordosh elder (cf. 1-E(b): bir boordum), instead
of bir tuugan elder: brother peoples
abiroy: fame (lit. kirg.: abiyir: conscience)
jemkor: éxploiter (lit. kirg.: glutton)
ereje: statutes (lit. kirg.: rule, decision,Y-960
akimchilik: self-government (lit. kirg.: attitude
typical for lords and VIPs)
cheberdik: technics (lit. kirg.: skill)
küjürmöndülük: heroism (lit. kirg.: determination
in tackling one's work); küjürmöndük: energy,
promptness (heroism in lit. kirg.: baatırdık)

erekchelik (lit. kirg.: ayrıkchılık): peculiarity
sala: a branch of knowledge
ese qosh- to make one's contribution to
jıldız tart-: to take root (lit. kirg.: tamır jay-)
bechel qal-: literally = to remain retarded,
speaking of a baby who does not walk → to remain
behind the times
bardıqqa keltir-: to carry through to a successful
conclusion
izchildeshtir-: to carry out
ortogo qoy-: to put forward (a proposal); Y-580:
to pool, to share something
qizuuluq: warmth, enthusiasm; Y-477: ardor, passion.
  A great many of these lexemes are not recorded
in Y: birdeylik: unanimity; taanım: knowledge;
achınarlik: offense; jalpı betkey = jalpı jüzdüü:
comprehensive.
  In particular, many suffixes such as /LIk/ or
/(I)š/: K-1054, 1252 provide derived nominals which
either have a special meaning (kelish: form ≠ lit.
kirg.: the coming) or are not recorded in Y: jazı-
lısh, oqulush. Same remark for azıqtıq idiya: ideological (lit. kirg.: ideyalık).
  - Conversely, Han loanwords and calques:
Besides local realia (lagman: noodles; momo: steam-
stewed bread) or old loanwords (tuu: flag; ayjang-
jung: top Han official) or proper names: Shinjang,
Shınhuashı: Xinjiang, Xinhuashi (News Agency),
most of the Han loanwords and calques are to be
found in journalistic/political texts (XVI-F,G):

hansu: ch. hàn zú 汉族   the Han people

lushiyen: ch. lùxìan 路线   (political) line

shyujengjuyı(chı): ch. xiūzhēngzhùyì 修正主义·
                                  revisionist

junghua: ch. zhōng huà 中华   China

junggo: ch. zhōng guó 中国   " (lit. Kirg.:
                                  Kitay)

fangjin: ch. fāng zhén 方针   (pol.) campaign

Idiomatic calques, such as chong jaqshı: excellent
(ch. dà hǎo 大好 , lit. kirg.: eng jakshı) pertain usually to the same field:

kagilgan miq: ch. dìngshǎngde dīngzì 钉上的钉子

'a hardened nail' = a hidden dissident

kalpak qiygiz: ch. zuò zhānmàode zhānzì 做 毡 帽　毡子

'to put a bonnet on' = to critize politically

boyun kötördü: ch. fān shēn 翻身　　'turned his body over' = emancipated itself

törttü zamandashdıruu: ch. shíxiàn sì ge xiàndài-huà 矢现 四个 现代化　　the Four Modernizations

tört kishilik top: ch. sì rén bāng 四人帮 the Gang of Four

kulach jaydıruu: ch. kāi zhǎn 开展　　to develop.

However, these 'hanisms' are by far much fewer than Russianisms in Soviet Kirghiz and, at least since the end of the 'Cultural Revolution', are not systematically introduced into the written language.

(El Geziti: 人民日报　　Rén Mín Rì Bào: The People's Daily

Shınhuashı 新华社　　Xīn Huà Shè: The New China Agency)

TEXT XVII

c)   FU-YÜ GIRGIZ

        A song in Heilongjiang Kirghiz collected
in 1980 by Prof. Hu from a 54-year old local Girgiz
woman called Yu Jima.

1   Erbe-serbe ibine be ?
           Erel-sarel garne be ?
           Saɠat namang jiti be ?
           Saɠat namang menda be ?

5   Erbe-serbe ibine joh,
           Erel-sarel garne joh,
           Saɛɠat namang jiti joh,
           Saɠat namang menda joh.

           Gününg-gününg ux Gas gerler yəlyə,
10   Ibining uxnar badarne odurlarda,
           Gününg-gününg sini surader yəlyə,
           Erbe-serbe ibine be ?
           Erel-sarel garne be ?
           Saɠat namang jiti be ?
15   Gününg-gününg sini surader yəlyə.

           Erbe-serbe ibine joh,
           Erel-sarel garne joh,
           Saɠat namang jiti joh,
           Saɠat namang menda joh.

TEXT XVII

TRANSLATION into Literary Kirghiz

Ырбы-сырбы үйүндө /бар/бы?
Ырыл-сарыл жакындабы?
Жаа-огуң /жага/ жетеби?
Жаа-огуң мында /бар/бы?

    Ырбы-сырбы үйүндө жок
    Ырыл-сарыл жакын жерде жок
    Жаа-огуң /сага/ жетпейт
    Жаа-огуң мында жок.

Күндө-күндө үч каз кирер эле
Үйүнүн батыш тамына олтурат
Күндө-күндө сени сурат эле
    Ырбы-сырбы үйүндөбү?
    Ырыл-сарыл жакындабы?
    Жаа-огуң жетеби?
    Күндө-күндө сени сураптыр эле.

Ырбы-сырбы үйүндө жок
Ырыл-сарыл жакында жок
Жаа-огуң жетпейт
Жаа-огуң мында жок.

TRANSLATION into Chinese

译文: 大雁, 额尔博。色尔博可在家?
跟前有没有额勒尔·萨勒尔马?
弩弓利箭这里有没有?
箭儿能否射着我?

额母: 额尔博。色尔博不在家,
跟前没有额勒尔·萨勒尔马。
这里没有弩弓和利箭,
箭儿把你射不着。

额母对儿子: 大雁天天飞来呀!
落在你房子的西墙上,
天天都来把你问。
说你在家不在家。
说跟前有没有额勒尔·萨勒尔马。
说弩弓利箭这儿有没有,
说箭儿能否射着我。

额对母: 就说额尔博·色尔博不在家,
就说跟前没有额勒尔·萨勒尔马,
就说弩弓利箭这儿并没有。

TEXT XVII

(Once upon a time, there lived a jigit
called Irbı-Sırbı. He had a horse called
Irıl-Sarıl. Each day, three cranes would
come to the West side of Irbı-Sırbı's house
and ask:)

1   Irbı-Sirbı, is he at home?
        Is Irıl-Sarıl near by?
        Can his bow-and-arrow reach me?
        Is there a bow-and-arrow here?

(Irbı-Sirbı's mother answers)

5   Irbı-Sirbı is not at home
        Irlı-Sarıl is not near by
        His bow-and-arrow cannot reach you
        His bow-and-arrow are not here.

(The cranes fly away. Irbı-Sırbı comes back
home. His mother explains that some birds
have come)

        Each day three birds would come

10   They would perch on the western wall of
             the house
        Each day they would ask for you:
        Irbı-Sırbı, is he at home?
        Is Irıl-Saril near by?
        Can his bow-and-arrow reach me?

15   Each day they would ask for you.

(One day, the cranes come back. Irbi-Sırbı
has been waiting for them. He tells his
mother to deceive the birds. One crane
asks the mother about Irbı-Sırbı. She
answers:)

        Irbı-Sırbı is not at home,
        Irıl-Sarıl is not near by
        His bow-and-arrow cannot reach you
        His bow-and-arrow are not here.

(The mother and his son deceive the cranes.
Irbı-Sırbı shoots at the bird which flies

406

away with the arrow that hit it. Irbı-Sırbı
chases it. The crane, upon being caught,
transforms itself into a beautiful girl.
Irbı-Sırbı marries her and they live
happily ever after).

TEXT XVII

COMMENTS

Two field surveys (in 1957 and 1980) by Prof. Hu
Zhen hua allowed linguistic circles outside China
to discover the existence in Fu-Yü (a small village
near Tsitsikar, 300 kms NW of Kharbin, in Heilong-
jiang/Manchuria) of a minute (about 600 people)
Turkic-speaking community calling itself 'Kırgıs',
the exact origin of which is not clear.
Although their language - the easternmost and the
sole yet undescribed Turkic idiom - must be considered independent from Tien-Shan Kirghiz (it is
a 'z' language: azah ≠ lit. kirg. ayak:foot), it
displays such features which makes it akin to other
Turkic languages of the Altay-Tuva range and thus
establishes a distant link with the 'historical'
Kirghiz who participated in the complex process
that gave birth to the present day (Tien Shan) Kirghiz nation. Fu-Yü Kirgis, heavily influenced in
the past by local Mongolian in a multi-ethnic
environment and now by Chinese, is rapidly losing
ground among the younger generation and may become
extinct in the near future.
A tentative synchronical description of this idiom
(on the basis of the limited data now available)
has been proposed by the authors:
    Hu Zhen hua, Guy G. Imart: "Fu-Yü Gїrgїs: A
    Tentative Description of the Easternmost Turkic
    Language", Papers on Inner Asia, 1988. n° 8,
    Bloomington, Indiana University (RIFIAS).
The Latin alphabet used here is a variety of the
Chinese Pinyin system as adapted at a time (in
the late 50s) for the minority languages of China
and as kept since then for scholar notation of
these languages.
The short song recorded here obviously is all that
remains of a probably much longer narrative - and
mythical - poem.

LEXICAL   DATA

ib: lit. kirg.: üy: house. ib + i + nı = üyünö
cf. in the above mentioned article the very
peculiar synharmonic system of Fu-yü Kirghiz.

bi: interrogative particle
garnı: near by
saǧat-namang: bow and arrow (+ng= your?)
jitibi = jit-i-bi = lit. kirg. jetebi
gününg-gününg: lit. kirg. kündö-kündö
ush : lit. kirg. üch = three
Gasger: lit. kirg. karkıra: crane + Plur.
       (Chinese: 雁 yàn) or (?) Gas: lit. kirg.
       kaz: wild goose.
gır-lır: lit. kirg. kir-: to come

^{y}ə l^{y}ə: lit. kirg. ele
ib+i+ning: Genitive or Possessive 2nd pers.?
ushnar: lit. kirg; batısh: West
badar(ı)nı: lit. kirg. tamdın bashı; tam+ı+na
odur-lar da: lit. kirg. olturar da
sini: lit. kirg. seni: you (Acc.)
sura-dır: lit. kirg. sura-p-tır-:to ask.

www.ingramcontent.com/pod-product-compliance
Lightning Source LLC
Chambersburg PA
CBHW060322100426
42812CB00003B/859